EGOALS

Exercising your ego

in high-performance environments

*What the back rooms of high performance sports can teach us
about ego in our professional lives*

egoalsbook.com

Martin Buchheit

George M. Perry

Illustrations by Christel Saneh

TABLE OF CONTENTS

INTRODUCTION

This is the book I needed to read 20 years ago.

Any endeavor has those things that you have to experience to truly learn and know. Starting out, I knew that I knew sports science, and I believed that was the only thing that would ever matter to my job. As long as I had the data and the science on my side - and I would ensure it was always on my side before stepping into any room - I knew that I could convince anybody of the right thing to do. Why else would they be in sports science if they cared about anything other than using science to improve athlete performance?

Twenty years later, as I realized that it was time to leave what should have been my dream job, I began to understand what I didn't know at the beginning and only slowly understood during my career.

Martin Buchheit, Ph.D.

Marbella, Spain

One of our contributors asks if maybe her willingness to answer Martin's questions and be quoted in this book was actually her ego's desire to have her name alongside so many of the luminaries of her field.

I have no such doubt about myself. When I saw that Martin Buchheit was looking for an editor, maybe even a collaborator, maybe even a co-author for a book about ego in high-performance sport, I absolutely knew that I wanted to be a part of it. Scratch that. I absolutely knew that I was going to be a part of it.

Sport? Writing? Ego? Are there three things I love more in this world?

George M. Perry

Broken Arrow, OK, USA

This book is about ego in high-performance environments. The overwhelming majority of stories - and all of the 100+ people we interviewed - come from sports, because that's the field we've spent most of our careers in.

Martin's original plan was not to write a book, but to ask a few of his colleagues how they deal with the dysfunctional egos that he encountered throughout his career in high-performance sport. Someone, amongst his peers in the backrooms of high-performance sports, must know how to develop a healthy ego and present it in a productive way, often in an unhealthy and unproductive environment.

He started asking around, setting up the conversation with some of the more ridiculous things he had seen and heard. "I am the only one in the world who can do that, so let me do it," or "I'll never learn anything from you because I already know everything I need." He quickly confirmed his suspicions: he wasn't the only one who had encountered people like that, and he wasn't the only one looking for answers, or at least a playbook.

Those early conversations shaped the survey that forms the basis of this book.

Once you get into Chapter 2, you won't hear too much from Martin and George. We'll set things up in each chapter and contribute a few stories along the way, but we're not experts in ego.

Throughout the book, any section in this style comes from one of the 110 high-performance practitioners who spoke to us.

> Sections in this style are from individuals with particular expertise at the intersection of ego and sports performance. Along with retired athletes and high-performance consultants, four performance coaches - psychologists who specialize in drawing the highest levels of professional performance from their clients, sports or otherwise - provide their insights on developing an ego capable of handling the highest ambitions.

You can think of *EGOals* as a guided tour, a curated qualitative research project or a playbook crowd-sourced from some of the most demanding sports workplaces. Given our background, we like to think of it as a playbook. Absolutely, you should go cover-to-cover in an attempt to get a handle on the whole thing. But sometimes you simply need to know what you need to know, and you go to that section and put some ideas in your notebook for the next training session, pitch competition, product launch or earnings call.

A NOTE ON PRIVACY

Not many people come out of Chapter 3 looking good. Other stories are very personal and may reflect the negative influence a coworker or employer had on a contributor. The people involved might not be too pleased to see their name in print, and might go right to the contributors list to see who they should never hire again.

Out of respect for both sides of every story, we have changed the settings, titles and names of people involved in those incidents at our contributors' request or our own discretion. We've also created two characters, Charles Vallejo and Antonio David Sanchez, as our all-purpose stand-ins for those times when we wanted to attach a name, but not a person, to a story.

Additionally, some of our contributors requested anonymity throughout the book, while others gave permission to quote them by name as long as the above details de-identified them in the more negative stories.

We were also wary that, at times, we might be committing a common ego f***-up from Chapter 3: free-riding on the fame and prestige of others.

Some of the most positive lessons we've learned about ego came from interactions with players who are household names in the sports world. We wanted to acknowledge their role as well as convey the message as accurately and completely as possible. But we didn't want anyone - especially these players - to think we were using them to boost our profiles or our sales.

Therefore, we ensured that each one approved of his inclusion in the book. If you came here hoping to read tell-all behind-the-scenes stories about your favorite stars, sorry, no refunds

1 | HIGH-PERFORMANCE SPORT: EGO'S SANCTUARY, ARENA AND LABORATORY

Sport is a sanctuary for ego. It's one of the few places we're allowed to have one, and, indeed, to celebrate and revel it.

Imagine... had US Women's National Soccer Team star Alex Morgan or Leicester City's Jamie Vardy gone into law instead of soccer, it's doubtful we'd see Morgan celebrate closing a deal by making the tea-sipping motion in her client's boardroom. Nor would Barrister Vardy react to a record-setting 11th consecutive favorable verdict the same way he celebrated his record-setting goal in 11 Premier League games: running in front of the courtroom gallery saying "It's all mine! It's all f**king mine!"

If people saw two co-founders chest-bump on the NASDAQ platform to celebrate the closing bell on the day of their IPO, it would be that hour's toxic tech bro culture outrage. But if two players chest-bump after a basket or two-run home run midway through a midseason game between two midtable teams, we barely notice it.

Professional customs and workplace propriety likely will never evolve to that point. For the best. But setting the line at physical celebrations and displays of visceral emotion, non-athletes are rarely permitted some outward acknowledgment of their present success and longer-term greatness. People look askance at even muted, internal acknowledgments of accomplishment. How bleak. All that ambition, education and effort to reach some point in your job or life, and if you dare to recognize it, you're branded with the Scarlet E of ego.

Sports will at least give back-handed compliments like: "He's got a huge ego, but at least he's got the skills and trophies to back it up." Commentary on ego in any other part of life, though, is all back-of-the-hand, no compliment.

Unfortunately, ego's safe space extends only to those who take the field, rink, court, diamond or track - the ones on camera and in the headlines. The practitioners in high-performance sport - the sports scientists, strength & conditioning coaches, nutritionists, physiotherapists and others - labor under the same confusion, repression, dysfunction and derision provoked by a word that once simply meant "I" and is now cast to represent everything from "the fountainhead of human progress" to "the enemy."

WHAT DID EGO DO TO DESERVE THIS TREATMENT?

The word "ego" is ubiquitous in sports and other high-performance environments, and in commentary about those environments. It is used so casually by so many people that it's easy to forget that it has a real meaning.

Nearly every definition of ego as a psychological construct has two features in common: the self, and reality. That's a bit ironic given that most modern definitions of ego trace their roots to the psychoanalytic theories of Sigmund Freud, whose self was regularly coked out of reality. That aside, Psychology Dictionary says ego is "the part of the personality which carries on relationships with the external world... a group of functions that enable us to perceive, reason, make judgments, store knowledge and solve problems. It has been called the executive agency of personality."

Encyclopaedia Britannica likewise roots their definition in psychoanalytic theory, saying ego "is experienced as the 'self' or 'I' and is in contact with the external world through perception." And at the more everyday level, Merriam-Webster holds ego as "the self especially as contrasted with another self or the world."

On the surface that all sounds pretty innocuous and a bit wonkish. It's hard to see how that carries over to common usage: "I'm so sick of his [group of functions that enable him to perceive, reason, make judgments, store knowledge and solve problems]!" "Oh, that's just your [experience as the 'self' in contact with the external world through perception] talking!" Merriam-Webster gets us closer: "He's got a big [self especially as contrasted with another self or the world], but at least he's got the chops to back it up."

Compare those to some from our contributors:

Alex Calder, Head of Sports Science, Houston Dynamo FC: Too high ego is having the inability to meet the needs or requests of others in order to please yourself. Specifically, ranking your own knowledge above others, regardless of outcome.

Duncan French, Vice President of Performance, UFC Performance Institute: To me, ego represents a primal characteristic that reflects an individual's default narcissistic tendencies. Now, sometimes, it's a positive thing to have an ego, and when managed correctly it can be a powerful psychological driver. But in too many cases ego is perceived negatively, and it represents a demonstration or combination of arrogance, narcissism and lack of value to others.

Nick Grantham, performance specialist and coach: Ego seems to have taken on a negative connotation in recent times: "They've got a big ego" or "They let their ego get in the way." I would see ego as a combination of my past, present and future and how each of those influences my actions and behaviours. It's how I perceive myself, and hopefully that is aligned with how others perceive me!

Adam Waterson, strength & conditioning coach, LA Galaxy: I feel there are different types of egos. All people develop an ego, this is human nature. The ego is in play whenever you feel superior or inferior to someone else. Extreme confidence or self-esteem can be viewed by others as an ego. I feel ego can help you become successful, but if it isn't controlled it can create your demise. Ego makes us feel a wide range of emotions: jealousy, angry, cocky, depressed, fearful etc.

STACKING THE DECK AGAINST EGO

Ego is a good punching bag because so few people will come to its defense. Some people are not fans of the self, for cultural, religious or social reasons. Others would rather not acknowledge the unyielding reality of, well, reality.

If you're not into the self or reality, you're not going to like ego. If you'd rather not ask questions of yourself because you have an inkling of what the answer will be, you'll reject the output of those questions *a priori*.

If all of that turns someone off, they are really going to resent anyone who embraces self, reality and those functions of perception, reason, judgment and problem solving. That is, anyone who displays an ego.

Or it could be simpler: strawmen rarely attract useful defenders, and common usage of the word "ego" consumes a lot of hay. This reached its zenith (or nadir, depending on your perspective) in Ryan Holliday's bestseller *Ego is the Enemy*. Holliday sets out his terms in the introduction:

"The ego we see most commonly goes by a more casual definition: an unhealthy belief in our own importance. Arrogance. Self-centered ambition. That's the definition this book will use. It's that petulant child inside every person... The need to be *better* than, *more* than, *recognized* for, far past any reasonable utility - that's ego." (italics in original) [Holliday, 2016]

Well. Siri, show me a definition of "stacking the deck against."

It's easy to say that something is the enemy if you create your own explicit definition in the most negative terms.

Holliday had a little bit more:

"It's the sense of superiority and certainty that *exceeds the bounds* of confidence and *talent*. It's when the notion of ourselves and the world grows so *inflated* that it begins to *distort the reality* that surrounds us." (italics added this time)

Who would stand up in defence of unhealthy beliefs, inflations, distortions of reality and self-perceptions beyond the bounds of talent?

KNOW WHO THE REAL ENEMY IS

The real enemy here is the package-deal. A package-deal "consists of treating together, as parts of a single conceptual whole or 'package,' elements which differ essentially in nature, truth-status, importance or value" [Rand, 1984]. It "[equates] opposites by substituting nonessentials for their essential characteristics, obliterating differences."

Let's try it ourselves. "Puppies are juvenile dogs" - so far so good - "at the moment they are defecating on a silk Persian rug." Whoa! Puppies aren't so cute and lovable when you conflate a specific occasional action with their objective identity and essential nature.

Bringing things closer to home: "Sports are competitive activities of physical exertion or skill" - well, we'd like to think they're a bit more than that - "that result in life-shortening concussions and severe injuries while attracting abusive coaches and corrupt businessmen and politicians." OK, maybe not that much more.

If we're going to expand the definition of sports to hint at some of the worst, honesty and integrity demands we include some of the best, that we visit what philosopher Tara Smith calls the "arena for admiration" as often as we peer into the courtroom or emergency room [Smith, 2018]. Or, better yet, we keep our definitions neutral and hand them over to the free will of the people (and the continence of the puppies) involved.

NO WONDER THERE'S SO MUCH CONFUSION

Many people share Holliday's definition and perspective. They rig the game against the ego. Some people know, at some level, that they are rigging it, which leads to contradictions.

They talk about the dangers of the ego, negative encounters with ego, their efforts to tone down or eliminate their own ego, they'll disparage an athlete or entrepreneur by saying "Ugh, he's so egotistical," then flip right around and say, "But you gotta have a big ego to do what he does." How so? Does the success of Zlatan Ibrahimovic or Elon Musk sentence them to carry a ticking timebomb, never knowing when it's going to explode? Or are they who they are because they are powered by something more potent than Zlatan's shooting leg and Musk's rockets?

Combine these contradictions with the back-handed compliment we talked about at the beginning of this chapter: "He's got a big ego, but at least he can back it up, but it makes him such a jerk, but someone like him needs an ego like that." Moving through that sentence, we have an assessment, a reality check, a moral evaluation and a needs analysis. That's pretty much the process of ego identification, a process people are willing to do when it's a negative for others but not when it's potentially a positive for themselves.

The difficult case is when you have someone who is not on the world's stage and who does not loudly proclaim his success or ambition, but who has a self-assuredness that brings to mind words like confidence, pride and arrogance - words that can be summed up as "ego."

SPORT CAPTURES THE ESSENCE OF EGO

The loss of ego as a reality-oriented concept is particularly unfortunate in sports. The story of sport is a story of competition and admiration, which makes it inseparable from ego.

ATHLETES AND THEIR EGOS, EXPOSED FOR ALL TO SEE

We shouldn't be surprised that the same people who gave us egoistic philosophy also gave us sports. The classical Greeks elevated humans by recognizing that we are capable of more than survival: we can flourish, in fact, we should flourish. And as far as our spiritual life is concerned, flourishing *is* survival. From those premises the Greeks built a culture that celebrated the ideals proper to an intellectual, physical and spiritual being. Their stars and celebrities were the philosophers and the playwrights, the thinkers and the makers, the poets, the builders, the traders and those men who competed, well-oiled and nude, at the games of Olympus [Perrottet, 2004].

This appreciation comes through in their art. Grecian urns are as much odes to well-formed pectoral muscles and ripped six packs as they are to thoughtful discussions in the Lyceum or victory in battle.

The Greeks were the first to understand that sports - in their days, running, jumping, throwing, wrestling and boxing - offered Smith's "arena for admiration." The Greeks, who took the mind and body equally seriously, understood the spiritual fuel that sport provides to its fans via the physical and spiritual achievements of its athletes. As Tony Perrottet describes in *The Naked Olympics,* the athletes competed unclothed not out of freaky exhibitionism, but as purposeful showmanship. The body doing the sport was as much of what the athlete had to offer the audience, was as worthy of admiration and applause, as what that body accomplished athletically. A classical Greek athlete transported to the modern day would be equally baffled by the rules of soccer as why Cristiano Ronaldo doesn't just take it all off during his goal celebrations.

Sport was no more a luxury or a frivolity to the Greeks than drama, epic poetry, sculpture or anything else "of the mind" that we celebrate them for. All of those activities were proper to flourishing individuals in a flourishing society.

The intervening two and a half millennia were rarely kind to Greek ideals. The Renaissance made it OK to celebrate the human body again, not coincidentally as the human mind was taking its greatest leap forward since the Greeks. After a few more centuries of downtime, sports made their way back into popular consciousness and everyday life. The modern Olympic Games resurrected the games' original sports, stripped of the original ideals (and clothed).

Popular sport, though, brought people back to stadiums, and, therefore, to the arenas for admiration.

The athletes wanted to compete and win, and the fans wanted to watch them do it. Fans wanted to cheer for their team, for their colors, for their boys, and the athletes wanted the applause.

The Greeks' appreciation for the aesthetics of sport does not mean they neglected its competitive and objective aspects.

Only one competitor in each event wore a laurel wreath on their journey home: he who threw the discus furthest, who ran the fastest, who wrestled every opponent into submission. Two learned Greeks could debate the relative merits of a play or a sculpture and never agree on which is better, but there was no debate over who won the race. Just as today, analysts can create hours of content debating which coach or player was most responsible for a win or loss, and can appreciate the tactics or execution, but there's no debate over who won.

The objectivity and transparency of athletic competition anchors sport in reality, and that's where sport meets ego.

REALITY ALWAYS WINS, IN SPORT AND LIFE

Even in the absence of fans (thanks, 2020), sport fosters a safe space for ego. The games are more complicated than they were for the Greeks, but they retain the attributes of objectivity and transparency. You either score or you don't, and everyone knows it. You were offsides or not, and everyone knows it. You jumped or threw far enough to qualify for the championships, or you didn't. And everyone in stadium or watching at home knows it just as soon as the athlete does.

There's no hiding from knowledge of performance or knowledge of results in sport. Truth is rarely so evident and immediate elsewhere in life. In sport, we can make assessments and pass judgments more confidently and clearly than in almost any other setting.

PERFORMANCE COACHES: PRACTITIONERS OF EGO

There is one member of the backroom staff for whom "ego" is an objectively meaningful term: performance coaches.

Over the last decade, performance coaches have become full-time must-haves for sports teams, hedge funds, real estate firms, law firms, tech companies and other high-pressure, high-output workplaces. Performance coaches are the practitioners of ego. When they say the word, they know exactly what they mean to say.

> Pippa Grange, psychologist and author, Head of Culture at Right to Dream Group. Former Head of People and Talent Development for the Football Association (England):
>
> Ego is the sense of I, the sense of me, of oneself. I like to call it our "I-dentity."
>
> None of us would be any good without it. We all need an ego. It's an energetic force, associated with drive, that helps solve problems.
>
> Ego is associated with resilience. It gives you the courage to face things, and the ability to tolerate adversity. "I am capable of" is very central in the ego
>
> It's not a dirty word, but oversensitive, immature, easily triggered ego becomes unhealthy. It's a bit like this lump of clay in the middle that, when overstretched, becomes out of shape. An inflated pride and inflated self-importance become troublesome when I am more concerned about the impression I make on others and am only concerned about me: my view, who I am, etc

> Joël Trébern, cognitive and psychology consultant, founder of JHT Performance:
>
> After 35 years working in high performance sport and in the industry, with head coaches, staff, players and CEOs, here is how I can define ego:
>
> Ego is a personified expression, that is ready to do the impossible to serve its own interest, that sometimes exaggeratedly affirms its singularity, often at the detriment of others or the group, and which may sometimes lead to its own loss.

It's the activation of a psychological mechanism that, via diverse defensive behaviors, strategies and actions, can use all mental and physical resources available to satisfy one's own beliefs. It's a very powerful energy that gets sourced by our fears (either conscious or unconscious) of not being able to realize ourselves, both in the short and long term, in relation to our environment that we may perceive as hostile (i.e., elitist, unstable, precarious). In other terms, this survival energy seems indispensable to most of us to reach our objectives during our career and life, both as professionals and human beings.

Most top athletes, irrespective of the discipline, manage to use this energy wisely, i.e., to get deeply involved in their long-term project, build intrinsic motivation, get over their own limits and develop strategies to improve, progress and succeed in the very competitive world of elite sports. This energy becomes less virtuous, however, when these competitors feel challenged in their primary values (honesty, respect, integrity).

Staff working in large organization around those athletes, in theory all meant to collaborate for the same overall project, irrespective of their social status or human values, are too often the activators of those egotistic behaviors. Fostering collective work, with all individual efforts put toward a unique goal and mission (e.g., working for the others and the team overall performance) is often the ultimate challenge in these organizations.

It's only attainable when staff manage to understand (either consciously or unconsciously) the operational plan and values of i) the organization (driven by the leadership), ii) their colleagues and iii) the athletes, that all together shape the virtual space at their disposal to express themselves, and where they can seed their art and qualities. Their security, their own professional and personal development and enjoyment may therefore be directly threatened by the context they work in. The level of their ego activation and its virtuousness is a direct function of their perception of the danger to their ability to act as professionals as per their job descriptions.

Michael Caulfied, sport psychologist:

I love a player or athlete with ego, as sport is based on belief. Ego can mean many things to many people, but to me it shows that a person believes in their ability to perform on the biggest stage. An ego can be destructive, but I believe some of the greatest performers had an ego, from Eric Cantona through to, say, Paul Pogba. Without ego, who would they be? How would they perform? But you have to manage and train the ego, too. That is the real skill.

Juan Carlos Álvarez Campillo, sport psychologist (Spanish National Football Team, Sevilla FC, Olympic athletes):

Ego, as a basic concept, could be defined as an excess in the valuation one has of oneself, an excess of self-esteem. It comes from the Latin meaning "I," but as we understand it nowadays, it is an increased - and, in many cases, disproportionate - self. That is why in sport it also implies believing oneself superior to or better than others. That is something that one cannot value by oneself alone. Other factors come into play, such as the opinion of specialists, statistics, the valuation of the market or even of the fans.

EXERCISE SCIENCE, BUT FOR EGOS

Athletes have objective reference points that they can use to reality check their own ability, and that we can use to reality check their public expressions of ego. They have their stats, salaries and transfer fees.

The backroom staffs of sports don't have those, but they are presented - perhaps confronted - every day with the egos of those who do. Some exploit sport's ego sanctuary and try to imitate the ego they see from the players, neglecting to establish their own objective measures to calibrate their ego. Others recoil from what they see, and make a conscious effort to dial down their respective egos, which may not always be the right answer.

Those efforts are what Martin wanted to hear during those first few calls, and what have since become this book.

Chapter 2 opens with Martin's up-close experience with two of the justifiably largest egos in professional sports: soccer's Zlatan Ibrahimovic and handball's Thierry Omeyer. Zlatan's public persona consistently toes the line between being a man who lives up to his ego and a caricature of the ego-delusional superstar. Omeyer is not as showy with his ego, but he never once shies away from the ego as the cause and effect of his achievements.

After meeting them, we head into the locker room to hear our contributors' ego success stories, those times when they used their egos as a positive in their lives.

It's a relatively short chapter, especially compared to Chapter 3: "Ego f***-ups."

All of the f*** ups in Chapter 3 were in the same direction: too much, too loud, too big. Not a single contributor mentioned a single time where they or a colleague f**ked up by not having enough ego for the moment, nor even regretted an unnecessarily self-effacing moment. Other than a few gentle self-admonitions in Chapter 2, we have very little evidence of anyone judging someone adversely due to an underinflated, sheepish, meek ego.

Martin says it's a selection bias: there are no underinflated, sheepish, meek egos in high-performance sport, and, if there are, they are overwhelmed and outweighed in every sense by people like those in Chapter 3.

George explains it as a cultural bias: he maintains our intellectual and cultural environment is anti-individual, anti-pride and anti-ego.

Martin also thinks that many of his peers intentionally tone down their own egos because they are surrounded by so many high-power egos. Or, they go through the motions of self-effacement because they think it's what they're supposed to do - "I can't be bothered with the team picture - go ahead and take it without me if I'm not around the training ground that day" - before plotting their next act of self-promotion, like calling the team photographer to find out the date of the team picture and then scheduling a hair appointment for the day before. True story.

George thinks the first type are over-compensating in pursuit of an empty goal at their own expense, and the second type are chasing vanity, attention or some other second-hand ego fuel.

Whereas Chapter 3 is outward facing and seeing what not to do by example, Chapter 4 looks within and all those times we learned by doing, often doing it wrong. Nearly all of our contributors come from the "hard sciences," fields rooted in biology and mathematics: nutritionists, fitness coaches, medical doctors, physiotherapists. Martin has his Ph.D. in exercise physiology and one of his three MSc.'s is in statistics. Before entering the sports world, George was a naval officer trained in nuclear engineering. Yet we all found ourselves devoting more and more time to understanding the psychology and philosophy of those around us, and making explicit our own, in order to do those "hard science" jobs.

Chapters 5, 6 and 7 are the "ego playbook": things you can do and things you shouldn't do to develop a healthy ego, manifest your ego in healthy ways and deal with the less healthy egos around you.

Chapter 8 arises from one of the most difficult tasks in sports. After a few years, you find yourself trying to explain to family members, friends and recent graduates one of the greatest absurdities of this industry: there are people in it whose personal ambitions are divorced from team winning.

You can't afford to make decisions casually in high-performance environments. Your decisions reflect your knowledge, experience, judgment and values. When a colleague questions or undercuts your decision, which of those are they aiming at? In Chapter 9, our contributors take us through how they approached situations where they first had to understand if they were being challenged on matters of opinion and implementation, or the values that define who they are and why they are there.

By that point in the book, you may be wondering why anyone would ever want to work in high-performance sport. Trust us, we've all asked that question. In fact, that question is at the core of why Martin conceived of this book and George ego'd his way into working with him on it.

Our line of work has some of the most recognizable brands and icons in the world, but what Jesus Olmo told us applies to the prestige and social cachet within some corners of tech, finance, law and many other fields: "The logo hides everything."

Chapter 10 is about recognizing when your life's work is irreconcilably in conflict with your job. Your ego is transmitting distress signals that you may not understand, may not want to hear and are afraid to act upon. Ultimately, you're left with the choice: their logo or your ego.

MEET OUR CONTRIBUTORS: WHAT IS EGO TO THEM?

Keith D'Amelio, performance and sports scientist, formerly Toronto Raptors and Boston Celtics: To me, ego is more than just what the actual definition says (a sense of self-esteem or self-importance). While I do think the ego has aspects of both self-esteem and self-importance, ego is self-identity. That is why so many people in pro sports deal with ego issues: their whole identity is tied to the badge on their shirt. Without it, they don't know how to function or know who they are.

Karim Hader, Performance Scientist at Kitman Labs, former Head of Performance at PSG Academy: The consciousness and the different representations of myself, depending on the domains. Ego may be interchangeable with self-esteem, pride, narcissism, power, need of recognition, need to feel unique, energy, fake life / objectives.

Allistair McCaw, author and speaker, team culture and leadership consultant: Simply put, ego to me is self-image. Our ego has everything to do with how we see and how we feel about ourselves. That's where I would start when it comes to defining and explaining ego. The way we think, act, behave, our reactions, our emotions, and how we view the world is closely connected to our ego.

Steve Tashjian, Head of Performance, US Men's National Team: I love Scott Barry Kaufman's idea of the ego. He describes it as "that aspect of the self that has the incessant need to see itself in a positive light." It is incessant, instinctive, primitive and has a role in survival. I agree with Kaufman that the ego should be controlled with a volume dial, not an on / off switch. When turned up too loud, it leads to self-directed decisions that are destructive and exclusive. When turned down to the right volume, it provides a confident mind that is at peace, comfortable with being vulnerable, comfortable with taking calculated risk, allowing for clear decisions that drive the greater good.

Lee Nobes, Head of Physiotherapy, Liverpool Football Club: I am a confident person and I have been taught that your background or what you do doesn't mean one person is better than another. In terms of ego, I like to keep myself fit, take pride in my appearance and wear nice clothes, but I don't feel like I have an ego in terms always putting myself ahead of others.

In my experience, there are two types of ego.

First, in this industry, many times I relate ego with insecurity. Individuals who are confident and back up that confidence with knowledge, skill and experience are less likely to have an ego. Insecurity breeds a lack of trust and the need to prove one's worth within a team or organisation. This, in turn, is exhibited by people exerting an ego in one way or another. In my mind, this type of ego does not portray the true picture of who that person is. It is generally false. This not a positive ego to be working within an elite team environment, but a person's way of creating a fanciful self-image to combat their own insecurities.

The second type of ego in this environment is not only positive but also necessary. Elite athletes have generally grown and developed an ego that is often the result of a self-fulfilling prophecy. Superstar athletes or coaches who have always been told how "good" or "special" they are, and have always been treated differently than others, actually start to believe the hype. If controlled in the right way, this type of ego allows players to thrive in high pressure environments. It allows athletes to continue to believe in themselves through all the challenges that their career throws at them. Whether it is a young player within a first team squad, coping with losses, lack of form or injury, the right type of ego is essential to cope and thrive in this tough terrain.

Paul Balsom, strength & conditioning and athlete performance coach: Understanding the meaning of ego is an important place to start. Everybody has an ego, but some egos are bigger than others.

Having a big ego is usually viewed as being negative, especially for practitioners working in team sports. However, there is still room for "big" egos even in team sports. The problem is that oftentimes such individuals don't have the knowledge and experience to justify their big egos, and they are referred to as egotistical.

Competent practitioners with relatively low egos can still be successful in team sports, although career pathways can progress more slowly. And, unfortunately, good practitioners with low egos, at least in the short term, can be overtaken by "average" practitioners with bigger egos. The importance of understanding and nurturing your own ego should not be underestimated.

Ben Ashworth, physiotherapist-turned-Director of Performance: Ego is about my personal identity. It can be used to describe my feeling of self-importance. In the high stakes environments that we work in, ego can often be deflated or inflated in relation to other people that we interact with in our teams and with the athletes that we work with. Ego can also positively or negatively influence the decisions that we make every day, and can be influenced by our position in an organisation's structure.

Mathieu Lacome, Chief Performance and Analytics Officer at Parma FC, former Head of Research and Innovation at Paris Saint-Germain: The ego is the illusion that one has of oneself, and which leads to two types of complexes. A superiority complex (narcissism), which pushes the leader to see only his qualities and to exaggerate them by denying his limits and weaknesses. And the inferiority complex (neurosis), which leads the leader to see only his defects and weaknesses and to ignore his strengths.

Doesn't mean ego is good or bad. Everyone, to achieve at high-level, needs to have some ego to believe in his qualities, to take risks and move forward. The issue is when ego polarizes people into a superiority complex, blocking them from seeing solutions / opportunities other than the one they had imagined themselves. Ego is bad when people hide behind their narcissism or their superiority complex to deny by fear that other people in the room can be smarter than them.

The level of ego - the amount of self-importance - has negative consequences on both ends of the spectrum. Too little can be just as detrimental as too much. And some ego is required for the world to progress.

Johan Swensson, Fitness Coach, Sweden Football Association: A reflection of the self-image that is translated into behaviour with more or less self-interest in focus.

As a player, a certain amount of ego was important to look after your own interests in order to survive among the competition. But as a coach, it's about doing the exact opposite and putting your ego (your own interest) aside and focusing on how to work together with players, coaches and other staff in the best way possible. This, however, also must relate to the family role where ego can be detrimental to relationships. We, as coaches / teachers, always can do "more," which is not necessarily better. Often, it comes at the expense of families / relationships. I once listened to a podcast who phrased it FOMO, fear of missing out, which sums that dilemma up pretty well.

Rafel Pol, fitness coach, Spanish National Team: I think ego is what separates you from all that surrounds you, and that is a double-edged sword. From my point of view, ego is a personal constraint which can be harmful, but at the same time is something you need to achieve top level goals.

I think is so hard to be able to do what you need to become a top player if you don't trust yourself more than any one. As example, it's hard to expect a goalkeeper would dare to play out from the back with short passes under the opposing team's high press in an important game without a big ego. As this goalkeeper thinks he is better than anyone, he can make those passes under pressure, both the psychological type and the football kind. But, at the same time, if he's not in the starting XI he will be deeply irritated. In fact, he thinks he is better than anyone, so it's not fair (from his point of view) to not be in the XI.

Other problems can emerge outside the pitch when players and people in general, which includes coaches and staff, are not able to control that ego, to stop him and to understand that their job skills don't exempt them from fulfilling certain obligations in life.

For me, ego is a state of being, which exists to an extent in everyone, tied up with one's personal identity and self-importance. It can inhibit doing the right thing for people or an organisation. In a highly hostile environment, such as elite sport, ego can also be protective, as it defends against exploitation from colleagues or the impression that you are "soft." (8)

I recognize an ego in somebody with "excessive gaze on herself / himself exclusively, loss of recognition and notion of the other, arrogance and deterministic attitudes that harm relationships and make coexistence in any field practically an impossible mission, somebody that has the assumption that he / she is always right, and that everyone else is wrong; or that he himself holds a position above the rest." Somebody that centers his /her entire universe around himself, lacking empathy and is probably protectionist, selfish and defensive. (10)

Andrew Wiseman, Director of Performance, OL Reign: More interested in thy self than being altruistic. Personal gain is greater than serving others.

Darren Burgess, performance coach, Melbourne Demons, formerly Arsenal and Liverpool: Ego is your need to feel validated in your actions and beliefs, regardless of their accuracy / relevance.

Steve Ingham, founder, Supporting Champions: Ego is where my own competitiveness, my urge to drive gets in the way of my own effectiveness.

Craig Duncan, Human Performance Strategist, Performance Intelligence Agency: Ego is the enemy and stops progress - it's that voice in my head that tells me I'm always right and others are wrong.

Adam Johnson, physiotherapist, Stoke City Football Club: I would define "ego" as a character trait whereby you lose clear sight of your own attributes (both positive and negative) and assume that your beliefs and opinions are the best and there is not another way to work or think. You also lose sight of what is important to those around you and become selfish.

Jo Clubb, performance science consultant, formerly Buffalo Bills, Buffalo Sabres, Chelsea FC: I think one's ego relates to their conscious perception of their self-importance. The ego itself is not your actual value but your perception of your value, importance or esteem. When the perception is not aligned with reality, it provides challenges in how you conduct yourself and how you interact with others.

As Ryan Holiday states in his book Ego is the Enemy: "If ego is the voice that tells us we're better than we really are, we can say ego inhibits true success by preventing a direct and honest connection to the world around us."

Garrison Draper, Performance Director, Philadelphia Union: In the context of this book / interview, ego is the drive for self-recognition within your role or job. In our field, there is no hiding from recognition. To get the next job, to get a raise, to bring in new/elite clients, to share your work with colleagues will all require a portion of your ego to be at work and expecting some recognition. Ego has its positives, its necessities, but there comes a point where it can also hamper relationships and productivity in the field, and this is where the management of the ego is important.

Colm Fuller, Head of Physiotherapy, Sports Surgery Clinic, Dublin: Ego is a person's sense of self-importance, by definition, but I would add that often it can be almost unknown to them; and the bigger the ego, the more unaware they become of it. I sometimes confuse ego with insecurity - in elite sport in particular, where weakness can be perceived as a problem, the reluctance to say "I don't know" prevents proper reflection. Ego can limit reflection and in the past, I was certainly more reluctant to show weakness than I am now. It actually requires confidence and self-assurance to realise its ok not to know the answers but to recognise how to find the answers by asking the right questions

Ego is that little monster that lives inside us all, that tells us that we are either better or worse than other people. The ego is always fighting to ensure its own survival, it is always hungry for more power, more money and more importance. Ultimately, if you live to satisfy your ego, you will NEVER be happy, because the ego is never happy with what it currently has, it always wants more. (6)

Paul Laursen, physiologist, sport scientist, entrepreneur: Taking a page out of Sam Harris, I define the ego as the illusion of the self. Inevitably, as creatures in the world that seek to survive, we learn from a very young age that when we protect our "self," and do "good" in the world, we are rewarded. This positive conditioning of the self manifests into a strong ego.

Obviously, sport is prime for conditioning the ego / self to very high levels: play or perform well and you are rewarded. This feels good, and why would you want to ever lose this? So we defend our ego, our worth, our self, in any way we can - pushing to always win, and when we don't, we place fault and blame elsewhere.

Sport is just one example. The same principles hold in academia, business, relationships and all across life. It certainly holds purpose, but it can get away from us. At the extreme level, we can observe Donald Trump's behaviours. Behaviours around politics, religion, even nutrition are other examples where an ego mindset often prevails over rational thought.

So I would define a person with a strong ego as one that doesn't appear to see a differing viewpoint from their own in the moment. Here, one appears locked into their one way / system of doing things, or in their belief system. The behaviour tends to be more reactive and less considered. They use fast vs. slow thinking. They provide an opinion or belief at the expense of rational thought. The ego or self is extremely useful for progress and achievement in life, however it limits progress in many contexts.

Sébastien Carrier, Director of Performance, Coach Corner: Ego is your constant willingness to be right, and feel more important than others.

Benjamin Kugel, performance coach, PSV Eindhoven, former German National Team: I see ego more as a negative than a positive. When ego drives, it's going to be a one-way street. But you need a minimal level of ego, as well, not to stall in elite football!

Paul Quetin, National Strength & Conditioning Coach, French Tennis Federation: Success in elite sport requires a clever mix of oversized egos and humility. Self-confidence is a great asset as long as it doesn't make you blind.

Steve Barrett, former Director of Sport Science and Research Innovation, Hull City: Ego should be seen as both a positive and a negative within our industry. It's the level of that ego and the management of it that will help provide insights into organisations and allow them to succeed.

egoalsbook.com

2 | EGO AS A DRIVE

Remember that competence freaks out most people.

– Eric Blahic, soccer coach, formerly Paris Saint-Germain, Bordeaux and French National Women's Team.

Claude Onesta coached France's men's handball team from 2001 to 2016. He holds one of the most successful handball coaching records, leading his team to gold medals in two Olympic Games, three World Championships and three European Championships.

"Ego is the petrol in your car," Onesta said [Onesta, 2014]. "The worse thing in a team is not to have egos. Without ego you don't have ambition, and people without ambition don't win anything. With ego, you showcase your ambitions – and the greater the ambitions you showcase, the greater your determination needs to be, and the greater the work you need to put in to achieve your goals and make success happen. The more you talk, the more you need to prove – and this is exactly what, as a manager, I use to get the most of my players and build up a winning culture in a team."

Onesta outlined the steps in positive, high-performance ego development: ambition, achievement, determination, work. It's a cycle, and each time you go through it, everything gets a little bigger. Including, rightly, the ego.

Thinking of ego as an "executive" frames the process of how ego links our past performance and current capabilities to the realities of the outside world, which includes what's out there for us to achieve next.

The executive ego evaluates what we've done in order to understand what we can do next. It weighs the potential rewards against each other and against what it will take to obtain them. It looks at the opportunity cost: what else could we be doing, as high-performance people usually have several options and ambitions to pursue. The executive has to convert the currencies of money, prestige and self-esteem to decide, organize and execute our priorities. Fame, fortune and fulfillment do not always come as a package. The executive ego chooses the desired result and lays out all the steps – all the little transactions and trade-offs – necessary to achieve it.

Then, in pursuit of goals far down the road with a low probability of success, the executive ego has to act at a scale that seems almost trivial.

For an athlete, it's things like knowing and committing to what to eat and when, and how much sleep to get. And evaluating who they should listen to on such matters, knowing how much is at stake.

ZLATAN IBRAHIMOVIC: EXTRAORDINARY PLAYER, EXTRAORDINARY EGO

Think you know ego? Meet Zlatan Ibrahimovic, the man who, when offered a trial at Arsenal as a teenager, told Arsene Wenger that he does not do auditions.

His confidence can leave people asking which side of arrogant he sits on. He forces them to compare his self-assessment to their assessment of reality: is he actually that good? Does he have the chops to back it up when he speaks of himself in the third person, says things like "I can play in the 11 positions because a good player can play anywhere," and calls himself Ibracadabra?

"I don't think that you can score as spectacular a goal as those of Zlatan in a video game -- even though these games are very realistic these days."

 Zlatan Ibrahimović ✓ @Ibra_official · Nov 13, 2017 ⌄

We are Zweden

🗨 1.9K   ⟲ 26.8K   ♡ 111.9K   ⬆

Ibrahimovic's self-regard is so high that when the Swedish national team qualified for the 2018 World Cup, Ibrahimovic made it about him, despite not playing any part in the feat.

Ibrahimovic is the ultimate reference for how a confident, forceful ego can be positive.

Martin: Having worked for two years with Zlatan Ibrahimovic, I have been privileged to understand a bit the dynamic of his personality. His ego is the pinnacle of self-confidence, which brings him an extraordinary strength and resilience both on and outside the pitch.

And since this ego, which he never forgets is all about him, is ultimately focused on performance and winning, it's difficult to blame him for it.

His confidence is transmitted to his teammates, staff, and all the people around him. The wind is pushing the whole team from the back. There is no limit. Everything is possible. It's pretty surprising how he can affect people's behaviour around him, and I would say it's for the best overall. His expectations are so high about everything that practitioners need to do their best to help and serve him. Cultivate excellence for him and the others will follow.

By far, he is the player who had the greatest influence on me as a practitioner. No one else comes close.

During sessions, he would always ask why we were doing one exercise and not another, so you had to be REALLY sure about why you had programmed X and not Y exercise. And if you did not have a good answer, he would simply destroy you in front of everyone.

On the contrary, doing the right things right was the standard, so he would never comment when things went well!

When I would f*** up something in terms of a decision for the team or the program, or not perform at (his) high standard, he wouldn't talk to me for a few days or weeks. When things were going in the right direction, he would be my best mate and provide me with (often good) advice.

One evening in 2015, we were playing in the Champions League at Chelsea, and he got a red card after 32 minutes of play. He came back in the locker room, really pissed, of course. Since it was just before half time, I was back there as well, preparing the nutrition for half time and adjusting our two light therapy lamps in the locker room.

The visitors' locker room at Chelsea is extremely small (like one you would expect in an amateur club, to be honest), which is very surprising for a club of this standard, but this is probably a way to add pressure to the visiting team. So it was very challenging to fit all of our gear - extra clothes, physio tables, warm-up equipment, etc - in there and still have room for the players and staff! As half time approached, I started to become a bit stressed as I realized that I would not be ready on time for the players' return from the pitch.

We were down to three minutes before the players would come back in, and seeing me dealing with the mess of my energy drinks and lamps in between clothes and boots all over the floor, Zlatan asked me:

"Hey Genius (that was the nickname he gave me, since I always had "great" ideas, he said)! What's the most important thing right now for the guys that are going to need to play 10 v 11 for another 45 minutes (it would, in fact, be 75 minutes since we went into extra time): to feed them well, or your f***ing hopeless UV lamps? Get them away now! Unless you have a good reason, and then I can help you fit them somewhere in this shit, but let me know and move your ass!"

Needless to say, we immediately pulled the lamps out and made some space for the energy drinks just in time for half time!

EXECUTIVE EGO GROWS THROUGH INVESTMENTS, NOT SACRIFICES

Nobody is going to put a limit on what I'm doing. I'm going to do what I want to do, when I want to do it...If I want something I am going to go and get it.

– Michael Phelps

When the ego does its job well, we generate a healthy return of self-esteem on our investment and effort - along with some amount of money, praise, promotion, prestige or whatever else we hope to get out of the endeavor. Those fuel a virtuous cycle of ambition and achievement. When the ego starts experiencing rewards beyond the ordinary, it develops ambitions beyond the ordinary. Working at that level becomes natural because it feels natural, it feels right - because it is right.

Yet once people achieve something there's this strange expectation that they should completely change their approach and mindset. Now that they've "made it," they should neglect or purge the driving force that got them there. What about their future goals? What about enjoying the rewards of making it as far as they have, while still striving for whatever is next?

So much for dancing with the one that brought you. If anything, the conventional wisdom to is sacrifice the one that brought you.

Sacrifice. Other than "ego" itself, no word pushed us to understand everything about this undertaking and each other than "sacrifice." Like "ego," it's a dangerously misused and misunderstood word that leaves you ruing what people would think, do and achieve if they really knew what they were saying with the word "sacrifice."

A sacrifice is when you give up something in return for something of lesser value (or nothing). You can sacrifice your money, your time, your effort, a relationship, some aspect of your ambition... whatever it is, as long as you're left with less, it's a sacrifice.

Within sports, saying that a player "selflessly" "sacrifices" for his team is a go-to cliché. Whether it's something they do during a game or how they live off the field, no one ever examines what that player supposedly sacrifices or to what end.

Baseball offers particular clarity. While many sports talk about sacrifice, baseball is the only one that has a stat for it. If the batter gets called out while advancing the base runner - either by hitting a fly ball that gets caught or hitting a grounder resulting in an out at first - he's credited with a sacrifice. It doesn't matter if it was intentional (as would be the case with a bunt) or unintentional (he hit a fly ball into the outfield). The idea is that he "sacrificed" his hit for the greater good of the team, by creating a more advantageous base running situation via the player(s) already on base.

If a player's ambition is to win games and titles - and that's what athletes are there to do, they're there to win - and he improves his team's likelihood of scoring, is that a sacrifice? Only if the batter values the base hit for himself over giving his team a better chance of scoring that inning and, by extension, a better chance of winning the game.

A sacrifice on the scoresheet is only a sacrifice for the player if victory is less important than some other measure in the game.

Let's go back to the night before the game. Did the player sacrifice playing video games until 2am so he could get 9 hours of sleep, or was there a greater reward on offer by turning off all electronic devices at 9pm before a 10pm bedtime so he could wake up motivated, alert and attentive enough to connect with a 95 mph fastball? Did he sacrifice pizza and beer on his off days (or for four years of college), or was that a worthwhile trade-off for the day his phone rang and the guy on the other end said "Pack your bags, kid. We need you on the mound at Fenway Park this weekend."

What does more for the ego: the video games or the home run, the junk food or the pro debut?

On our side of the touchline, you can barely get through a podcast or conversation without hearing a sports performance practitioner talk about all the sacrifices they make for their athletes. Once again, what are we supposedly sacrificing and to what end?

Our purpose and ambition is to make the athletes under our care better. Are the long hours, late nights, weekends on the road, a sleepless night because you noticed a subtle hitch in an athlete's stride the week before a key race and the occasional "that's not my job, but I'll do it anyway because it needs to get done and I think it'll help" really sacrifices? Not if our purpose is doing everything we can to the best of our abilities to maximize each athlete's performance.

When the athlete wins her race or simply steps to the line for the first time after a prolonged injury, when the season ends with a record low number of injuries, when your mentor says "That was amazing work you did these last few months," the inputs seem insignificant.

As long as you can say "Worth it!" then it's not a sacrifice. It was all worth it because your ego has more now than it did at the outset. It has one more reason to positively contrast the self to another or the world, and to have a high assessment of one's abilities against the demands of the external world. That reward, the satisfaction and self-esteem, is what fuels high-performance egos to say "On to the next one!"

Sacrifices truly are selfless and anti-ego. We see this when we get it wrong.

Sometimes the executive ego misreads the situation, overvalues things like prestige and makes poor choices in pursuit of lesser rewards. Only after we start noticing that we're unhappy and unfulfilled do we realize that, yes, we have made a sacrifice. We sacrificed our happiness and our ego to the brand, the logo, the unappreciative player or colleague. Even with the job title, the status or authority, we have less than we did before, and what remains of the ego is sending distress calls. We'll see plenty of those moments in later chapters, along with how to recognize when you've allowed your ego to become the sacrifice on the altar.

All talk of sacrifice is ultimately talk about trade-offs: what you're willing to do now in order to have and be something better later. Only someone with a strong ego will be able to recognize the sacrifices from the investments, and then act in pursuit of the greater value.

Zlatan Ibrahimovic and Claude Onesta epitomize the essential relationship between ambition, achievement and ego. They have their critics, but any objective reality check - whether by their egos or ours - leads to the same conclusion: they've earned it.

THIERRY OMEYER: PERFECTION IS THE STANDARD, CONFIDENCE IS THE WAY

Martin: Thierry Omeyer is considered the best handball goalkeeper of all time, and was selected best player in the world in 2008. He is a five-time world champion, three-time European champion and twice an Olympic champion. Overall, he has won 59 trophies. At his former club THW Kiel, his nickname was *Die Mauer*: The Wall. A member of the French national team for more than 15 years, he also played at other prestigious clubs in France, including Paris Saint-Germain and Montpellier.

As a former (and failed pro) handball player myself, I trained for two years with Thierry in the late 90's, when we were adolescents at the talent training center in Strasbourg.

From my memories of him at that time to watching him later competing at the highest standard on top of the world, what has always been incredible about him are his extreme focus on his game and his unwillingness to accept conceding a single goal. I remember him getting furious at himself, hitting the goal posts with his hands, slamming his shoes on the ground, throwing water bottles and towels all over the court just from seeing a ball fly into the net at the end of a simple training session, where there were no stakes at all. On the other side, if, during a training session, I couldn't manage to score a single goal (I was two years younger and not as talented), he would completely destroy me and take the p*** out of me for a week. He would repeat how good he was... and how sh** I was. This mental game was pretty frightening, and was part of his approach to destabilize his opponents on the court.

In the heat of any match - competitive or friendly - you see him very often pumping his arms in the air after a save, staring the shooter straight in the eye, making sure the shooter knew that he - Thierry Omeyer - denied him a goal. It could just be one save among many others, but to watch Thierry you'd think he just made the save to win the team the cup.

Just about anybody watching this would think it was extreme arrogance, inflammatory boasting and all the other marks of a very egotistical attitude.

But when you know Thierry, you know that it's everything but this. He is an extremely nice guy and full of humility. He uses self-talk and pushes his self-confidence to the highest possible level to give himself every advantage to perform better.

In Thierry's own words:

> You need a constant process to succeed. It's every day, in everything that you do.
>
> I have always wanted to be the best during ALL matches - that is my standard. Although it actually happened once during a friendly match against an amateur team (23-0!!), not conceding a single goal is impossible when playing elite teams. But to be honest, I take every goal as a defeat. I simply can't accept feeling responsible for the team's defeat. When I reached the peak of my career in 2008, what motivated me the most was being able to remain where I was, for as long as possible. Playing well for one game is easy. Repeating top performances over 2, 3, 4 matches in a row is something way more difficult. Consistency. When you win the Olympics, you are walking on the moon. It's so good you just want to win another one. When you have also won the World and European championships one after another, if you really want to leave something behind, you need to keep winning over and over. People expect you to win again, to save more goals. The pressure increases each time, but I have always responded positively and it has always helped me to progress. It's this willingness to last and leave something unique, both as an individual and a team that has helped me to keep working again and again every day to remain the best.
>
> Today, many people think that they give 100% and they believe they're doing it right, but in reality, they are only at 90%. This is not how you become the best. It's about being at 200% ALL the time. Teammates say this also about me. I have such high expectations for myself that I expect the same from others - it is sometimes difficult for the others to cope with me on their back all the time, but in the long term I think it clearly benefits the team.
>
> It's something you have in you from a young age. I have always sought an extremely high level of excellence in everything I do. Looking for perfection in every aspect of my game, but not only at handball: playing cards, football with friends... every single game, it has always been impossible for me to lose. I can't tolerate defeat.
>
> I have a twin, Christian. It was incredibly competitive between us when we were kids. We were always competing against each other, whatever we were doing. I also certainly needed to prove to our parents that I existed as a part of our brotherhood.
>
> This attitude likely also comes from other frustrations I went through when I was younger, like not winning matches in the youngest categories and not being selected to national teams in the younger age groups. My brother and I played in a small club, and we couldn't compete against the larger clubs where most of the young talented players were playing.

I was not being recognized by others as I thought I should be. In the end, you end up putting yourself in this mindset to prove to yourself and others that you can make it. I realize that, in my career, from youth national teams to the senior French National team, every non-selection, match-related frustration, poor playing performance, defeat... every negative has always been almost instantaneously the trigger for me to work harder and, in turn, take a step forward and become better. Many of the coaches who managed me knew this, and used this strategy to make me react and perform when needed.

When THW Kiel - the best club in the world at the time, where the two goalkeepers were also the best at the time - contacted me in 2006, I said: Never mind, I can do it. I thought, if "The Kielers" want me, they must also believe in me. Their confidence that I could make it added to my own. Your self-confidence helps you risk things when opportunity comes. You need to challenge yourself to be better.

When there is no challenge, there can be no progress.

Every match, when people were congratulating me, I was happy, of course, but always saying no, no, I can do better - just wait and you will see - because really I knew I could do better. You know yourself and know what you can do. Knowing yourself is key to controlling your ego and what you can achieve.

We won everything, especially with Kiel and the French national team and I am proud to say that I had an impact. But the numbers say it - not me, not my ego.

EGO NEEDS ACHIEVEMENT, NOT HEADLINES

Martin: Summer of 1999. I was the strength & conditioning coach and a player for a handball team in Strasbourg, France, competing in the fourth tier of the sport.

I was right in the middle of my post-grad studies and already at the height of the left part of the Dunning-Kruger curve. I understood everything about human physiology from the books of A.V Hill and Per-Olof Åstrand. I knew everything about the Russian training block principles. And I was just craving to make an impact on the court with my team and hopefully reach the elite level as a coach, since I didn't succeed myself as a player.

But I also wanted that impact off the court. Via the university's first internet connections for students, I had just found access to all this growing sport science literature, which was fascinating to me. I was also enrolled in a strength & conditioning master course, where the lectures were only given by professional and well-published sport scientists working in top clubs like Juventus and Inter Milan. They were lecturing us on how things worked on their side of their pitch, far from the university bench! Too good!! I was just ready and dreaming to be part of this world. I just needed to find out what would be the entry point.

I understood that I needed to be creative to be noticed, but being only 21 with little experience at the elite level and a native French speaker with pretty limited English writing skills, I had a few early obstacles.

I then started to study more English and put myself in the habit of reading 5, 10, sometimes more papers a day, to understand the vocabulary and the rhythms of a scientific publication. This only made me progress higher on the Dunning-Kruger curve.

In parallel to this personal journey, I was somewhat mentored and deeply influenced by three great men: Alain Quintallet, who a few years later would become the strength & conditioning coach of the French National Handball team and win the Olympics, and the World and European Championships alongside Thierry Omeyer; Michel Dufour, my lecturer at the university and a strength & conditioning coach for many first division soccer clubs in different leagues; and Philippe Lambert. Ten years later, Lambert would start to work with Laurent Blanc at the French National Football team and then at PSG, and he would be the one enrolling me in all those adventures with him and Blanc.

Those three guys were incredibly influential to me at that time, and while I was as full of ideas as I was of self-confidence, they gave me the extra support to undertake the process of creating a new fitness test. I had found the flying ticket to my dream. The rest was only a matter of physiology and sport science!

The idea was simple. For many reasons that aren't important for this book, the typical fitness tests we were all using in team sports were lacking sensitivity to each player's individual profile: some are heavy and tall, other are short and light, some are quick, others lack explosive power, some have good coordination skills, others not, etc. It was clear that we, as a community, needed another tool. That tool would allow a more relevant player evaluation, but, more importantly, help all of us to better individualize athletes' high-intensity interval training.

It took me more than a year of further readings, talks with my mentors and trials to seal the definitive protocol in July 2000 [Buchheit, 2010]. On different surfaces, at different venues, I personally trialled more than 30 different versions of the test, based on different increments, stage duration, recovery periods, etc! For many reasons detailed elsewhere, I came up with the following formula: repeated 40-meter shuttle-runs lasting 30 seconds, interspersed with 15 seconds of active (walking) recovery, and a speed increment of 0.5 km/h per stage [Buchheit, 2008].

Twenty years and over 200 publications later, the test has become the reference test to assess fitness in team and racquet sports. From Champions League soccer to the NBA, top 14 rugby clubs, Handball, Futsal, AFL, NHL or top tennis players, the test is used in every sport and in every part of the world.

It has its own app, which had 2000 downloads in the first 15 days when released in 2018; audio files in French, English and Spanish; various versions of the test, including different starting speeds and adapted protocols such as 28-meter shuttles (the length of a basketball court), along a 400-meter athletics track, and, of course, the ice hockey version. People can find the latest news about publications, use cases and users' testimony on the blog, Twitter and Instagram accounts we set up to keep people informed and engaged about the test.

The lessons from this journey?

While I still don't know where this strong internal drive to make an impact really comes from, what is sure is that I could count on the strength of my ego. I had the courage to put myself out there to create a new test, going up against a bunch of well-known and valid tests already in use, all of which were supported and promoted by some of the big guns in the industry.

My ego helped me to preserve my self-confidence and faith in the project despite people telling me that I was going to re-invent a wheel that a new test was not needed. I have been able to use those critics positively and in turn, reinforce my ideas: I truly believed that creating an intermittent shuttle test would solve a specific problem for me first, and that of a whole profession later.

I also probably had the naïveté to believe that I could do all of this while I was only 21, and when I knew nothing, in reality, about how to train top players. But all this helped me to put the work in and make it happen.

Looking back, I am obviously proud of this achievement, and the fact that the test has changed the way practitioners test and train players in so many sports. I am satisfied if my work continues to help athletes perform better. And I am fulfilled if, in fact, my work has had an impact on other people's lives.

I am also happy that while this was driven by my motivation to reach the elite level as a coach and sport scientist, I did it in order to solve a problem and help our community.

There was one other thing I knew I wanted for this test: I did not want it to become known as the "Buchheit test." Many of the other tests in sports science (and elsewhere) carry their creator's name, e.g., the Leger tests, the Conconi test, the Gacon test, the Lambert test… Whether these were self-given or bestowed by the test's users, this could never be an option. So, before this idea could germinate in a user's mind, I named it the "30-15 Intermittent Fitness Test," which simply describes what it is.

EGO IS NECESSARY TO COMPETE

If you are too nice, you will just get eaten alive. The football world is not always a nice place.

– *Zlatan Ibrahimovic*

Ego can be necessary, when well-managed, because having a high opinion of oneself obliges you and makes you work harder and better than others to maintain that "status," to show that you are really better and not to disappoint. This process also raises confidence and results in high performance. To obtain challenging and ambitious results, in general, it helps more to have an ego than not to have one, as long as it forces you to work harder. (Juan Carlos Álvarez Campillo)

It has been suggested that the best athletes cannot make it to the very top without such ego. LeBron James calls himself a king, Zlatan Ibrahimovic calls himself a lion, and Muhammed Ali proclaimed himself "The Greatest," to name a few. (Jo Clubb)

Every single person involved in elite sport (participants or support staff) step across the white line and put themselves up against the very best athletes and practitioners in their chosen sport or field of expertise. They relish the challenge of working with and competing against the best, often in a very public arena. (Nick Grantham)

Sport is based on competition. You are only successful in competition at the highest level if you have confidence in your ability. Add money, fame, and the desire to compete, and I feel that grows egos subconsciously. (Duncan French)

Sebastien Gardillou, national coach, French Handball Federation: The competitive spirit that characterizes elite sport eventually translates to staff, who identify themselves with the game. In turn, they show increased self-confidence and ego.

Iñigo Mujika, sports physiologist, coach and academic: Some degree of ego is required to succeed in elite sport.

Frederic Bougeant, handball coach: To me, ego is too poorly perceived. But if you don't have any, there is no way you can succeed at the elite level in sports.

Yann Le Meur, sport scientist and entrepreneur, AS Monaco, French Agency of Sport: Without ego, you simply can't exist in elite sport! You need to involve yourself at 200% at all levels to succeed; you need a strong ego to do so.

To be successful as an athlete, you must be SELFISH. You focus most of your energy on becoming the best you can be each and every day. You don't let others distract you from your goals. (6)

I think you need to be selfish to get to the top as an athlete, and there is no problem with that, but some can't differentiate between the selfishness to get to the top, and how it can affect others (Andrew Wiseman).

Tom Vandenbogaerde, Lead Physiologist, Swimming Australia: It's not so much the desire to win but absolutely hating to lose in elite sport. One might need to be self-centred to be the very best. Winners take control. They look where they can improve and they know what they need to win. Obviously, self-belief and getting things done is super important in this regard.

Ego and self-confidence go hand-in-hand, and to stand up in front of people who are deemed the best of the best, you need to have a little of both to be taken seriously. (Garrison Draper)

The pressure and tension in elite sport is brutal. I would argue that only people with ego volume control can survive. (Steve Tashjian)

Working with the athlete population that I work with right now, big egos are everywhere. I would go so far as to say, more than any sport I have worked with, these athletes have the biggest egos. Not because they have the most money and all the fancy shit, but the ego to know that when they go into a fight they are simply going to beat their opponent up! Add to that the promotional side of prize fighting, where you are trying to drum up fan engagement and interest (for which Conor McGregor is clearly the best in the world), and it's a melting pot for big egos! (Duncan French)

STRONG EGOS CONNECT AMBITION, EFFORT AND PERFORMANCE

A PERSONAL DRIVE FOR IMPROVEMENT

I think I am difficult to satisfy, because when I win something, I'm already thinking about the next step, and that is maybe a problem for me. I'm not enjoying the moment. I'm already on the mission to win the next trophy.

— Zlatan Ibrahimovic

Franck Kuhn, strength & conditioning coach, French Basketball Federation: My ego has always helped me progress in such a way that I tend to never be satisfied with my knowledge, my skills and my current situation. I constantly question myself and tend to believe that others do things better than me. To be able to show my confidence to others, I need always improve, while obviously understanding my limits.

Being competitive to succeed, driving to get good, investing hard in reflecting and learning, being willing to connect and explore things that no one else is. (Steve Ingham)

Jonny King, rehabilitation physiotherapist: I think my ego allows me to go into work every day with the question "What does excellence look like?" at the forefront of my mind - even "What does world-class look like?" My ego drives my personal standards and provides me a motivation to provide the highest quality of care possible for the athletes I work with. However, for me - and I have learnt this through experience - the art comes in appreciating that not every colleague you work with will have the same mindset – personal mantras and philosophies differ, and being appreciative and respectful of this is key to making sure your ego does not negatively impact team dynamics.

Of course, there is a "positive side" of the ego or FOMO ("fear of missing out") that enables you to invest time and resources in yourself. In education, for example. This means, for me, not being satisfied if I have a university diploma, but rather seek opportunities to educate myself. For example, by setting a certain amount of my salary aside as a personal development account since 2008, investing private savings to develop further with EXOS international mentorships, World Football Academy courses, etc. etc. (Johan Swensson)

Working in sport at a young age, getting recognition for doing well in sport and triathlon. Ego was stroked. Made me work harder, more success, work harder again... until I reached an endpoint realization. Ego crushed - time to shift to doing something else :) (Paul Laursen)

Ivi Casagrande, sports scientist and performance coach: When I started coaching, I spent two years coaching for a college team. At the end of those two years, I started to understand and realize I was good enough to be working somewhere else. I don't think it was a negative ego guiding me, but the type of ego that I knew my worth and knew that I was not getting the recognition I deserved financially; and, also, the understanding that I was at a point that I was not learning anything and hitting a plateau. So, I was brave enough to leave a place where I was comfortable and was really passionate about the people I worked with, to go to something unknown that would challenge me on a different level.

The world of academia. Grad student. Learned to publish or perish. More publications meant more success. Fast promotion through the ranks of academia, more opportunities, more confidence in myself. Lecturing to 100's. The great Professor Paul. Conference invitations and world travel. (Paul Laursen)

I started to work at the top level so young. Nevertheless, my ambition to be better and better (even the best) and nonconformist pushed me to work and study every day to become it. I think, at least in part, that desire is fed by ego. (Rafel Pol)

Jeremy Sheppard, Integrated Support Team Lead, Canada Snowboard / Senior Advisor to Canadian Sport Institute: I had enough ego / stubborn confidence to overcome a poor undergraduate experience and less than stellar academic pedigree to complete advanced degrees. I've also published a fair bit in academic journals, which was mostly driven by my ego to rebel and do what was not expected of me.

I feel like having confidence in my abilities, knowing that I have put in the work (and will continue to put in the work to better myself) has allowed my whole career progression. Having a bit of ego is essential for success - it is only when it hinders you from improving that it hurts your progress. (Keith D'Amelio)

Mmmmm, I think there may have been times where my desire to be better than others forced me to work at my craft, and even getting a Ph.D. was probably highly related to ego. (Craig Duncan)

Adam Douglas, sport scientist and strength coach, Catapult Sports and Hockey Canada: I'm sure it played a role in going back to school to complete my Ph.D. part-time while working at a university and with Hockey Canada... along with raising a young family. There were times where I felt overwhelmed and overloaded with no end in sight. Internally, I wasn't going to let myself quit - I did not want to suffer that blow, too.

Alexandre Dellal, strength & conditioning coach and sport science researcher: My ego is a constant drive to examine, test, trial and discover new things, read and look deeper into whatever is related to my work. It pushes me to progress endlessly. That's how and why I leaned new training techniques, skills and languages. All this work is self-driven, self-organized, and I got a lot from chats with people with more experience than me. I am using every opportunity to learn from others, whatever their background, confirmed or young practitioners, etc. Exchanging opinions and listening is key to being better, regardless of whether you think in terms of being "the best."

Stuart Yule, Head of Strength & Conditioning, Scotland National Rugby Team: My ambition has helped me progress, along with my dissatisfaction for a status quo and mediocrity. This may come across as ego, which may very well be the case in the "frustration phase" of not making progress. However, I moved quickly from this phase to the systematic process phase where rational thought and interaction takes over.

Julien Robineau, strength & conditioning coach, French Rugby Federation: Each day, your ego motivates you to do the best and to be the best. I try to maximise my ego to make the absolute best of myself.

EGO, THE FATHER OF SELF-CONFIDENCE

Stuart McMillan, lead short sprint coach and CEO, ALTIS: I think it is difficult to succeed in high-performance without a healthy dose of self-importance - which is on a similar continuum as self-confidence. The ability to believe that I am able to do something has underpinned everything I have done, and this wouldn't be possible without an ego.

A certain level of ego can be beneficial in some circumstances in professional sport. For example, having a level of ego can help relate to professional footballers and create a sense of commonality. Although this isn't a specific situation, I believe illustrating a sense of egotism, balanced with humility, has helped me develop a level of respect amongst professional footballers. (Alex Calder)

Pierre Lassus, strength & conditioning consultant, former coach Top 14 Rugby and PSG Women: The high self-confidence I had, especially when I started, helped me get respect and gain trust from coaches and players. It helped me progress in the hierarchy of the different clubs I worked with.

Andrew Young, physiotherapist and fitness coach: I have not always had a naturally high self-confidence but with age I have become more confident. I definitely had to manipulate my ego (change volume) when dealing with Usain Bolt at the Central Coast Mariners in Australia. He was taking a great deal of reputational risk in attempting to transition to professional football. And myself, I had to be in a leadership role so that we could transition him into the program and that he could trust me to help him do so. I needed to display my confidence to him in the project so that he could trust me to help him. Those great athletes like Usain can see weakness in your eyes in a second, so I worked on my ego volume so that he could see that I was confident in what I was doing and that I was also very calm. This shut down any potential communication barriers between us and built respect between us.

A portion of your ego is your own self confidence. We, as practitioners, must believe in ourselves if we expect the coaches we work with and athletes we train to believe in us and adopt the recommendations we are giving. Many of our athletes have great self-confidence / self-belief, which is why they can pull off extremely difficult tasks in high pressure situations. (Garrison Draper)

Andrew Murray, Chief Medical Officer, European Tour, Ryder Cup Europe: Having a degree of self-confidence is, I think, almost necessary in performance sport, whether you are competing or whether you are helping athletes to be their best. I don't know if believing in yourself is ego, but if you don't think you will succeed, you won't. Having confidence in yourself gives you a chance.

Again, this is probably similar to rehabilitation cases where there are strong time pressures and demands. I would look to fill the player with confidence that I am the right therapist for their case by being confident and firm that I believe I can get them better on an aggressive time scale, reinforcing with previous positive outcomes. This may come across as having an ego, as it is an unquestionable "arrogance," even if maybe you yourself have doubts deep down! (Adam Johnson)

Especially at the beginning of a new process and facing difficulties to convince athletes to work hard consistently. They will test you every day until results show you were right to push them. (3)

Every time the management changed (coach and sporting director), my role and responsibilities were challenged. People don't know you. You need to be active to handle the situation and survive. Without a strong ego that gives you the energy to show you value and defend your position, you may struggle into those circumstances. (2)

When you coach important teams it's easier for your ambitions to rise and your dreams come true. But before getting to coaching those teams, my dad was an amateur player and I started as a PE teacher. My ego gave me the strength of conviction that I could make it - starting from very far away. Without it, it would have been impossible in the highly competitive world of elite sports!! (Frederic Bougeant)

Tom Little, performance coach, Preston North End: My ego means I have a fine line between assertiveness and aggression. When working with a group of ego-driven young men, and driving many things they don't want to do, you need that air of consequences. You may lose the odd battle when you spill into aggressiveness but you win the war.

At the start of my career, I was often perceived as arrogant. One of the biggest problems in France is that someone who openly shows his ambitions is perceived as arrogant. When I started coaching, I kept saying that I was doing my job to win titles and trophies, and that I wanted to be the best coach. I didn't see the problem since it was my (and everyone's) objective. But it cost me just to make it public. We ended up (so far) winning 16 titles in 16 years, and every time I mention this, I am described as someone with a big ego!! In French, we say about someone with a big head (big ego) that "he has a melon," like the fruit. I prefer the melon from Spain. (Frederic Bougeant)

Dave Martin, professor of exercise science, Australian Catholic University: When presenting and defending research findings or training concepts to elite athletes, a strong, confident approach can be beneficial. Although ego and self-confidence are strongly aligned, I think the positive aspects of ego are good when a strong lead and conviction is required.

Johann Bilsborough, Director of Performance & Rehabilitation, a National Football League team: Unsure if it was ego, but having the confidence to stand up for what you think is right when everyone else in the room is too scared to have an opinion or tell the truth because they are scared of losing their job.

Andrea Belli, performance sport rehabilitation and return-to-play specialist, FC Inter Milan: Years ago, during a staff meeting concerning a complicated injury and recovery, I expressed my point calmly but firmly arguing with my Head of Department, explaining that, working with the player for months, I knew his conditions and I could tell that he was not ready to return to training with the team even if his clinical situation was good. At the end, the HOD followed my suggestion. My ego helped me support my ideas in that case.

It's difficult sometimes to split ego and responsibility. The staff and I were talking about whether an injured player would be available for the next game, and eventually play if the coach decided it. They were not convinced, but I insisted that, because he worked with a plan and given his evolution, he could make it. I could have said nothing, just to be on the safe side. Ego or responsibility? The player started on the bench and played the last 30 minutes without problems. (Dave Martin)

Knowing my strengths (for example, training periodisation and S&C planning) helped me handle discussions with over 100 international coaches and players, where I would be telling them I did not agree with what they were saying. I have always been respectful and open, which overall helped me gained their trust so we could progress. (Mathieu Lacome)

Being prepared to take on a speaking engagement early in my career. Standing in front of an audience and speaking about strength & conditioning has led to so many other speaking engagements, conferences, courses, lectures. Taking that initial step opened up a whole new avenue in my career. It afforded me the opportunity to travel the world and meet the clever kids in class! (Nick Grantham)

CRUCIAL DECISIONS: GOT EGO?

Pierre Mangin, coach, French Handball Federation: I've made some very difficult coaching decisions, which wouldn't have been possible without a very strong level of confidence related to my ego. Had the outcome been different, it would be considered a failure today! I have, for example, decided to bench players for various reasons, hoping they would make the difference when entering as subs later on. It was my ego against theirs: if they responded positively, the team would win. If not…. But overall, it taught me how two egos, if well-managed, can do incredible things together when trying to prove the other wrong.

Marc Quod, sport scientist and high performance manager: Ego is probably a large part of the (my) internal driver / motivation that helps overcome the fear of speaking up, of providing a dissenting or alternate view and of trying something different. Although a sport scientist / coach should always make decisions on good quality data, there are inevitably situations where no data exist, yet we need to make a decision. I think ego helps us deliver that decision, helps us go forward knowing that the outcome may not be what we expect. And when the outcome is a failure, to then front up and do it again the next time. OR maybe overcoming that failure is actually overcoming your ego...?

Darcy Norman, physical therapist, performance coach and athletic trainer with the US National Team, Kitman Labs: Your ego helps you progress when you have to make real-time, quick decisions and apply the correct response in the right situation. Whether that was a decision to hold someone out because of injury or be able to push someone harder in training while taking a risk and everything working out. It has also been helpful in defending my positions based on my values in times when the management group did not see eye-to-eye on various decisions or outcomes. I have gone above a superior to voice my opinion on what I thought was right in a specific situation, which earned me trust and competence within the staff. When I feel extremely strong that I am correct in the situation I will say it, but if I have doubt at all I will typically try and seek a better understanding of the context before my ego pushes on the information.

In the Summer of 2014, we returned to the United States from England. In September of that year, I joined Gregg Berhalter's staff at Columbus Crew Soccer Club as High Performance Director. I used the rest of the season to evaluate the needs of the team and the high-performance department. Together as a high-performance staff, we made the decision to implement several new platforms. But the decision to implement one additional platform was mostly mine. It was a total break from convention. It was a massive risk that needed total "buy in" from everyone. I decided to implement a low carbohydrate, high fat nutritional periodization model for the senior team. I had researched it thoroughly, starting even before I returned from England. I had experts in the area guiding the proposed plan. But in the end, the decision was mine.

At any given moment, decisions are a choice that are mainly influenced by our own perception of risk versus reward. Calculated risk is the most liberating decision anyone can make. I had turned up the ego volume just loud enough to give me the confidence I needed. But just low enough to make sure I could hear everyone's voice.

We implemented the plan during pre-season 2015. Although the ups and downs were predicted, it was still unnerving. I remember at the end of the first week of preseason, Gregg was not pleased with the quality of training that we were seeing. The players were all in carbohydrate withdrawal and it was evident. I vividly remember the meeting we had at the end of that week. Gregg singled me out in the middle of our staff meeting, in front of everyone, and asked, "Are we doing the right thing (with this new nutritional model)?" I did not answer immediately. I was calm and composed despite my racing heart rate. I went through my checklist. My mind was focused on the group, not myself. I knew that what we were seeing was normal. I turned up some ego volume and said, "Yes, this is all normal. Keep going. You'll see, next week it will turn." The truth is, there was doubt. There was no way of knowing for sure. But that added ego volume in combination with a very present, thoughtful review of our circumstances gave me the confidence to answer Gregg directly. (Steve Tashjian)

In 2012, I was coaching a triathlete for her third Olympic participation. With only a few weeks to go, she felt her training was not going well, she was unsure about the training program and cried after swim sessions almost every day. I had been coaching her for nine years by then, so I knew her well, and I was so convinced that the training program was right for her, that I trusted my own assessment of the situation more than I trusted hers. She arrived at the Olympic Games better prepared than ever, and she had a great race and an excellent result. Maybe my ego can take some credit for that result. (Iñigo Mujika)

We were about to play the cup final against Nantes in 2004. The coach asked me to get the opinion of colleagues on how to best prepare this match, while still managing to perform in the league at the same time over the preceding month. I made those calls, but without really listening, since I was pretty sure about my ideas… which we ended up implementing… and we won the final… but does that really prove I was right? (Eric Blahic)

BIDDING FOR A NEW JOB? TURN THE EGO VOLUME UP!

My first steps in pro football would not have been possible if I hadn't had the confidence to step up and put my ideas upfront.

I was living and surfing in a beach town. I was doing some personal coaching during the Christmas break, and one of my clients happened to be the president of top-tier team. During the sessions, we were discussing various stuff and at one point he asked me my opinion about all the injuries that were occurring in his club at the moment.

I put on paper my ideas and sent it to him. Didn't hear from him for six months, and five days before the next preseason he called me and offered me a job!

A few years after he hired me off the beach, I was with the national team at the world championships!! (Benjamin Kugel)

Somewhere within ego there is a part that is about self-confidence. I have never lacked this, so this has helped me to compete successfully for several roles that have progressed my career. (Ben Ashworth)

Joseph Coyne, exercise physiologist and coach, formerly UFC, Chinese Athletics Association, Chinese Olympic Committee: I definitely believe you have to have some ego to progress in this line of work. There are so many people wanting to work in sport, but you have to believe you are one of the best in the world. Call me egotistical, but I do believe this about myself and it helped me when I first went to China and was basically only working with Chinese Olympic gold medallists. Because of my belief in my ability and knowledge, I had confidence that I could work at this level from the get-go. I would like to think this helped in my initial time there.

I think that this is a fine line between using your ego and trying to exude confidence. I have tried to approach job interviews in a confident manner where I am able to show what knowledge and skill base I have. (Adam Johnson)

Pretty much every decision (good, bad or indifferent) has been driven by my ego and will have influenced my career progression. As a new graduate, applying for two vacancies that, probably at the time, were roles that I shouldn't even been considering is a good example. At some point, I must have thought "I'm good enough to do these jobs," despite not meeting all of the essential criteria. I felt that if I got to interview I could demonstrate my skill set. (Nick Grantham)

Selwyn Griffith, Head of Strength & Conditioning, Melbourne Demons: When I was starting my career in elite sport, I worked in the medical department but spent a lot of time in conversation with the strength department and made sure to assist whenever possible. One of their staff members left mid-season and, while I didn't necessarily have the previous experience to take over the role completely, I approached the head strength coach and high performance manager to offer my services to cover the role for the rest of the season and, if they thought I was good enough, then look to continue in the same role the following year.

Andreas Beck, Head of Physical Performance, Prevention and Rehabilitation, Eintracht Frankfurt: My ego gave me the self-confidence that I could join Borussia Dortmund after working for a minor club, and helped me to progress in different positions, becoming the head of performance at the end.

I believe a big reason that I have been able to progress through our club into a leadership role is that I believed in myself and my ideas. I believed that I was able to apply these ideas in that setting to get results. Without the confidence to step into a staff that had already been in the club for five years prior to my arrival, and say we are going to make some changes and this is how things will go from here on out, my career and experience with my current club would not have the positivity that it has. While speaking with ownership about my new role, I had to pull on previous successes and show why it is applicable to this situation and how I can reproduce it in this setting. These conversations required that I have the self-belief, as well as the know-how, to get the job done. (Garrison Draper)

During my studies, I had been advised not to take two masters classes at the same, alongside my full time job in a small club. "You won't be able to do both." My ego pushed me to do them anyway. In the end, I managed to go through, with pretty good marks on top. (Alexandre Dellal)

Julio Tous-Fajardo, strength & power coach, formerly FC Barcelona, Juventus, Italian National Team: I received a call from a well-connected colleague warning me about the uselessness of applying to a position where the board had already pre-selected their candidate from over 500 people. I responded with something like an outburst: "OK, let´s still compete and maybe they change their decision." I got that position, despite later realizing it was not for me.

Perhaps my ego in part helped with career choices and advancements. For example, when being offered a role in a different sport (that I knew nothing about) and a different country (which I had visited, but not this specific area), there must have been some level of ego that told me I was capable of fulfilling the requirements of the job. In that instance, a role was being created rather than replaced, and to bring me in, I would need a sponsored visa along with assistance moving across an ocean. So my ego must have told me, rightly or wrongly, that I was worth this investment. (Jo Clubb)

When negotiating a contract with a world-class professional team, and after several meetings discussing the job description, duties and responsibilities, the time came to discuss the annual pay. The amount I was offered was in accord with the going rate for similar positions in other teams, but well below the amount I felt I deserved. When asked why should they pay me such an amount, my ego replied "Because you are trying to hire the best in the world, and I am the best in the world." Well, my ego got his well-deserved salary. (Iñigo Mujika)

Any job that I have applied for, I have almost assumed that I would get it in advance of the interview. That helped me prepare for the position and the interview. (Colm Fuller)

Every time, I know I have achieved stuff and my ego told me that it was OK to go and see my boss to ask for a promotion. (Mathieu Lacome)

This is a shitty response, but I think I use ego every time I'm trying to move into a new job role or up the career ladder. I think in applying for roles your ego has to almost tell you you're the best and that you have all the tools necessary to succeed in the role. I mean, there are thousands of people competing for the highest jobs in high performance sport. If your ego doesn't tell you that you're the man for the job, I feel you won't be very successful. (Duncan French)

Ideally, the negative connotation to ego, being overly self-centered, doesn't support progress, but confidence does. In reality, perception matters. Job interviews are often panelled by people who don't really know your area of expertise, so ego can make a difference in getting the job or not, by selling yourself well. I think my moderate ego has helped me work with people who are more self-centered and self-important. (Tom Vandenbogaerde)

Andrew Gray, founder & director, Athletic Data Innovations: I actively sought a role at a club that had been going through a very tough patch. They had finished last in the competition and were embroiled in an illegal supplement scandal so it represented a huge challenge, or risk. However, I had enough self-belief to feel that I could make a positive change to the organisation / environment, so I went after it. The decision turned out to be a very good one. We won a Premiership in my second year at the club and it helped to progress my career considerably. I now believe that if I had not decided to "back myself" and had chosen a safer role at another club, this would have been a lost opportunity.

Frederic Demangeon, Head of Player Support, French Handball federation: Self-confidence. I was only a semi-pro player. But without this self-confidence, no way I could be where I am today, delivering coaching courses to top coaches and also CEOs in big companies and for the government. All my experience, both as a player and coach, helped me convince myself that I was able to do all this

I do think in interview situations, or where you are trying to make a good first impression on a person who has access to more decision-making power than you, it is often helpful to be able to "fluff up your feathers" and act in a confident manner. General managers are often looking for people to solve problems for them, to take the problem off their hands. So if they ask you the question "How can you reduce injuries in our team next season?" and you answer 100% honestly, that you can do some assessments and put intervention plans in place but there is no way of knowing if it will work or not until the next season is over, they do not want to hear that truth. So here, allowing the ego to act, to over-estimate your confidence in your plans and skills, can help you to get the job. But getting the job and then actually being effective in the job require two different sets of skills. (6)

Creating my own business was a personal challenge that I was keen to develop and try to succeed at. It was a gamble and fraught with risk, going from an executive position at arguably the leading sports institute in the world. (Steve Ingham)

David Utrera, strength & conditioning coach and physiotherapist, formerly Aspetar, OGC Nice, Krasnodar: I started in professional football as a physio. You have no credit within the performance department. I asked the club for my chance as Assistant Physical Coach. They were not convinced. Neither would I be. I had no experience. But it was clear that was where my future was. Based on what I saw from others, I would not make it worse. And it worked.

I remember the 30-year old Thierry Omeyer leaving Montpellier Handball in France, where he was the #1 goalkeeper, to play for THW Kiel in Germany, where there were already two international goalkeepers. When I asked him why take the risk if he might not be playing, he responded "I don't care since I am better than them." (Frederic Demangeon).

STRONG EGOS REFUSE TO STAGNATE: ADAPT AND IMPROVE TO STAY ON TOP

> That's my hunger. If I start to relax, and I lose that, then I had better stop my football. I need that hunger. I still feel I need to do things 10 times better than other players. Just to be accepted and to improve myself.

– Zlatan Ibrahimovic

My ego has helped me to stand up in our difficult and competitive world, and to be where I am at the moment. It pushed me to go to the university and learn about strength & conditioning when teachers in high school were saying that I wasn't good enough for this. It then helped me to get a job in a sport I didn't know much about (ice hockey), and finally have pretty successful outcomes and gain trust and recognition from top players of the sport. Working in pro skiing, it then gave me the confidence to work as I wished and not as others wanted me to. (Sébastien Carrier)

It is easy / safe to follow what other teams do or what has always been done or what is ascribed as best practice. However, if, in sport, the goal is to increase performance, this will not be achieved by copying everyone else. I think ego has helped me to try many new things in athlete preparation. More specifically, my belief that I know something / have understood something that no one else is aware of and then making that change. (Marc Quod)

The level of self-confidence I have has also given me the strength to repeatedly find new working strategies / areas and build an economic model, like moving from being an employee in a large structure (economically safe) to being a freelancer for big organisations. (Yann Le Meur)

David Joyce, sport strategy and performance consultant: Ego, at times, has helped me be successful in getting a positive outcome when perhaps my skill, knowledge or experience was lacking, as it allowed me to have the self-confidence to motivate and engage other talented people along on the journey.

Ian Beasley, sports physician, Aspetar; medical consultant, Global Performance Team, City Football Group: Yes, I took on challenges that were scary, with a potential to fail, but took them on partly aided by self-belief.

EGOS GET KNOCKED DOWN, BUT THEY GET UP AGAIN

After each failure, my ego helps me bounce back and regain confidence in my abilities and, in turn, my actions. (Paul Quetin)

Meeting roadblock after roadblock, the ego gets punched in the face. But perhaps it's the ego that allows me to stand up again and try a different way. (Paul Laursen)

Antonio Gómez, fitness coach, Poland National Team, former FC Barcelona and Liverpool: Probably, when the results have gone wrong, my ability to believe in my work has been decisive for not quitting. This environment is very hard and exigent, especially in top level clubs and teams.

A high self-esteem has helped me a few times to progress, to continue my job, to maintain a high level of motivation, perseverance and activity on a daily basis while I had to cope with repeated criticism and denigration by head management. Self-esteem is key. (Karim Hader)

Amelia Arundale, physiotherapist and researcher, Red Bull Athlete Performance Center, former role in the NBA: I think it might be more self-confidence, but potentially ego, when, in some situations, I have been able to "pump myself up" to have the courage to do certain things like introduce myself to someone at a conference.

Andrea Azzalin, Head of Fitness, Ukraine Football Federation: It helped since the beginning boosting my confidence and keeping me positive during bad times. If I have to give an example, I would say that at the beginning of my experiences at high level it helped a lot building relationships and dealing with people in a professional way, even though I was the youngest of the staff.

Chris Barnes, football scientist: When I entered the world of elite sport (football), my colleagues had little or no exposure to sports science, which was fortunate as I had little or no context for how my academic knowledge would translate into applied practice. The fact that the mistakes I made in trying to introduce a scientific way of working to football were not really noticed was due mainly to the fact I managed to stay one step ahead, and, fortunately, didn't seriously injure anyone. For every positive intervention, there were probably three f*** ups, but, with hindsight, I am delighted that my ego meant we kept trying new things and, in doing so, hopefully made a small contribution to the development of our industry.

KNOW YOUR WORTH, AND PROVE A POINT SO OTHERS KNOW IT

When people criticize me, instead of putting my head down, it gives me energy to do even more.

– *Zlatan Ibrahimovic*

Martin: I worked with an assistant coach who had diametrically opposite visions of strength & conditioning, nutrition and monitoring practices than mine. Pretty difficult situation overall, when you have to collaborate for the team's best interest and respect the coaching staff's ideas and decisions. It was even harder for my ego, since the practices that he systematically rejected had been working so far, and were largely backed up by both internal and external research. His overall denigrating attitude of my work and me as a person didn't help my feelings and increased the frustration to unprecedented levels.

This period is behind me now (although a lot from that period awaits in Chapters 9-10), and now I am actually, truly thankful to him. He directly pushed me to research more and provide more evidence to prove him wrong and show that my beliefs had greater value.

Consequently, over a three-year period, I ended up publishing seven papers (with one more in preparation as I write this), each centering on one of the areas of disagreement.

In fact, I realize only now that I used this complex and painful situation as an incredible and unprecedented source of both inspiration and motivation to get some great studies done!

Since the studies we conducted and wrote up in these papers unequivocally confirmed my positions on all topics (and, I promise, that as a good sport scientist I have ALWAYS committed the greatest possible level of objectivity to the analysis and results), they even allowed me to close the ego loop: ego threatened → hard-working ego to prove the other wrong → satisfied and reinforced ego upon seeing the results.

Now I feel better, of course. But more importantly, those seven papers have all contributed to a better understanding of sport science and strength & conditioning practices, for the benefit of our entire community.

George: When I first came into the world of track & field, there were some well-known, respected "old hands" that I connected with early and sought to learn from. As my network expanded I relied more on other people, but I still deferred to the individuals in this first group because I was new, I knew I had a lot to learn and they were well-connected and well-informed.

While talking to one of them, I asked whether it would be worth it to reach out to a particular person who once had been involved in the sport. The reply I received was "He's a flawed man. I wanted him to succeed. I tried to help and guide him, but he wasn't willing to listen and learn, so it was never going to work."

I was appalled as I saw things very clearly. This person I'm talking to had never created any new value, had never taken a risk, had never actually worked in the industry, had never encouraged others to go beyond the absolute failure that was the past. A custodian of an unsatisfying status quo, he had the gall to disrespect one of the most successful executives in American sports, a bulldozer and an innovator, and presume that he could tell this exec what's what and how to be.

At that point, I realized I didn't know everything, but I certainly knew more and had a better sense of direction and value than the people from whom I had been seeking help. If that wasn't the last conversation I had with anyone in that group, it was definitely the last one I took seriously. After that, I raised my threshold and screening process for who I would seek counsel from and how I'd weight their advice.

Maggie Bryant, Director of Rehabilitation, Los Angeles Clippers: I used my background and degrees to help argue a point of me being worthy of making a decision. I was arguing with a very egotistical person and I had to demonstrate my ability to be included in the decision / process. It ultimately demonstrated confidence and competency, I believe, and I was involved.

I worked with a player who, after a bad ACL injury, was released from a top team. The following season he played for a second division team. We all thought his career at the top level was over. He worked very hard, and two years later he was recognized as the best French player in the first league. Without a strong ego, I don't think he would have recovered so well and become even better with time.

I also knew a player who had been terribly blamed by a coach, who told him he was rather made for volleyball and that he didn't choose the right sport! He suffered a lot, but it clearly made him react. A few years later he signed a contract in a pro team. (Franck Kuhn)

EGO IS A TOOL: KNOW HOW TO USE IT

It can help you dig in on certain issues that you feel are important, as well as prop up your confidence when you need it. Personally, I think it has helped give me confidence when I need to walk into a room full of coaches and management and deliver plans and preparations. It helps when you face elite-level athletes to take them through training sessions. The key is being able to know when to check your ego and when to have it take a back seat. (Adam Johnson)

There are many situations where a decision needs to be made. Ego can help summon the strength to take the lead and make the decision. The trick, of course, is knowing when it's the time to suppress your ego and listen and be humble, and when it's the time to "take over" and make the call. In some important meetings, I believe my ego has served me well and has come across as confidence, not arrogance. (Dave Martin)

Chris Tombs, Performance Lead, Seattle Seawolves: Recognizing when to push and pull, when to compromise and when to really stand up for a specific inclusion or element of the programming takes into account all the elements of ego. However, being respectful of the ownership group and head coach is always going to be a challenge. I personally kept pushing for investment in things that would help the playing group. I wanted more resources because I have seen what truly high performance environments look like and I wanted my current team to rise to those standards. It was a long-term process, but, inevitably, improving takes manpower and financial investment. I did, however, compromise, and believe having a small ego helps here. There is frequent conflict in sport. How you manage and present yourself matters. I believe I had a positive experience because of my ego, not despite it.

My ego has definitely pushed me to work harder and do more. I've always believed that if I was to put the work in, it will pay off. However, being able to control my ego has allowed me to stay lucid and realistic about my objectives throughout my career. I had a strong drive to succeed and enough self-confidence to know that I would make it, but I always tried to keep in mind my limitations and the areas I needed to work on to progress. I always tried to have a plan related to the context of the moment to direct my energy to where it was needed. (Yann Le Meur)

Grant Downie, OBE, consultant in medical and performance solutions, formerly Manchester City, Rangers FC, the Football Association: I think when you have been around the block and are grey-haired like me with national honours you can story tell in new situations, which will always open the door more quickly to new organizations or clubs. I like to think I get my ego under control and readily talk about my vulnerability and situations I got wrong. However, I learned from these and I will always still be able to make performance and pressure decisions. I think you "earn the right" to talk this way and, done correctly, allows progress and connection.

I see ego as something that can be very positive because of the self-confidence that it can provide for you to confidently and honestly speak your truth. But I do believe that your ego needs to come from a good base of emotional intelligence, an authentic experience based reasoning, empathy and the ability to listen to others. (Andrew Young)

When time are hard and there is incertitude, it gives you confidence to move forward when you're not following the mainstream (Martin Buchheit)

OK, BUT HOW DOES ONE BUILD EGO?

"He was born with his skates on." "She came out kicking a ball."

These are cute clichés, often from family members who can't remember a time when the athlete in the house wasn't immersed in their sport, but sometimes we hear these from pundits and journalists trying to describe the combination of natural talent and years of practice that go into being the kind of athlete that has pundits and journalists searching for words.

Cute clichés, yes, but yet another dismissive back of the hand. Whatever physical traits and natural talent an athlete is born with, they do not reach a noticeable level without incredible levels of drive, ambition, determination and effort. They may have been "born with" skates or a ball, but the only reason we're talking about them is everything they've done since. Outside of sports, "born leader" is probably the most common phrase to erase and evade what it takes to lead.

In the same way, none of us are born with an ego, just the capacity to develop one. Having an ego that properly reflects what we've done and who we are requires a similar amount of work to whatever we had to do to get to wherever we are.

> The good news is that our confidence is something that can be worked on and improved. This can be achieved by simple practices like self-reflecting in a positive way and by recognizing our strengths. Learning to celebrate the small wins on a daily basis helps us improve our self-confidence.
>
> Another way we can build our confidence is by surrounding ourselves with more positive people who radiate a vibrant energy.
>
> Growing up, we are a direct result of our environment and family upbringing. For example, our behaviors, attitude, values and personalities will have been nurtured and developed in the home. Already, there we see one of the reasons why, even as kids, some might already exude a confidence or a lack of it. (Allistair McCaw)

Children playing sports often see themselves as their favorite player. You hear it on the playground. "Messi… dribbling through traffic… he shoots! GOAL!" "D-Wade for the THREE!!!" They identify with what they already know is the pinnacle of what they are trying to do.

Again, we don't recommend a knee-slide celebration across your co-working space when your app leads its category on the Apple Store. But visualizing yourself as that highest self, viewing yourself within your own arena for admiration, can help bring your ego up to the level it deserves.

> Reinforcing the ego is equally as complicated as lowering it. For people lacking self-esteem and self-confidence, exercises to reinforce their ego include the active visualization of the maximum they could achieve if they prepare well, if everything goes as they would like, if there were no impediment to perform at their best. If the perfect day happens. In short, dream big!
>
> Don't make any excuses to be the ultimate expression of yourself and succeed. There are many people and athletes who are "afraid" of success. I have seen it in my work. They do not believe they are capable or deserving of it, they think that is for others.
>
> It also helps to really believe in the good moments they have had in their career, value them and not downplay their importance. Also take into account the opinion of those moments of those people who are important to them.
>
> In short, believe that you are worth much more than you think. See yourself not only as you are in your current state, but imagine how you could be exploiting your full potential, succeeding, succeeding again, and being better than others. (Juan Carlos Álvarez Campillo)

TAKE AWAY

On two occasions I have been asked, "Pray, Mr. Babbage, if you put into the machine wrong figures, will the right answers come out?" ... I am not able rightly to apprehend the kind of confusion of ideas that could provoke such a question.

— Charles Babbage

Charles Babbage is one of the fathers of computing and, as such, may have been the first to articulate the principle of "garbage in, garbage out." A computer can only do what you tell it to do, and the quality of the output depends on the quality - indeed, the basic coherence and literacy - of the input.

Our output - the things we say and do, and the emotions we experience along the way - is not strictly computed from the input. Until science fiction becomes a reality, we alone are sentient and have free will. Part of that free will is in writing the "assembly code." We have to build our own egos, deciding what values are important to us, what our purpose is, how we'll react to our own successes and failures. If we decide on a lousy purpose or choose flaky ways to go about it, or if we get our ego hooked on cheap hits of prestige... garbage in, garbage out.

On the other hand, as we saw in this chapter, when you put good ideas and good work in, you get better things out. Ego powers the cycle of motivation and reward. You start to understand why we have this thing that often seems so troublesome, perhaps even more so than it's worth. Perhaps you're even wondering why and how ego has such a dismal reputation. Among other reasons: it's hard work. Really hard work, lifelong work, the kind of work that requires you to look at things very honestly and learn some difficult, maybe painful, but essential lessons.

Garbage in, garbage out is easy - a million monkeys on a million computers can write garbage code all day. Nothing will get done. But it just takes one person to come along and set things right, and when it comes to ego, there's ultimately only one person who can do that.

3 | EGO F*%# UPS

I suspect that ego, in some way, contributes to most fuck ups. If you get beaten by someone better, well, you get beaten. But if you made an error, if you have fucked up, that is because decisions were made in the lead up to that error. And, certainly, ego played a part in those decisions. (Marc Quod)

Fans are lucky. They get to enjoy all the entertainment value of ego - the commanding performances, the press conference fireworks, the social media swagger - with only a cringe when an ego flare-up becomes an ego f*** up.

People with uncontrolled egos tend to speak without any filter and act without restraint. For them and those around them, ego outbursts are a regular occurrence, so much so that it desensitizes their colleagues.

Consequently, the difference between an ego flare-up and an ego f*** up is usually only a matter of degree and perspective.

Zlatan Ibrahimovic's ego has done great things for him on the pitch and as a global brand. But no one player can raise a trophy: it takes a bare minimum 11, and usually twice as many. Even when an individual with a large ego is an overall positive for the team, he can still be divisive and leave a few lasting bruises.

"For the national team he became too big, too important. The team spirit has been rebuilt since he left, something that the Swedish side always was famous for," said Swedish football expert Gunnar Persson.

"When a player has such self-assurance, he treads a fine line between being a major catalyst for his team or a serious weakness.

"In the long run, his team-mates—or, rather, the other players—became wary of him," Persson recalls. "It didn't take them long to realise they were now only a supporting cast to him. The team had no tactics, just the intimidating presence of Zlatan. Every attack should go through him.

"It didn't matter if he was up for the occasion or not. When he was on, maybe it worked. When he wasn't? Absolute disaster."

The players at least have a platform and outlet for their egos, and objective standards against which the world can assess their grip on reality. The backroom staff on a sports team, like people in almost any other profession, have none of that. But that doesn't mean they don't sometimes have Zlatan-sized egos.

Ordinary levels of achievement and recognition justify each expansion of their self-generated mystique until their ego becomes self-perpetuating. They don't need new successes because they already have the ego to prove their greatness. Why should they ever pause, consider, listen, reconsider and engage, when - obviously! - their first instinct was impeccable? Well, because sometimes their first instinct is to say things like this:

FULL OF THEMSELVES OR JUST FULL OF IT?

"Do you believe in god??? Then you believe in me!"

"Forget all what you have learnt so far. Football, it's me!"

"You must be perfect like me."

"I think I'll need to put the shirt on again." - Coach saying he'll need to play himself since the players are not good enough.

"In the world, I am a star. I am not an outsider, I am simply ahead of everyone."

"You should write my biography and all about my success." Coach to a journalist.

"Only one method works: mine!"

"I'm the best coach in the world because I worked with (insert name of high-profile athlete or team)."

"The world record will not be broken in my coaching lifetime." Needless to say, it was not his team that broke the world record two years later.

"What an idiot, he has no clue what he's doing!" right before "the idiot" won a World Championships gold medal and destroyed the world record along the way.

"I do what I want today. It's my birthday." Head coach to a player asking why he was on the bench for this match.

"I'm a coach, I don't carry bags."

"This business class is shit. I've been in way better." First team head coach

"I can't be bothered going to coaches' conferences. They don't know anything."

"You don't need to go to any more conferences. I pretty much know all that there is to know about performance, so you can just come to me." High Performance Manager, when I asked to attend the European College of Sports Science conference.

"If you were an expert as your pretend to be, you shouldn't need to go. By the way, it's the people from the conference who should be asking us to give talks, not the other way around." I once asked the sporting director for permission to go to a conference for a couple of days on a very timely topic. I obviously did travel to that conference!

"I don't care what the science says, I know it works!"

"There is no one in the world that I can learn from anymore. I have hit the top!"

"I'll never learn anything from anyone else, since I am the only who knows what I need to know. And, at the moment, I know enough."

"I don't need anyone who had never coached in the league to tell me what to do and how to prepare teams for competition."

"The only things that matter occur on the field, and this is where I coach."

"In my career, I have always done it this way. Why change?"

"I know more than you about this because that was the topic of my Ph.D."

"Why are we measuring what we do on the field? If we do or not do a good job, we know it! No need to measure it."

"I know what I see with my eyes. You don't need to measure it."

"I smell the situation and I know how to handle it."

"I know he is not injured. He can play. Trust me." MRI shows a clear muscle tear.

"You all need to act and work every day like your job is on the line, and I am not seeing this from you all, and I think that is why we can't win."

"We don't need outside help for this. This should come from the head coach." When speaking about developing team culture.

"If the coaches would listen to me, we'd have won that game."

"The greater running performance of our players is directly related to the supplements I give them." Team doctor

"I saved the club! And after carrying everything on my own, I have sore shoulders!"

"The players I train do more intensity than all English Premier League players." The team he coached was at the bottom of the Premier League table. My world is more complicated.

"You see this player? Without me, he would be nothing."

"You see, I told you he was a top player." Two months ago, he didn't want to hear about him.

"I can prevent all your injuries if you hire me."

"I am the second-best physio on the planet - and I can tell you who is the only one better than me."

"I am the only one who can treat you."

"I can get any hamstring injury back on the pitch training with the team within 10 days."

"I'll treat you only when you manage to lift heavier than me." Physio to a young player.

A strength & conditioning coach who insisted on referring to himself as "the difference."

Premier League manager telling the whole team that he's the best-looking bloke in the dressing room, the best footballer and the only reason why the team is successful.

"The grizzly has done a great job today," "The grizzly is hungry," "The grizzly needs to talk to you…" I worked with a staff member who talked about himself in the third person, and calls himself "the grizzly."

"Never present data that contradicts my opinions… I am your boss."

"I have the power to make your life hell. Don't f*** with me."

"I could help you get a job… in return for 10-15% of your salary."

"You owe me your job."

"Don't f@#k this up, because you work with me, and that will reflect badly on me."

"My plan is to have your job in a few years." A colleague to me. Not a job similar to mine - my actual job! It was his stated goal.

A "famous" athlete: "Don't you know who I am?" The response: "No."

"Hello, my name is XXXX XXXXX, and I am better than all of you."

"I know you'll need me to get to the world championships." Handball player to the national team coach.

"If you guys want to win, just give me the ball and I'll make it happen." New player, standing on a chair during his first meal at the club, in front of all his teammates, coaches, backroom staff and president of the club.

 "You don't understand the sport since you not part of the 100 caps group!" A rugby player with over 100 international caps to a player with over 30 international caps.

"You know, I haven't scored for 18 months only because, you know, I am so strong, that all the opponents have to defend against me. They know how dangerous I am and that they need three players to defend me."

"Do you know from which club I come from? I can't be a substitute here!"

"The coach really doesn't understand anything. I am always better in second half." Player substituted at half time.

SOME EGOS ARE STRANGER THAN FICTION

Martin: Ibrahimovic talking to me in the locker room just before his last match at the club (he is actually already late, adjusting his pony tail in front of the mirror, the referees calling him for the second time):

Ibra: "Hey Genius… you are going to miss me, right?"

Me: "Of course, you've been such a great human being to work with, and it's been gr…."

Ibra: "I have a match to play, I can't be bothered listening to your reply." And he leaves the locker room!!

One of our top players came to me and said he wanted to have an important chat with me in my office. I imagined it would be related to the fact that I substituted him at the last minute in the previous game or something like that. The reality was that he complained about the fact that he was not on the posters in the city to announce the home matches to the public.

Many years ago, I worked with a well-known German athlete who is extremely famous in her country. Even though she was an Olympic medalist, she never liked coming to the United States to compete and never performed well there, so I asked her why. The answer was quite interesting! She said it was because, "In Germany, people know me and recognize me. In Germany and most parts of Europe, I get special privileges like where I can park my car, free meals in nice restaurants or gifts from fans. In America, that doesn't happen." WOW!

After a team title, one of the athletes asks for a greater portion of the bonus, because he believes that without his contribution, the team wouldn't have won.

I once witnessed a Director of Performance, whom I worked for, pull the janitor into his office and insisted he be called "coach." The justification was due to his "years of getting to where he is at."

A former manager made me sit and watch YouTube clips of his playing days for over an hour.

A manager wanted to hire new staff, and referenced Google Images (and his own image) to say it's important how many trophies the person has for them to do this role. This was the most shocking: basing decisions on trophies and images on Google rather than their actual experience to do their job within a performance team.

I worked with a famous manager who, when you were walking to him in his office to say hello, was able to give you his left hand as he kept watching videos on his computer.

Some of my colleagues would only say hello or good morning to players and ignore the rest of the staff when entering the restaurant.

It's clearly hard to believe, but once a coach asked me to meet the world champion of a non-physical sport (can't name it to remain anonymous, but it was like the world champ of chess or darts...) to discuss nutrition. It was suggested to me that we at the club should follow this guy's advice and eat like him. Because, of course, football has very similar demands.

One colleague insistently pushed for an MRI for a suspected muscle injury to a high-ego player, who flatly rejected it while complaining in a mocking way about - in his opinion - the excessive alarmism of the doctor. The next day the player had pain, and now imperatively requested the MRI. When a muscle injury was revealed, he blamed the doctor for not having been persuasive enough and not having "his confidence." The doctor was eventually fired for "not having the confidence of the players."

One colleague was pressured by a high-ego player to give him a medication, and then blamed when there was a problem with this medication: "You are guilty of not holding out against my pressure."

The ego person telling you that you have an ego. I've been told that self-care is ego. The same person told me that having personal goals (like running times, playing sports outside work), even if it has no impact or conflict on work, is ego.

One of my colleague still claims everywhere that what he does is the best possible, while his winning and injury records are the worst in the league

I worked with a manager who consistently dismissed the opinion of some of the more junior staff from the club, while he was always following more senior and experienced colleagues: "it's a fantastic idea, thanks!" as the senior repeats what the junior had said two minutes before.

THE GLORY HUNTER: IT'S ALL ABOUT ME!

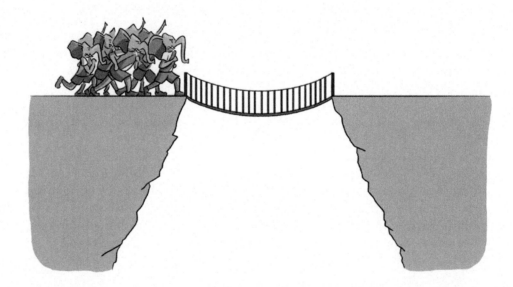

Many of these reactions are emotional and impulsive, and are motivated by the need for attention. Not the mission, not their place in the big picture… them, front and center.

These are many times the same people who show their disappointment over not having been informed, consulted or just simply involved in every decision-making process. They feel it is 100% legitimate that they should be part of the situation, even if it's not in their area of expertise or part of their job description. This often happens when the job descriptions are unclear, or people decide themselves what their mission is. For example, a doctor might get petulant because he is not involved in research projects looking at some injury or his imagined field of expertise. A physio might be upset that the team bought new strength machines to use on the training pitch without his direct input.

Sometimes, though, it's nothing more than attention FOMO.

When we get started in our careers, we crave real accomplishments. Those are the moments and contributions that drive the success of our team, our company, our organization, even our family.

As we start to feel like "Hey, I've figured this out and I'm more than a little good at it. I've made it!" we want other people to know about it. In itself, that's not a bad thing. Sharing our accomplishments with others and accepting recognition is a valid reward. Who knows, maybe we can even teach, motivate or inspire someone through our example.

But if we're not careful, we lose the connection between the accomplishment and the pride, between the work and the reward - between the cause and effect. We confuse attention with recognition. The plaudits become an end in themselves, overtaking the accomplishments they celebrate and represent. The money, job titles and media attention didn't bring us to that point, but now that we're here, damn it, I've earned it and I'm going to get what's mine.

Some people will want to skip over the work and go straight to the higher paying job. Others will look for the individual spotlight without first achieving the team's goal.

When things really get out of control, they go zero-sum: either the group succeeds or I do. If that was simply an inane thing to believe - how can anyone in the sports world think they are doing well personally if their team is racked with injuries, infighting and debt while at the bottom of the table? - it would be one thing. But if validation supplants achievement, then staff members just grab what they can.

Like so much else in this chapter and in this book, it's easy to chuckle smugly at our contributors' stories and say "I would never do that, and as a leader I would never allow it to happen." You know who else said that? Just about everyone you're reading about in this chapter.

Delivering a presentation to the team that keeps their attention and communicates all the relevant information is enough of a challenge. Some practitioners and players decide information is not enough if they do not get a personal shout out. One colleague complained that he was not mentioned by name when his specialty was mentioned in a team presentation.

Players were starting to lose consistency in their use of recovery strategies after matches. I decided to put a poster in the locker room: "Score 100 points and win your recovery!". They had nine items to select from, and each item was worth 20 points, which meant that if you were to do five of them you'll be good to go and optimally recovered. The same evening, we were flying out to an away game. I was sitting and reading quietly Ego is the Enemy when I received a paper ball in the neck. I unfolded the paper. Two physios had taken the poster from the locker room and were now shouting at me since I had given their massages as many points as a recovery protein shake or a cold bath. It was an insult to them and their profession. It took months for one of them to talk to me again.

During a short presentation to the players, the team nutritionist used a picture of one player to illustrate which supplements would improve his various capacities. Some of the other players wouldn't look at the slide, because they didn't want to hear anything about him - they would only listen if it was about them. Solution? Next time around, the nutritionist made 22 slides, one with a picture of each player, each containing the same content. Indulgent? You bet. But the nutritionist's fear of them missing out on useful information outweighed his concern about giving in to their ego FOMO.

One case I will never forget came in the run-up to the World Cup. Two physiotherapists started fighting about who would march in the opening ceremonies. Egos were so big that when the decision was finally made about who would go with the team to the big event, the physiotherapist who didn't get to go broke down in tears. As a result, a few days before competing, the country's best chance of a gold medal ended up consoling the physiotherapist who was in tears, and even offered up some of her World Cup gear to make the physiotherapist feel better.

I once heard an argument between a colleague and our head coach about whether we should do 200-meter runs with our players in 22 seconds or 23 seconds. It lasted 20 minutes. It was unbelievable. It was a heavyweight bout between two of the most stubborn people I had ever met.

Highlighting the silos that the nutrition and physiology teams were working in, the nutrition team at one time took it upon themselves to run a field experiment that involved taking blood lactate levels in rowers. We're not sure what the premise even was, but all that was seen from the dock was floating blood-soaked gauze and complete confusion by practitioners with no experience in blood draws, and meaningless, invalid data. Once again, ego fucked us up. Little to no trust between the teams at that time.

A group of four coaches / team managers had worked together in different organizations for about 20 years. They were good personal friends as well as colleagues, with a lot of shared triumph and failure between them (personal and professional). They were now in control of their own team, a dream situation. While there were always some tension and disagreements in the group, it was because they had different points of view - that was a major driver for the group's success.

Unfortunately, due to ego, one member felt like he was not getting enough "say" in decisions. This led to a growing rift over months and a negative impact on the team's performance.

When it all came to a head at a meeting to resolve the issue, an emotional and confrontational discussion for everyone, each of the group acknowledged their role in the current issue and a willingness to put it behind them. Except for the one individual. His ego would not let him acknowledge his role. As a result, he left the team. All that was required was an acknowledgement, as each of the other members had provided before him, and the group would have been able to overcome this issue.

The group genuinely wanted to overcome the issue. But because his ego would not let him, he was without a job and lost a group of very good friends.

A certain player was solely focused on individual success and not the team's. If he didn't score a goal or make an assist he did very little to celebrate with team members. At half time, he would strip off players for not adequately getting him the ball, and if a player didn't make a specific pass in a goal scoring opportunity, it would be World War III. The confidence of all players dropped, and so did motivation and performance.

Two riders on the team had a very similar profile of strengths and weaknesses, and consequently shared goals and target races. In cycling, strategy and tactics are the only way you can beat stronger opponents, and two riders working in tandem can be very powerful. Unfortunately, because of ego and the team's inability to manage the ego of both riders, not only did we lose both riders to different teams because they refused to work with each other, we were not able to utilise their combined strength to win races.

A player talking himself up in the media about how he was much better than anyone had seen because the team was holding him back, demanding a trade and holding out for more money. That put him in a massive hole, and lost him a lot of money and friends.

A player who caused trouble for a staff member (stopping him from being able to work) just because the staff member did something that was better for the whole team and not for this player. The player did it knowing, as well, that this staff member was someone whose wages allowed him to have a normal life for his family.

During away game meals, staff were dispatched as a function of jobs and responsibilities. A table for the kitman, one table for physios, one table for the big guns (head coach, doc, etc..). One of our colleagues, although not being a big gun, in fact, was always trying to get a seat on that latter table.

A colleague in a previous club was systematically - and without being asked - telling the entire group of players and staff everything he had done in his day: the new gym machine he had just fixed, the individual training program he had just developed or whatever could help him be recognized by the others. While this was likely coming initially from a perception of insecurity, this constant willingness or need to be acknowledged and stroked was just ridiculous.

I've seen a lot. Take one coach I worked with, who was historically super successful but hadn't had much recent success. So it wasn't so much one massive f*** up, but just consistent moments - almost always unsolicited - where he would have to show other coaches or athletes how much he knew and could help them... to feed his ego. From this, and it happened over time, other coaches and athletes started getting sick of always being given advice on how they needed to fix things or make things better, and they would just avoid this coach, put him down or not want to work with him.

The big Professor Bensman presenting on football physiology performance!!! Here's a researcher who, when he gives a talk, presents only his work. OK, he has done a lot, so he can talk for hours, but don't expect to see any other finding or results from any other researcher. There's only him, and what he has done. It's pretty impressive, and every time I have been watching him I was very uncomfortable with this practice.

Once I was invited to a round table with Professor Bensman. The round table was meant to be 30 minutes long, with approximately 20 minutes allowed for the three speakers to successively present their findings (so seven minutes each) and then 10 minutes of discussion for the group. Professor Bensman started, I was #2 and a female colleague was to speak third. He spoke for 17 minutes. I then presented two slides in five minutes, and let my colleague finish to present what she could. There was no discussion after, not only because we ran out of time, but because he had already left at the end of the third speaker's presentation.

Several scientists giving advice on how to eliminate injuries in football. They have only limited data (such as GPS tracking during sessions and matches) and claim that those data are strong enough to predict injuries, completely overlooking the importance of myriad other determining factors that they don't handle (physical capacities, non-tracked off pitch activities, history of previous injuries, fatigue, nutrition, mental state). Full of themselves? A little.

WHO NEEDS YOU WHEN WE HAVE ME?

With accomplishment comes a growing pressure to pretend that we know more than we do. With success and power, more often than not, we begin to overestimate our own power. Then we lose perspective. And there begins our downfall.

– Ryan Holiday

Egos are part of nature, so we can think about them in physical terms.

Some egos get so big they develop gravitational fields, attracting others to their orbit, which can be a good thing unless they become so big they implode and become a black hole from which no light, hope, *esprit de corps* or careers ever escape.

Others max out at an equilibrium point and just roll along on their own inertia. They don't shrink, they don't grow, they don't rejuvenate - they just bloat. These individuals will maintain their place and their ways unless someone intervenes to push them onto a new course or moves them out of the organization. They don't have to become actively malign to harm the team. A stale ego trading in old accomplishments traps the organization at that level and in that past, while your competitors evolve, improve and look at you and laugh.

Ego inertia explains the practitioners who have developed their own "analytical" methods over the years. They assess players' freshness and injury risk based on everything but scientific, reliable and valid methods. Self-video, the "eye-o-meter," eye-balled observations, chats, feelings, smell(!), hair cut meter(!!)… these all happen.

They can see everything except themselves. Whereas some of their colleagues are obsessed by what people think of them and are therefore constantly cultivating their public image, the inertial ego can't see outside of itself. Even when results unequivocally show how much is going wrong, it can't see its own role in creating those outcomes. If such a person holds a powerful position, they tend to have an ego echo chamber to help impose "their" methods, assign blame elsewhere and ensure that the ego in motion stays in motion.

Veteran personnel and managers should always bring their experience and anecdotal data to the problem at hand, but nothing about their past relieves them of their responsibility for the work today and the results tomorrow.

It's a very common fact. New staff arrive at a club and want to impose straightaway all their methods without taking a minute to look at what was in place before their arrival. It's an incredible way to show how self-centred they are and, more importantly, it's disrespectful for the others who have done the work before.

Another example is that of a staff member - could be a coach, assistant, sporting director - who requests to take over or at least have a word in every decision of an entire department that they judge is not functioning optimally, despite that person not having any real competence and experience in the domain. Instead of trying to improve the situation via teamwork and using the strengths and experience of the people in charge, their (too) high confidence pushes them to take responsibilities they can't assume and execute correctly. In addition to showing a very large level of disrespect to the people in place, it's unsurprisingly the recipe for failure.

When a coach, despite substantial evidence confirming the positive impact that the support team (sport science and medicine) had on performance outcomes (player availability, injury levels, etc.), decided to break up what had been a highly functioning back room staff.

As a newly appointed fitness coach to the club, the head of the medical team made it clear from the beginning he had no interest in working together with me. His view was that he worked with injured players from the moment the player got injured until he was almost ready for full training. Then I could take the player and do some heart rate-based conditioning before the player entered the full team training again. He was extremely hierarchical and "protective" about his part of the work, and he didn't want to cooperate because he felt I was threat to how he usually did things. This made the process slow and also very ineffective, since a lot of the interventions were based on his gut feeling and anecdotal evidence (it worked for that player so it must work for this player) rather than evidence-based methods. He also had very little interest in the daily monitoring of the players, and the lack of documentation made discussions very hard.

I worked with an assistant coach who believed that how he had always done something in strength & conditioning or rehabilitation was the only way to do it. All athletes are different, all injuries are unique and all environments have different cultures. But he never got that.

Many coaches or S&C coaches don't accept advice or debate about different topics. They have their own philosophy (that is good), but they often refuse to discuss anything with each other.

Believing you can take a program from one successful organization with one group dynamic and replicate the exact model in a new, unsuccessful organization with a completely different playing group and have no adverse reactions.

Refusal to change the structure of strength training programs at an NRL club after being there for 10+ years!! Ended up getting sacked.

One distinct memory I have is being lectured by a manager on monitoring fatigue where he believed his "old school" methods were far superior to our scientific, evidence-based approached. I remember leaving the meeting thinking it was time to change professions!

I spent most of a season doing my S&C at the start of each training session. Eventually, I noticed the head coach was doing another S&C portion later. One he believed in. His way. The best way. The only way.

During a session I was doing with all the players, an assistant coach asks me to change the number of repetitions.

The worst ego f*&% up I have seen was a collegiate Director of Performance talk down to every single staff member in the Performance and Medical departments. For instance, this individual made a clear statement in a team meeting that players should not see athletic trainers if they are injured or sore. He consistently insisted that he knew what was best because he had "worked in the NFL previously." He inevitably got fired from his role and hasn't worked in college or professional sports since.

EGO F***-UPS CAN HAVE SHATTERING CONSEQUENCES

New, first-time manager - an ex-international player. We were D-1 of an international game and the manager was feeling that our players were not "ready for combat." We were training on an artificial grass pitch (a crappy one) and already had a heavy week. So we recommended an intense, non-contact, very short session to peak for competition - the usual stuff. He did not accept it, and asked to do a 2 x 8-minute session of opposition play with full contact... on artificial grass. Our key player - now an international player - tore an ACL that day. Season over. He couldn't play in the European and World championships that year. The manager said we were unlucky.

Start of pre-season. There were a few older players in the squad who had been at the club for many years, and we knew from experience that they needed to be looked after and given special treatment to go through the increased load of this phase. This included, for example, removing them from some extensive running sessions and favoring other forms of exercise (off-field gym, cycling, etc.). Despite some clear warnings, the new management suggests that we have been too protective with those players in the past and that they should train with the others. Second running session, two injuries among those "special players." Ego 0 – 1 Common Sense.

One morning, the assistant coach asked me for more data on players' training status after a hard session the day before. I immediately prepared a new report, and 20 minutes later he had all the info in his inbox. Meeting with the whole staff, the question about players' recovery was obviously on the table. I mentioned the document that "WE" just prepared, which suggested a bit of general fatigue. The assistant coach started by saying he didn't think the data were worthwhile and what mattered was what he felt earlier that morning at breakfast. He believed we were good to keep on training as planned. They actually ended up doing more than planned that day. Two days later, two of the most important players injured themselves during a league match and were out for six and eight weeks, respectively.

I once watched a goalkeeper coach implement a five-day plyometric phase in the second week of pre-season despite my colleagues' recommendations to reconsider. He told his strength coach to mind his own business. His number one goalkeeper ruptured his patellar tendon doing 36" hurdle hops on day three of the plyometric phase.

Against common sense and our suggestions, a new manager extended a pre-planned training session by 15 minutes, which resulted in a 300% increase in very high speed running and directly resulted in two long-term hamstring injuries.

Manager at a massive professional football club in Europe who simply would not listen to anyone because he knew best. He overworked the team, they had four hamstring injuries in the space of three weeks and was sacked after three months (and six losses in a row).

Sadly, injury-related again. I had a player with an ongoing hamstring injury who convinced the coach he was ready to start playing again, even though he hadn't completed the return to training criteria. The egos of the coach and player convinced them they were right, so the player started. After 12 minutes, he reinjured his hamstring, and both blamed me in the press!!

For various reasons and ego battles between decision-makers, we had a player coming back from a bad hamstring injury who ended up being given the green light to return to competition without having done a single assessment of his hamstring strength. Thankfully he had done multiple fitness tests!!

When I first arrived to head up performance for this team, I implemented a team-wide heart rate monitoring system, which was a new concept for our coach.

During one of our early training sessions, which was relatively easy from both a volume and intensity standpoint, one of our best player's HR showed well over 200 beats per minute, maybe 220+. I walked over to him to check on him and he was fine - no issues whatsoever. I assumed it was interference in the system.

Shortly after, same thing: HR was around 220 bpm. However, this time when I went to check on him it was a very different situation. He struggled to speak and was clearly in distress. I immediately removed him from training and monitored the situation. After a short while his HR returned to normal, yet he did not feel well and understood something was not right.

I immediately called a meeting with our head coach and medical staff, and asked when the last time this player had a cardiac exam. It had been over two years. I explained the situation, and we had him examined by our team doctors and cardiac specialists. The initial response was that he would need a heart transplant and never play basketball again. After several different medical opinions and evaluations, it was determined that he needed a corrective procedure on his heart and would miss the season. However, barring any further issues, he would be able to play basketball again the following year.

I was quite happy that we might have saved this athlete's life by identifying an underlying issue and prevented a potential disaster from happening on the court.

Our coach, however, could not see this and allowed his ego to get in the way, being upset that one of our best players was out for the season. He ordered me to never use heart rate monitors again, as it cost us one of our best players.

I could not and, still to this day, cannot get over the fact that he could not put his ego aside and now viewed HR monitors as a negative thing.

One coach tried to "make" a player get into an ice bath. The player did not value the ice bath as a recovery modality and challenged the coach's fragile but large ego (not me, incidentally, LOL). It ended up with the very well-known and truly elite player wrestling with the coach and almost throwing him into the ice bath. Totally unnecessary conflict, but funny now looking back at it.

I worked for a head coach who was a good guy, and I do believe that he did what he thought was in people's best interest even if it made no logical sense to everyone around him. The issue was that he felt as though he knew it all, and really struggled to take on information and see things from a point of view that was not his.

I helped a player get his weight and body fat down. He wasn't playing much, and the coach emphasized that one of the reasons he wasn't playing was his suboptimal physical condition. We decided together that he should reach a specific target for his body composition. He was working hard both on the pitch and in the cafeteria to reach his objectives. While he was improving but not completely fit yet, several players got injured in the squad. The coach had no choice but to make him a starter for a few matches. The player did really well, with three goals and two assists over three matches in two weeks. Following the third match, he came to see me and said "Your weight-loss program sucks. I can't be bothered following this anymore. It's hopeless and I don't need that, anyway." He put on three kilograms in the next three weeks and didn't start any other match during the rest of the season.

World Cup. One of the young athletes in the squad wasn't happy with the way he was ranked within the team, and decided to race with what he thought was the best strategy, violently dismissing all advice from the different staff. First race, he hit his head and didn't finish. Even worse second race: torn knee, career over. Nothing more to comment on.

DID I MENTION I KNOW EVERYTHING?

One day I sent around a scientific paper, which was the first published comprehensive analysis of the effect of kinesiotaping on muscle function and pain. As soon as I clicked on "send," one of my physio colleagues came to me and said that I didn't need to send stuff that he already knew 20 years ago, because he had been in the business for way longer than me.

We worked hard to organize various internal courses or workshops. The invited speakers and practitioners were high standard and would obviously bring some light to our practices; help people with questions about their work; open their minds to techniques they would already know. Staff might even learn something new. The reality is that, most of the time, almost no one would show up even for a 30 minute workshop. They knew it all. This happened many times until we stopped organizing these events.

"You are not a marathon runner. Don't bother going to the race. You'll fail." This was the "wise advice" of the sports medicine egomaniac "expert" to an endurance runner right after finishing a blood lactate test on the treadmill, five days before his marathon debut in a world-class event. Not only he did not fail: he finished 14th, in a time of 2:13:43, and subsequently went on to run 2:09:55. Not bad for someone who is not a marathon runner.

A fitness coach wanted to know my strength training methodology and visit for a workshop. Before long, I started consulting at the football club where he worked. Curiously, he didn't want to learn anything then. He already knew everything and did everything right. My role didn't make sense. I didn't understand!

SUPERMAN > A SUPER EGO

The club performance coach had sent the individual summer programs to all players. I found out on Instagram that many of the players were doing other exercises than those prescribed. I then told myself that they may have hired personal coaches, external to the club, and would do their own program with them. That's something we don't control, and that's OK. I found out, however, a few months later that it was one of my physio colleagues at the club who had been sending out those programs… without letting anyone else know, of course.

A physio preparing and delivering a rehab session on his own. The session turns into a technical session with more players involved, which should be under the supervision of the technical staff. But who cares, right? Practitioner and player were happy with the session, and, more importantly, they had pictures for social media at the end of the day.

There are a couple of examples of injured athletes working with a massage therapist or strength & conditioning coach who has such a big ego that they wouldn't refer the player to medical staff.

They honestly believed they could fix the athlete on their own, with no additional support required. I also have seen many physiotherapists, strength & conditioning coaches and massage therapists with big egos ignore their colleagues with expertise in nutrition and psychology because... they know it all!

Medical staff asked a colleague not to perform a physical assessment on a player because it would put the player at great risk, as they were not ready for it. The person ignored the request and performed the test anyhow. The player got injured, the staff member got sacked. Reality 1 - 0 Ego.

Without consulting the medical team, a fitness coach proposes to a player back from hamstring injury to do change of direction and repeated sprints training after eight sets of small-side games in the first session with the team. The player suffered a reinjury at the exact same place.

STAND TALLER BY STEPPING ON OTHERS

Some people with uncontrolled egos are simply mean. They're just jerks who get off on putting other people down to feel more important themselves. They will disrespect a fellow professional simply to reinforce the hierarchy, not for any minimally justifiable technical reason. They indulge primal attitudes - they probably look in the mirror and think "alpha male" - to show their own superiority over others, which reinforces their own impression of grandeur.

"This food is shit. You'd be better off giving them Snickers." One of the assistant coaches, who had some very particular views on nutrition, to the nutritionist who had ordered some high-end, healthy club sandwiches.

"You know, you were writing papers when me, here, I was doing the team warm-up in front of 80,000 fans." An old fitness coach to me, when I was trying to help him by showing him data and research findings.

"We don't win matches with a computer!" Same old fitness coach after a win, to the sport scientists on their laptops.

The manager threw the training session plan in the face of one sports scientist. In front of the entire staff. How do you react and recover from that?

"Remember that I'm am the manager and I'm up there, you're down here." Head coach, pointing to the floor, to one of his assistants.

Someone I work with who is unwilling to recognize value in people with less experience, or experience that they don't deem as worthy. For example, even though I have been a physio for nine years, continuing to tell me that I only have three years' experience, because for four years of my time as a licensed physio I was working on a Ph.D. (yes, I know that math doesn't add up!). This, among other things, has led to struggles in our interactions, because now we react to each other emotionally and defensively. I have struggled not to let my ego get in the way because I feel put down.

I began to work in judo, where I had no real previous experience and was called a white belt by one of the coaches in spite of having significant transferrable experiences from other sports. It was a clear attempt to devalue my input / influence in a sport where, at the time, the coaching and programming had a major influence on the number of injuries to key athletes.

A colleague humiliated the best player on the team during the first fitness session, because he didn't turn with his foot on the line. "Not ethical," he said. He lost the player forever and struggled the entire season to get work done.

The regular coach tactic of making players train by themselves because they want to get rid of them, even though they signed them. It's inhumane and should not be permitted. But the fact is many coaches are actually not a coach, they are just a player that had no other life plan.

One day the head coach told me that he will be in charge of the conditioning for the day instead of me, who had already prepared everything. He asked the players to do a crazy session, likely double the volume of what we would typically do. He was about to destroy them. Half way, he stopped the session and told the players that they did really well and deserved a rest. Then he looked at me and said, "This is a conditioning session, and this what you should do. You need to adapt the session when it's needed." Overall, the players ended up doing exactly what I had planned but it looked like the coach had made the right decision, not me.

It was his last meeting of the day, one that he kept delaying, until I sat down and he said "I don't know if I should bring you back next year. You are only 26 years old and already working in the NBA. It has taken me 20 years just to make it as a coach," as he puffed out his chest. He wanted me to grovel at his feet and show him that I was worthy of his presence. Needless to say, he didn't hire me back for the next year (although he didn't last much longer after that, either).

I was told a job was becoming available in an organization and applied for it. Another practitioner who was my equivalent went directly to the CEO and effectively got the opening removed because he didn't want me to be his boss.

Assistant coach who started to coach thanks to the head coach he was working with (doing a very good job). At this level, he started to receive a lot of praise and people were telling him he would manage, etc., because his job was brilliant and he arrived the moment he felt he could manage the team. He started working as always, but when the dynamics of the team started to be bad and he thought he could be sacked, he changed his behavior regarding his role, talking with players about their thoughts and what was going wrong the head coach. After having this information, he talked to the board behind the head coach, to explain what he would change if he became the head coach.

A couple of colleagues (their egos, really) try to "kill me" like in a gangster movie. They trapped me in a bathroom and "advised" me (while they smoked...) to stop working with one athlete. Only he could work with them: "Be careful or you are out..."

In the club, the women's team staff and men's team staff shared offices and gyms. Men's team performance staff was going through an intern education with their interns in the room, and I was next to them in the same room. The interns were asking about long term athletic development, something I spent the last few years focusing on and came from an environment where I led a youth athletic development culture. The staff knew about it because one of them was in the committee that hired me. This guy never really had a great amount of experience coaching kids, and instead of asking me to join the conversation because I could add something to it, he completed ignored that I was in the room and did not allowed me to share and collaborate in the conversation.

GENDER DYNAMIC

And yes, gender egos are very prevalent the other direction. I have probably had a harder time being accepted by the females in the field than by the men. Seems to be pretty situation dependent - some woman that I work with are amazing. There are only a few of us, though, only two females in the traveling party for the team (which makes up about 60 people) and I love the other female who travels. But not always the case!

That's very interesting that the other female contributors reported that gender dynamic. That's not something I have encountered directly, to be honest, but I do see a pattern emerging where a majority of teams now have one female on their performance team, mostly a medical person, physio, etc, and just one. No more than one. I guess it's a pattern of the "token female," which has been seen in the American boardroom in business for a long time now: "We are diverse because we have one woman on our board," but really that woman's voice is not heard.

I think it depends a lot on the outlook of the women in question. If a woman comes into a professional team position with an attitude of scarcity, meaning there is only room for one woman on each team, and that woman will be her, forever, and if any other woman comes along she might threaten her position, then I guess I can see how that woman may not help other females around her.

On the other hand, if you have an attitude of abundance, where you feel there are lots of jobs on these performance teams with 50 staff members, and plenty of room for women, and plenty of injured athletes who need help, then I think you are more likely to help those young people you meet.

There's a quote from Madeline Albright, an American politician, that I am reminded of with our current conversation: "There is a special place in hell for women who don't help other women."

I try to maintain an attitude of abundance, and I truly believe the more that our performance teams look like our diverse society, the better.

In Switzerland, where I am from, there is a really good female physio who I always looked up to as an example to follow, being a female coach. She actually was close to my family as she treated my dad in the past. When I was going to spend some time in Brazil for summer, I reached out to her to learn from her and be able to shadow her for a day to talk shop and collaborate. At that point, I already had made a good name in Switzerland with the work I was doing, and being a reference coach in youth development where I was from. She was really rude to me, and kind of cut me off and never really responded to my text and said she wouldn't be able to meet to talk or let me shadow her. As a role model for me as a female coach this was extremely disappointing, and I mainly think this was because of her ego and competition from having a good female coach emerging in our town.

DON'T FORGET WHO'S THE BOSS: ME! ME! ME!

Head coach arrives late at most of the meetings. Of course, we have to wait for him. He is so important!! But best of all is that when the most important players are not on time for training or matches, the coach gets crazy and hammers them!!

One doctor reported a higher than normal rate of perceived exertion in a player's training session, suggesting we check for a possible fatigue problem and increase the recovery measures. The doctor was strongly reprimanded by the head coach for criticizing the coaching staff's training methodology, which was supposed to have all the players constantly in perfect condition and in the highest performance state with no fatigue. The doctor was eventually fired.

In my first year as performance director, I was given a very big name (within the elite sport industry) consultant to utilize within my staff. It was a huge deal to have access to him full time.

A player in our club reported back from off-season with complaints of shin pain and, upon further review, we saw he had a tibial stress fracture. This was a big name player, our highest paid player, with serious injury history.

The consultant, in one of our first staff meetings, stated that the entire staff didn't have enough experience to handle this situation and stated that HE will be handling this case alone. Not only did this immediately separate him from the newly formed team, but also removed unique assets, which could have strengthened his ability to perform his role. Obviously, having to manage this as a young leader was difficult and put me in quite a predicament.

I had a colleague in the medical department who couldn't tolerate seeing the sport scientists dealing with anything related to what he believed was "medical stuff" and most importantly within his area of expertise. He warned me that if I was to ever write a paper with "those" data, he would write a letter to the editor to say how poor our work was. Twenty papers later, I am still waiting for his letter.

Working in pro cycling, during the Tour of Britain, the owner of the team wanted to stop for a lunch / drinks with all staff despite the fact the staff didn't really want to, and the riders were already back at the hotel. So we ended up drinking late and riders were desperate for treatment.

It's a repeated story of players who are not selected for a game for various reasons and then they take it badly. Then, when the coach selects them for another game, they fake an injury, as a way to say "ah really, now you need me? I decide now if I can play again."

BLAME IS FOR THE LITTLE PEOPLE

Anyone working in a high-performance environment has seen their colleagues sacked - or been sacked themselves - for little or no cause. When there is a good reason for a sacking - an injury crisis, a run of bad results, a decline in fitness across the season, relegation - poor egos put up the deflector shields.

I like this one inspired from Raymond Verheijen. It's about subjectivity in football, and the huge culture of blame that comes with it. Subjectivity in a subjective world creates chaos. The only way to survive in chaos for people who actually can't explain why they do what they do, is to blame others or something else, as long as it's not them.

The Football 90° rules. People put their arms up to claim ownership of positive outcomes and down to let others take the blame when things go wrong.

Yes. I have somebody in the staff who thinks he is so good at what he does that the reason the team fails is because of all the other staff members, never because of him. Not being able to self-reflect, blame others instead, not giving attention to constructive criticism. I think it's a big characteristic of somebody who has a big ego in this field. Also, the majority of staff tends to be really selfish and are always blaming others before reflecting on their own actions. That creates a really negative environment sometimes.

A Spanish colleague started to work with us at the club in an English-speaking country. After studying English for some months, he thought - his ego made him think - he was able to manage his meetings in English, without anyone having to do the translation. When he had to talk in front of the people, he wasn't able to say much. At the end, he missed the most important information. One day, he came back to me two days after an important meeting, pissed because I didn't give him all the information he needed! Of course, everything was discussed and agreed during the meeting, and many decisions had been taken since. But it wasn't his fault, of course.

"I think we should push him on." This doesn't always work, and is driven by the ego of the "pusher," who often wants to use "instinct" rather than anything measurable. Only one person suffers when it goes wrong - the player - and the "pusher" usually hides behind a veil of blaming others!

This happens all the time. Physio on the bench during a match. Players requesting whatever sort of often non-urgent tape or material, and the physio has all of the gear with him except that piece. Instead of running back to the locker to get it, he blames his hopeless colleagues who have not prepared the bag correctly. In fact, it's 100% his responsibility. He simply takes the radio and requests a kitman to bring it to him URGENTLY.

A training session that is poorly prepared (e.g., last-minute decisions) ends up - unsurprisingly - a disaster: wrong timing during the exercises, unclear rules, time gap between sequences, players pissed. Coaches stop the session, blaming the players who are not in the right mindset, and keep talking about their poor attitude for weeks after.

Lot of injuries happening six months into the season, load is clearly poorly managed, etc. The manager's staff starts to blame the club staff who have been in place for many years, during which injury rates were super low. Instead of adapting their approach to the player group, the new staff simply rejects responsibility and says they can't do much because they inherited poor players. They keep blaming the nutritionist because some players are borderline with their body fat percentage and she prescribes what they say are hopeless and even dangerous supplements. Sure, the research is conclusive on the fact that the supplement is highly recommended in periods of overload and there is nothing that links it to injury occurrence. But apart from that, their program is ideal and there is no need to change AT ALL. WTF?!

I think carelessness is another source of watching an ego f*** up! If you are going to delegate you have to be supportive in helping the person you delegate to have the correct information to perform a task. If that doesn't happen and you fail to even check that individual's work prior to taking it as your own, that for me is a big ego f*** up. What would be even worse is claiming it is yours, someone else identifying the mistake, then you blaming the person you asked to do it: "throwing someone under the bus."

THE EGO THIEF: STEALING OWNERSHIP

Certain staff have a habit of trying to claim a form of ownership over things that have been developed during their time in the structure, whatever they were involved a bit or a lot. This could include training programs, sport science processes, facilities extension and development, all the way up to player and team performance. Doing so, those persons forget (unconsciously or not) the teamwork to anchor their individual actions and ideas to the broad end goal.

His team won the tournament. The following day, the head nutritionist tweeted something like "Best performance of the team ever, outstanding playing style, greater running performance and fewer injuries in the league, records at all levels…I think I can be proud of my work." I am not saying this guy didn't have an impact, but it's a lot to be proud of.

A certain colleague I worked with was invited to speak at a prestigious conference in Australia. Just before going on stage in front of 3,000 people he bumped into the chief executive and academy manager from the club, something which made him really twitchy. He informed the guys that "this being the US, you do need to big up the messages in your presentations," before delivering a presentation in which he explained how he virtually single-handedly was responsible for the trophy the team won the previous season. The following day he gave the assembled throng an insight into how "he had made player X (a product of the club academy) an international player." Ouch!!

I've seen guys I worked with make claims at seminars about what they were doing and gains or improvements they were making, that were not inaccurate - they were complete lies.

Coaches assuming credit for injury reduction when the new head coach was the reason due to a change in training philosophy.

A nutritionist had worked for a few months with a goalkeeper to help him lose a bit of body fat. The player got in shape finally, and during his first match after the post-intervention body composition assessment, he stopped a penalty. It didn't take long to hear everywhere that the penalty stop was attributed to the change in body composition and, of course, her amazing work.

Before an important match, a physio who was in charge of player rehab tells the coach: "When I give you back the player, he will be ready." As if he had been the only one in charge and responsible for the return to play process, overlooking the work of about 12 colleagues!

LEGENDS IN THEIR OWN MINDS

Staff have this feeling of self-importance since they work in prestigious clubs. But don't assume that self-regard correlates with expertise.

I believe that there is a preconceived idea that reaching the "elite" and professional level makes those coaches better than everyone else just because they are there.

Lack of quality leadership has allowed it, social media and bullshit drive it. Therefore, based on supply and demand, ego has been used to raise the status of some individuals.

An ex-international player, now manager, after a speed testing session: "We only have one player below 10 seconds on an 80 meter. In my time, all the backs where below 10 seconds! This is shit." Without him knowing, we got our hands on the data from his time: no player was below 10 seconds. Not even one was below 10.5!!!

A colleague who had been working in other clubs kept praising the work that he had done there, which was supposedly better organized and, more importantly, allowed those teams to stay fit and healthy throughout the seasons he worked there. It was simply impossible to discuss with him why we were doing things differently here.

Despite the good track record we had, he couldn't imagine changing his philosophy. So we adopted his approach. Things quickly went pretty poorly, with a lot of injuries and a disappointing year in terms of results. His reaction to that was, of course, that it wasn't his methods but many other elements in our context that f**ed it up. The next season, the same thing happened, and he had the same response. Interestingly, in the meantime, I managed to chat with some of his ex-colleagues at his former club, and they told me exactly the same about him. More importantly, they said they had similar problems with his unwillingness to change and unfortunately, this had led also to a lot of injuries there.

This made me realize that this guy had been able to carry with him an ineffective methodology and approach for years, and the biases and stories he had in his head sadly prevented him from seeing the reality of things. I can only imagine that now, if, by luck he gets a good season in the future, he will just say "I told you, my method works!!"

A colleague of a peer who, every time he would raise a question or try to discuss an intervention with his superior, would receive a dismissive reply of "well I've done it this way for 30 years." For me this is a clear example of an individual being gripped by their ego. They believe their experience from the last 30 years overshadows any evidence, be it scientific or anecdotal.

"We have always done it this way and it worked fine." For example, youth national teams playing games with only one day apart with an 18-player squad. They say that to protect their egos from having to consider change / development.

Junior World Cup. Before an important game and after two weeks of competition, we pulled together all of our screening processes to discuss one of the key players. We were up until 1am analyzing his creatine kinase, making sure we were the first awake so we could collect his wellbeing report and discuss it before the day's jump tests. We skipped eating so we could be on time to deliver the report. The player was identified as being tired: his well-being was low, creatine kinase was high, countermovement jump was lower than expected - all red flags. We asked the manager to reduce his workload. I went directly to him and still the coach didn't plan to rest him. His reply: "U20 players are not tired! They are young. When I was a young international, I could play every game without fatigue blah blah blah."

Our key player trained... and got injured.

The manager: "Bad luck!!"

I particularly recall a job interviewee I was interviewing for a position. He had been messaging me for weeks before, thought he had all the credentials, thought we were friends, and therefore thought the job was his. His efforts and antics in the interview were ridiculous! Trying to half-ass things, tell us how we had to hire him, telling us that he knew more than we did. Lo and behold, he fell from a great height when we didn't give him the job.

BLINDED BY EGO: WHO NEEDS THE OBVIOUS WHEN YOU HAVE ME?

Those who have excessive faith in their theories or ideas are not only ill prepared for making discoveries; they also make very poor observations.

– Claude Bernard, physiologist

I worked with a coach who was very good at interpreting match data to support his work and protect him. He didn't have a problem using the same data to explain and attribute credit or blame opposite outcomes!! Obviously, this strategy worked against our collective ability to learn and improve. For example, while in the first year when the team was having very good results, the limited running activity of the team during matches was supposedly a reflection of the coach's very good tactical strategies. But the same low match running performance was used to blame the physical coach of the club the following year when results were poor.

Errors don't enter into the development process. We don't document them as, for example, the aviation industry does so we can learn from others' mistakes. Rather, they are immediately swept under the carpet by those who commit them as a protective mechanism.

Facing a period of increased injuries, a meeting is held to discuss the possible cause and remediation strategies. The head coach reacts immediately saying that if players are getting injured it's simply because that are not ready to play how he wants them to play and we just need to be patient. In the long term they will adapt, and it helps player selection on the weekend, anyway. So where is the problem?

A response to an "injury crisis" was to buy more equipment for the weight room rather than really reviewing the facts as to why "the crisis" was there in the first place.

An assistant coach, for unknown reasons and despite an incredible amount of evidence, both scientific and "best practices", didn't believe in the efficacy of some specific gym exercises to mitigate injury risk. One day, he noticed that another team in another league was facing a lot of injuries. Without having a clue what that other team's actual training was like, he told our staff that the other team were surely doing it wrong, just as we were doing it wrong before HE joined the club. This was also without admitting that, at the same moment, his own team was showing the worst injury record of the past 10 years.

We had been testing and training players for many years on a track at the club. A new coach came in and was sometimes running with the players. After a few sessions, he started to question the actual length of that track, which looked a bit shorter to him. Despite the fact that we had measured it many times with appropriate materials, and that every single session was monitored with GPS, confirming the exact length of the track for years, he decided to measure it on his own one early morning. We never heard any complaints since. But obviously, he never tried to apologize for doubting our data.

I saw a head coach ban all GPS and sport science data because it was "making players soft." The truth was it was evidence that he was training the team improperly.

I went to see a colleague to debrief his return-to-play session, showing him a GPS report. It was obvious that the load of the session was a bit too high if we were looking at the overall progression. I just wanted to make him aware of that, so that he could adjust accordingly the following days. Nothing more. As soon as I started to show the data and he realized the "issue," he dismissed the report and said that GPS were unreliable anyway, and it was a waste of time looking at those numbers. Needless to say, a week before he had asked me to build a specific GPS report to help him to monitor his training and showcase his work to the sporting director, and was very thankful to me for putting this together.

I once saw a fitness coach go outside a planned session, which was 4 x 2 minutes of 5v5 with two minutes recovery. When I reviewed data later there were 12 x 2-3 mins. This was GD-2, and after being beaten easily the coach was interviewed and stated the team was just so "flat." Furthermore, from this one session, six players had an injury during the following three days. Moronic. And no responsibility - they continued on their merry way. I remember asking, "What have you done?" Fitness coach said they got what they deserved. Sadly, this person still gets work.

I was watching a colleague in the gym working upper body exercises with a player in rehab. They were working with a little bit of weight on the exercise. As the player started to struggle with the load and blame my colleague for not selecting the appropriate weight, the coach just said it was expected from him and, instead of simply reducing the load and dropping a few kilograms, he assisted the player while pulling him up with a band. The colleague clearly didn't want to admit his error and tried to hide it like that, but overall it looked even more ridiculous.

After an executive in our club told ownership, media, players and staff that a specific player (Player X) was not good enough for "his" desired style of play, the executive gave a presentation on KPIs in our optical tracking data.

To give some context, Player X joined the club about three years earlier under the former leadership team. He was a vocal leader and told leadership and the media how he felt if he felt something was unfair, but was always a professional in his actions and work ethic. One such occasion occurred between this player and executive, where Player X told him that a decision he made was not good for the group, and he said it in a semi-public forum (a team meeting).

Within the presentation, the following data points were discussed and were given as the KPIs for our style of play: Distance Covered, Player X ranked third; Forward Passing Index (some number he created), Player X ranked second; Passing skills (by-passed players), Player X ranked first. This was not decided with the entire staff or with insight from the data or performance staffs.

All measures presented except for high speed running had Player X evaluated as one of the top players in our team. Even with the public presentation, this executive stood by his decision and stated that the player was not suited for the style of play and would not survive its intensity.

Reviewers who do not assume that there may be opposite results to those of their study, and then reject a paper that was, in reality, pretty good. But at least nothing that could get in their "way" gets published.

EGO INTELLIGENCE AGENCY: CONTROL THE INFORMATION, CONTROL THE ROOM

Sir Francis Bacon (supposedly) taught us that knowledge is power. G.I. Joe cartoons taught a generation of children that "knowing is half the battle." And economist George Gilder linked information to the complexities of the economy in his straight-forwardly titled book "Knowledge and Power."

Clearly, they're all on to something.

Fragile egos need all the protection they can get, and the power of information can be a useful shield. Micro-managing is not just about depriving those around you of input and agency, but information. The less someone's colleagues and subordinates know, the more dependent they are on them for their input and the less able they are to challenge their ideas with something better.

Hoarding information confers a certain level of immediate control, but it also provides the delusion of broader control. You can wield your private stash of information over your colleagues, but what you don't know will always exceed what you do know, so you'll never be able to control everything. It's what economists call the "knowledge problem." Sooner or later, the nature of reality will take events in your team, company, classroom or other organization beyond the reach of your information. And when it does, and your boss wants to know who is responsible, everyone will happily say that you and you alone had control of the process.

And even if you could perfectly control the information flow to control the people around you, you can never control nature and its addiction to freak events. Your tightly-held data and minutely scripted plans are useless when a player trips on his way back to the locker room after a routine training session, fracturing his ankle.

If you want to take credit for your control, you have to be on the hook for the chaos. Over the long term, which do you think will win out?

I worked with a doctor who never wrote anything down and used to choose which information should be given to which staff, so that he would always need to be consulted. It was, in fact, impossible to make decisions without him in the room.

We had a team doctor who didn't want to share any data with the sport science department in the name of confidentiality. It was pretty harmful practice since we couldn't do any retrospective analysis of injury rate, etc. He kept pretending that he was doing the stats himself, and that he didn't need to share anything and he could respond directly to all of our questions on the topic in person. "Just ask me what do you want to know and I'll tell you."

This year we had a very well-known practitioner appointed as a consultant by the board to help us "smoothing out" the return to play process at the club. After the consultant had decided that the staff could work with other members of staff, a set of protocols and procedures were developed to guide decision-making and progression. Upon "mastery" of specific movement qualities, and before progressing to the next stage of reconditioning, there was a testing battery to objectively rate the movements.

At one point there was a split camp as to where our next steps should be in the progress, so we decided to evaluate the athlete's abilities to decide if there were any gaps in the qualities built up in the previous stage. Internal data comparisons, along with scientific articles, were utilized to compile normative data for each assessment. Following the testing and analysis, data showed that he had markedly improved upon the quality which was the focus at that time, which led a majority of the group feeling as though this athlete could progress. The consultant felt differently. Having not been in the facility for a few weeks now, he felt that the athlete should have to prove to him and spend multiple days being "reassessed" with him present, to prove that the athlete could do this again. Obviously, staff and the player felt this was a large waste of time, as it was well-communicated in meetings and emails that we would conduct testing and progression assessments the previous week.

This was a difficult situation which created much angst in our group, and decisions were made to remove the consultant from day-to-day work with the group as there was a lack of confidence within the day-to-day staff.

The department leader who is the "lone ranger": does not interact with his staff, does not delegate, does not seek opinions, does not admit mistakes, does not share information! Extremely dangerous and destructive!

I was working with a team manager who would select which information would be sent to who, would retain information or only release it at a certain time so that he would always need to be consulted at some point. As a matter of fact, his strategy allowed him to keep a central function and to know everything about everyone, which was often beyond his role and responsibility.

I've stopped counting the times when I realized that a meeting had been held without me, while my role and function would have implied I should have participated. Typical responses from colleagues: "Don't worry, we know you're busy, we sorted the problem, it's OK." without even letting me know what they talked about!!

When I worked at the university, I had a manager who could not get out of his own way. He thought every single issue was something he had to deal with, and the only correct path was his way. Unfortunately, he ended up spreading himself so thin that he couldn't accomplish anything, which ultimately led to his downfall. Again, this is another example of how someone's ego clouded their ability to do their job to their strengths.

It's the whole approach - questioning, comments, not sharing information, reluctance to work together although you are in the same performance team - which can almost be compared to bullying in school.

ENTITLEMENT COMPLEXES: WHY EVEN BOTHER?

With accomplishment and fame, lots of athletes and staff develop a belief that they deserve to be given what they want, when they want. They completely lose their sense of reality.

Our club photographer was once invited (on a non-working day) for the birthday of the kid of one of our top players. He obviously understood that he was expected to take pictures, which he did nicely. But when it came time to eat the cake, he was requested to step back and wait for two hours in the kitchen, but still stay until the end so he wouldn't miss the last moments of the party. The next day the player complained about not receiving the pictures quickly enough. Obviously, he never offered a compensation to the photographer.

While all the information possible about players and programming was available on the club athlete management system or shared drives, some colleagues (mainly coaches, heads of departments or others in high positions) couldn't be bothered logging in. They were still requesting the info, so we had to send separate messages to each of them, based on their own preference: email to one, text to another, WhatsApp to a third...

A coach called the yellow pages and asked them to book a table at a restaurant. They told him they could just put him in touch with the restaurant, but he had to book himself. The coach replied, "But I'm Diego Munoz!"

I've seen coaches remove players from a first-class upgrade seat on a flight because they felt they should have it instead. Crazy.

A player working long hours on his rehab was late for lunch at the club after having spent a bit too much time in the cold bath post-training. The kitchen being closed, he got pissed for not be able to eat, but rules are rules at the club, and the kitchen had to close. Seeing the situation, and thinking that I still had to do some intense work with him in the afternoon, I asked security for the restaurant key and prepared him a sandwich myself, which is completely out of my job under normal circumstances. I remembered more or less the type of sandwiches he would order sometimes, so I put a lot of effort into it. I then brought him the sandwich, explaining the story a bit and why it took me 30 minutes to get that done. He looked at me and said that he wasn't hungry anymore and pushed aside the sandwich. There was a very odd feeling during the session for the rest of the afternoon, but I did my job until the end.

Most teams have kit men, at least one but as many as four at some teams, whose job is to set up the locker room and assist players (and staff!) with anything you can imagine. Basic jobs are preparing players' uniforms, installing whatever is required for the locker room to feel "like home" (especially during away games), unpacking some gym materials, putting on a music speaker, a coffee machine, etc. The kitmen may be changing studs on a player's boots and distributing warm-up shirts for the players while also pouring coffee(!), making sure iPhones are charged and that a player's friend playing with the opposing team gets his signed shirt at the end of the game.

Kit men are everything.

But because of their presence, players (and staff!!) feel entitled. They think they don't have to do anything at all other than chatting and looking at their phones. Most players throw their stuff on the ground at halftime and shout for a shirt replacement and changes in boots while everything is on the table 1.5 meters in front of them. Staff ask for their piece of equipment from the kitman 45 seconds before the kick-off, as the kitman is already running everywhere in the locker room to find the credit card of a player who forgot to leave it to his brother before the game, who is now waiting in front of the locker room (how could he reach this place with all the security??). And this is, of course, more urgent than anything else.

After the match, once players and staff have left, the locker room looks like a battle field. Dirty shirts and socks everywhere, food leftovers on the benches, and energy drinks bottles in the shower, used strapping bands on the wall…. and the kit men have to clean it entirely before leaving.

Do players and staff need to behave like this, all while being served like they are in a five-star hotel?

Elite sport and all the bad attitudes that come with it create these behaviors. I once asked a player if it was that difficult to throw his used socks in the container and put the paper of his cereal bar in the bins rather than on the floor. He said: "Kit men are here for this. This is their job, mine is to score goals." The next day I came to the manager and asked him if he wanted to say something about that. His response was very clear and somewhat understandable: "Players already hate me for so many other and more important reasons, such as why I didn't select them to play x or y game. There is no way I need to add that on my back. But please tell them something."

I tried with some individually, but without great success, and every time I did, I lost the player for a moment (with the greater his ego, the longer the loss).

So, in order to act, or at least show my disagreement, I renamed my iPhone "Sweep your shed." When we were all together in the bus, plane or locker room, everyone searching for a shared connection would see this anonymous reminder. A bit passive-aggressive, but it was my way to show my displeasure while keeping my job!

The first day after summer break, we were doing testing at our club's training ground in Germany. Players received their testing schedule the day before. One player who was scheduled in the morning called and said that he was on his way but he will be a bit late, and asked if I could schedule him later that day. I said I will, without arousing too much attention. Later on that day, I was getting nervous, as management and coaching staff started to ask for him. I had no choice, since I couldn't get him on the phone, to tell them that he called and said that he is on his way. They called his agent who said that the player was on his way - but not from home. He had called from the Miami airport!

PARANOIA AND COMPLETE LOSS OF SELF-CONTROL

The conditioning coach of the team came to me at the end of session and told me that I shouldn't talk to the sporting director on the side of pitch: it was disturbing for everyone, and everybody had understood that I was criticizing their work. Interesting, since we had a simple discussion about the catering cost of the next away match.

A lot of people tend to get offended by - and take personally - informal research dissemination within the club. Once I shared a new paper about injury prevention, and a large portion of the staff took the email as an attempt to criticize their own work. They didn't want to talk to me for a few weeks and, obviously, they didn't make the time to let me know why.

I have seen many of my colleagues reacting in an inappropriate manner when someone would tell them something about their work. They'd get completely pissed off for nothing, start shouting at the others and getting ready for war, while the comment was pretty insignificant. They ended up being ridiculous and saying things they don't even mean.

One of the club physios and I were watching a rehab session. The conditioning coach was running with the injured millionaire player. In between the running intervals, the physio, who was closely watching the live heart rate trace on the iPad, commented on the running intensity. He suggested it could be, in his opinion, increased slightly to challenge the player a bit more. Hearing this, the conditioning coach got completely mad, and started to shout very loud in front of everyone, the player included. He said it was disrespectful and totally inappropriate for a physio to comment on his work.

This showed a very poor image of our professional unity to the player, which is obviously everything: what you need during those return-to-play phases is for the player to trust the process. My colleagues didn't talk to each other for weeks after that. And I still don't know how a simple comment on heart rate could have led to such an escalation.

One morning I asked a colleague some information about a player. He said he will not respond to me since he knew I will use this information later in the day to dismiss his work.

One of my colleagues at the university completely lost it when his scientific papers were rejected. He would start swearing at these hopeless reviewers, then criticize every single point of their comments, dismissing every single argument: again, the journal had picked the wrong people who had been incompetent to examine his work! He was so loud at commenting about this that colleagues in the other offices knew when a rejection had landed in his inbox.

IT'S NOT NARCISSISM, I'M BUILDING MY BRAND!

Take the job titles in elite sports. It's become a circus. There's plenty of confusion about the actual roles of those performance professionals, i.e., which domains are they really in charge of, who do they manage and what level of contact with the athletes do they have (operational vs strategic planning). To add to the confusion, there is little, if any, consensus about those titles. They are often self-given, so that there are (almost) as many job titles as practitioners and structures; and there are large variations in actual roles across people with the same job title!

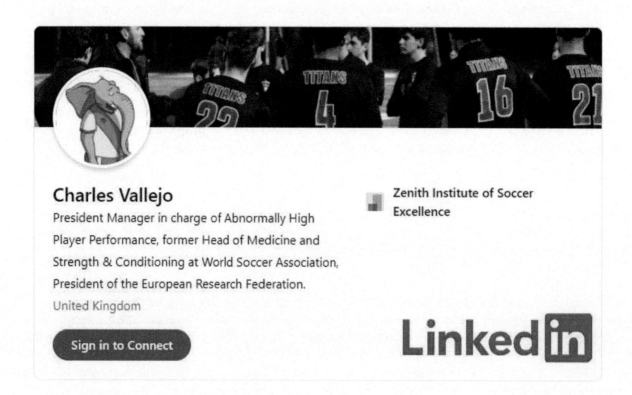

Charles Vallejo
President Manager in charge of Abnormally High Player Performance, former Head of Medicine and Strength & Conditioning at World Soccer Association, President of the European Research Federation.
United Kingdom

Sign in to Connect

Zenith Institute of Soccer Excellence

Linked in

The lack of a clear framework [Buchheit, 2019] has allowed anybody to become somebody - or at least make other people believe they're somebody "important" or "consequential." Everybody now is "Head of High Performance" or "High Performance Manager," and it nicely feeds their egos. People chase the title, rather the job itself.

But the truth is that performance is about winning or losing, so those "prestige" titles should be reserved for the coaches, not for supporting staff. But who wants to hear that?

"Performance engineer / architect" or just the title inflation where people who are fitness coaches are now "high performance managers," but have no skill in management or leadership.

You call yourself a doctor (or Ph.D.) everywhere.

Insisting on the need to run outdoors with a star who was in a return to play situation when it was not his duty, arguing about the confidence the player has in him. I said no problem and, at first, I did not realize why he was so keen on asking that. Then someone showed me the photographers eagerly shooting the player's first steps after a long injury.

This year most of the pre-season sessions were open to the media. The head of performance then decided to move the whole gym outdoors and he said he was happy to be more hands on this season.

I've seen so many professionals that pay more attention to being near the camera than improving their skills.

Producing and thinking as a teammate becomes far less important than communicating to the head management and skilfully pretending to be essential.

I've seen a fitness coach who had a work-related private registration plate - something along the lines of FIT COACH 1. Not sure that's something I would ever consider having on my car!

A colleague, a well-known researcher who creates a new lab and decides to give his own name to the lab (generally the institution may decide to do so, not the practitioner himself!!).

It's a sport scientist who creates a "new physical test" and decides to name the test after himself.

One day I received an email from a tech company. They were selling new products on the back of a few experts in the field. One of them had worked at the club a few years ago, in a field operating type of position. In the email, he was introduced as the head of one of the departments in my club and another where he never worked, and his job description was, in fact, an exact copy-paste of mine from my LinkedIn profile.

@TRAININGROOMEGO #EGO #NARCISSISM #SMH

Social media is a lot like ego. At its best, it communicates who you are, and how you view yourself and those around you. It can help you gain recognition from your peers; lead you into conversations and relationships you otherwise wouldn't have; and help promote your career.

But how often is social media at its best? Even less than ego, we'd say.

Social media provides sports performance practitioners with two ego temptations. First, they can put themselves where they don't belong: in the center of things. Pictures from the training ground or - worse - post-game celebrations let practitioners poach some of the team's and players' popularity. If we wanted to be on camera, we either chose the wrong line of work or we're doing it for the wrong reasons.

Second, a single social media post can get more engagement than a practitioner's entire corpus on ResearchGate. Will the fans liking, faving and retweeting actually remember who that practitioner is, or care about what they do? Probably not. Is that what your years of school, continuing education, self-study, 18-hour days, trials and lots of errors were building towards? No, but look at all those retweets!

#INSTAEGO #WINNING

I am in the locker and trying to be as small and discrete as I can after a bad defeat to a much lower ranked team. I see players coming back in, looking down. One of them, truly responsible for the second goal after a poor pass that was intercepted by the opponent, shows a bad face but keeps moving on his bench... looking for his phone.... He then starts to shoot a few selfies, 1, 2, 3 more... asks his teammates to join, then there's a whirl of photos and funny faces... post sent. I am so surprised by the scene that I hide myself in the toilets to check his IG account: 6,000 likes in three minutes! Not bad.... the players' comments on this to his teammates... what a great pic!! The defeat is forgotten... the pass to the opponent, too, apparently.

A colleague of mine used to retweet / report on Instagram every single picture where he would appear with players and staff. The moments were also always well-chosen: the better the match results and the more significant a victory would be, the greater the number of pictures of him working with the team he would post. When we won the title he even added pictures and montages that he took himself. The best was that he even added TV screenshots where you could see him... imagine the work for that. Funnily, however, he never posted pictures of himself with the team or players after defeats.

It was the day before the cup final. All the staff from the department were congratulating each other on LinkedIn, posting group photos and saying how proud they were to be working together. "I'm not used to writing things on social media, but I am so proud of what we achieved," wrote the head of the department. Likes, re-posts, shares everywhere. The next day, we lost. Their LinkedIn accounts have remained silent since.

#BUILDINGMYBRAND #EGO-FLUENCER

Now with the omnipresence of social media, it's like you have to have an account to post videos and photos of you working with athletes to be perceived as a true professional. When a new head physio was appointed to the club last year, I was surprised - but it's a fact- that we all checked his Instagram account when we heard about his signing. When we saw that he had more followers than most of us combined, even though we hadn't met him yet, it pushed us to implicitly feel that he was competent!!??

MARTIN BUCHHEIT
@mart1buch

...

 Hey Twitter please help, respond and share 🙏🙏

 I am curious to know how much the number of followers influences the credibility that people give to someone 🤔

Not important at all	**44.5%**
Ok, but content matters	40.6%
The guy must be relevant	10.7%
Credibility = following	4.2%

384 votes · Final results

I have witnessed many practitioners who, as soon as they are appointed to a now role, the first thing they do is add their new title to their Twitter profile. Most of the time I bet that the organization doesn't even know it, and if they were to ask they would probably not be allowed to do so. I also like the people mentioning their previous role in their profile, especially if now they hold a position in a less prestigious club.

I have an ex-colleague who was very active on social media as long as he was working with us. Pictures of him on the pitch, video of his work laughing with players... Now he works in a smaller club and surprisingly his account has remained inactive since.

During the COVID-19 crisis, I have been astounded by the sell that Dr. Henrik Petersen has made of his position and book. It is a daily social media bombardment and self-righteousness that has propelled him to new levels of arrogance and egotistical behaviour. This may sound surprising, as I'm sure you know him. However, I'm sorry to say that he has very little impact on the team at ground level and presents a mirage on the outside to demonstrate his effectiveness.

This is possibly not at f***-up levels yet, but he seems to be completely unaware that the more he promotes himself and his book during the absolute crisis when players and coaching staff are looking at redundancy, the more respect he is losing from his colleagues on the ground. He has not visibly coached anybody in his position since he started, bar a few speed sessions with the national team squad! He had zero impact on the national team in preparation for the World Cup, and when he visited the competition camp, he wasn't even staying in the team hotel! He just travelled to say that he was there.

Certain staff desperate for photos with superstars to put on their social media feeds, looking to be on camera all the time during live games, etc. "The higher the monkey climbs, the more you see it's arse."

How to increase your number of followers? Just add pictures of you treating or training players on Instagram A staff member gained >2,000 Instagram followers in a few days with a couple of pics!

I had a colleague who used to post on his own Instagram some pretty cool infographics that I had made for the players at the club. It was my personal work, club-branded by a great marketing agency, and he was hunting for likes on his account. I still haven't figured out how he even had the idea to do so.

The Gym Performance God ✔
@liftyourlife

🏆🏆🏆 ! 🏆🏆🏆 ! 🏆🏆🏆

I don't think I can win more trophies.
Running out of space in my office to
store them all!

#sorrynotsorry
#highperformanceproblems
#uwishuwereme

7:12 PM · Feb 7, 2021 · Twitter for iPhone

78K Retweets   **25.4K** Quote Tweets   **102.4K** Likes

Physio.Dream88 · Following
Spain

Liked by **Michael_Curry** and **22.145 others**
Physio.Dream88 🏀 Happy birthday to @Steve_Bryan, the
best player, person and #bff I ever coached. (We spent a
lot of time together in the gym at the World Basketball
Foundation and I know you always said I was the best gym
coach you had)
#PleaseRT #CallMe #Thirsty
View all 5523 comments
basket4skin 🎂🎂🎂 HB @Steve_Bryan!! #legend
Mary_sexy 🎂 Happy Birthday!! @Steve_Bryan!! #thebest
7 MINS

Bretrand.Martin_LifeCoach
France

"REMEMBER, IT'S NOT ABOUT YOU
- STAY BEHIND THE SCENES"

Bertrand Martin

Liked by **mart1buch** and **2.598 others**
Bretrand.Martin_LifeCoach 🔑 Another great conference,
so many people willing to talk to me after the show, I
couldn't talk to everyone so please follow me and leave a
message. I am probably the only one who can help you by
the way…
#LikeAndRT #YouNeedMe #LifeCoach … more
View all 1256 comments
Mathieu.dubois 👏👏 What a talk
@Bretrand.Martin_LifeCoach>!! #thebest
3 MINS

You see many people, when they want to say happy birthday to a famous player, they put a picture of them with him as a way to show that worked with him.

I follow a few people who put a lot of cool content on social media, self-improvement types of quote, but I don't see the value of having their face in each photo.

The odd self-promoting tweet, where people auto-congratulate themselves for having reached a certain number of paper and number of followers!! Is this necessary?

I like when people retweet/repost/like their own content, or even better when they quote themselves on a tweet/post. I understand they are trying to promote their ideas, but ideally you would like people to quote you, right? There may be a way to tell what you have to say without the need to post a picture of you, and quoting yourself on that same picture?

How often colleagues tweet instinctively, reacting to another one where their contribution wasn't acknowledged, so they react like "hey I did it too, but before and better."

It's incredible the number of people you see who just tweet a copy of the acceptance letter of their last paper – without adding any content. What is this for? Since they don't share anything to the community, it's just about stroking their own ego, no?

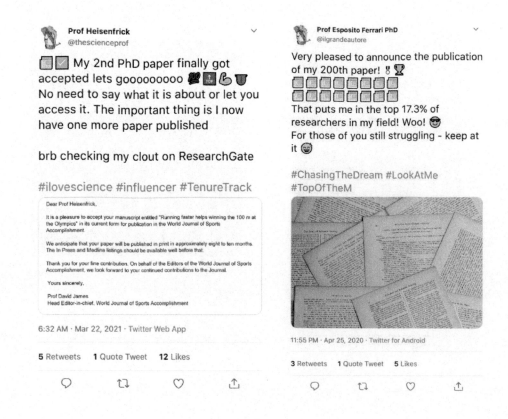

Feeding one's ego with social media is one thing. At least it's kind of harmless, you are not harming everyone else physically, but the question is: is this really necessary?

EVENTUALLY THINGS WORK OUT 😌

In my world right now, it's pretty black and white to see the consequence of bad ego. We have one or two fighters in particular who deliberately go out their way to demonstrate arrogance and ego. When that person goes into a fight and gets knocked out or their jaw broken so that it has to be wired shut and they can't talk for a number of weeks, that's a pretty powerful demonstration of your ego getting you in trouble.

A few years ago, the club signed a very talented young player from a top five European club. He had been in the U21 national team for his country, and people were saying everywhere he would soon be a superstar. When he arrived at the training ground for the first day, it was a bit as if Jay-Z and Beyonce had arrived in town. Expensive cars, designer clothes, hot girlfriend following him at every press conference, etc. He wasn't very friendly with the staff, and not speaking the language didn't help his integration, either. But above all, his attitude toward most of us was poor. He felt superior and entitled about everything. When the season started he clearly underperformed and even ended up being sent on loan for the rest of the season during the Christmas break!! When he came back to the club the following summer for preseason training, he still had the same car and clothes, but not the girlfriend anymore. His attitude changed impressively and he showed way more empathy with all of us. We started to connect. He trained with us for a few weeks, and then went on loan again for the season. The next summer, back with us. He couldn't even be bothered wearing fancy clothes anymore. We got even closer and he became one of the few players I managed to see outside of the club context!!

I do think that the lack of team success, for example, not having good results on the court for the past decade or more, dampens down the ego a little. Many players have been discarded by other teams and picked up by us. They have failed before, and now have a point to prove. We have no recent history of success. So I think there is less ego at play within our team than in more successful team environments I have experienced.

TAKE AWAY

These are the people and the moments that give ego a bad name. If these are your defining encounters with ego, then ego looks like a synonym for things like hubris and narcissism.

Laurent Schmitt, in *Le Bal des Egos* [Schmitt, 2005], traces these malformed expressions of ego to "the current ego-system, [where] popularity and image have become the end goal in itself. It's about people's notoriety per se and power. What matters is to make sure you outperform your rivals in terms of job and social status."

Schmitt's "ego-system" is a competition for emotional, psychological or professional resources and rewards. The competition is either zero-sum or no-win, because even if the mutant ego gains a temporary advantage, it comes at the expense of "the meaning, the why." And without those, we're on a treadmill instead of journey towards a goal.

Schmitt recognizes that people with these tendencies or characteristics are completely tangled up with others. Their only reference point is the person next to them: am I better than him, do I have more followers than him, did I get a better performance evaluation than him, is he getting paid more than me? They're not selfish. You can be selfish all by yourself. They, on the other hand, always need someone else, someone they will "perceive as inferior, incapable of anything or as threats that then need to be eliminated." Many of the quotes and incidents in this chapter come from an attempt to overwhelm others with a grandiose sense of self-worth, often from a position that allows them to speak with impunity.

That reaches the core distinction between ego and narcissism. Ego is about how the self contacts, perceives, relates to, judges and contrasts with the external world. Narcissism is the obsession with how others do all that to us.

Hopefully by recognizing the difference, we can prevent ourselves from doing the one thing worse than being on the receiving end of an ego f*** up: committing one ourselves.

4 | LESSONS LEARNED

Graduation day plants you at the peak of the Dunning-Kruger curve. New graduates know more than enough to get their first job in sports performance, and landing that job confirms what they are already primed to believe.

What's the best way to program in-season strength? I just graduated, I know that. What's the most effective rehab and return-to-play progression for a meniscal tear? I just graduated, I know that. Do you really know what you're doing? I just graduated and now I'm here, aren't I? Why should I listen to you? <awkwardly long, tense silence> Uh-oh.

Our classroom educations fill us with confidence and certainty. Then there's the post-grad boost from the clinical residency or internship with Prestige Experience FC, where you followed around that magician of a physio who treated that star player. Follow that up with a few early publications and conference presentations, and it's understandable to think we know it all and, therefore, can do it all.

I had no problems telling the 15-year veteran that he could be doing something better, when I was a 19-year old intern. I probably still think I was right, hahaha, just not very culturally sensitive. (7)

Miguel Ángel Campos, strength & conditioning coach, Cadiz CF: When I started as a professional, immediately after university, in a team that was highly successful, I believed that I was responsible for those results. It's only later, with more experience and working with people who were actually more knowledgeable, that I understood my value. I realized that being with such people was good for me. In the end, now, I even believe that if I've had more ego I would have been further in my career.

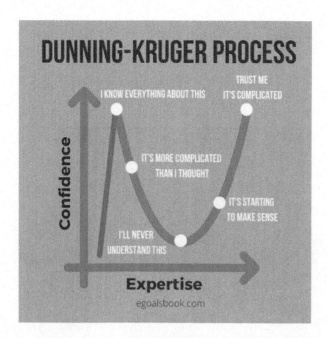

But the classroom, the lab and those first few steps are pretty well-structured. Someone else is managing the chaos so you can learn the basics that you need to learn. Those of us who make the jump from research to practice know that when they say "controlled study," the key word is control. That imparts a false sense of security and competence, one that makes it difficult not to think you're that good and that you'll always be able to exert that level of control and influence.

And this is where you start to do very questionable things, both in your work and your self-assessment.

All the certainty of an evidence-based education comes at the expense of context and communication. Even the most practical program cannot simulate the daily unpredictability of a high-performance environment.

Most training plans will change from one day to another to accommodate either simple physiological principles (e.g., the player is still sore from Tuesday's session), unplanned events (e.g., the plane was delayed after the away game, resulting in a shortened night of sleep) or external factors (e.g., family needs, press interviews). Classify those under "things you don't learn at school."

Classrooms also have no way of preparing students to communicate with the kind of people - the kind of egos - they will only encounter in a high-performance environment.

At the individual level, top athletes build up their own habits and beliefs. Training staff need to respect those practices if they hope to build trust and gain the athlete's buy-in. Even if we learn in school that that is the case, we can't know what those habits and beliefs are until we meet the player. Until we get to know the player, we can't know how to work within those habits and beliefs to induce them to do what we want them to do. Some of what they'll be doing - with the compliance of the current training staff! - is at odds with important physiological or programming considerations.

Handing down "the science" from the Dunning-Kruger apex will bring no one over to your side, which means even if you're right, you won't be able to improve your team.

Hierarchical environments present the danger of rank or position giving the illusion of control, and the opportunity to substitute control for competence. The worst possible answer to "Why should I listen to you?" is to (metaphorically or literally) tug on the rank insignia on your collar or point to the title on your door.

Having encountered a few overly rank-conscious officers in the US Navy, George came up with a saying that helped him handle his interactions with them and set the standard for his own conduct: Your rank entitles you to a salute and a "sir." You have to earn the rest.

Photo: Christian Gavelle

"I am trying to convince Zlatan Ibrahimovic to take a shake at D+1 instead of the BCAA he wants. He tells me to bring what he wants, not what he needs. And he has scored 256 goals without my shit anyway." (Martin Buchheit)

These are things we don't know that we don't know as we start our careers. Sometimes we learn them only to forget them along the way, or think that, at some point, they no longer apply to us.

Professional development is about context more than content: recognizing where we belong in a high-performance environment, appropriately deploying what we know and creating the relevant context for the players. As coaches and practitioners, we are communicators. We have to give our coworkers and athletes what is behind the methods, results and statistics to show why we and our ideas are worth their time - and, if we're wrong, their careers.

Our answer to "Why should I listen to you?" is how we deploy our ego in the workplace. The previous two chapters showed some of the right ways and a lot of the wrong ways people answer that question. This chapter and the few that follow are what our contributors learned about this "job within the job."

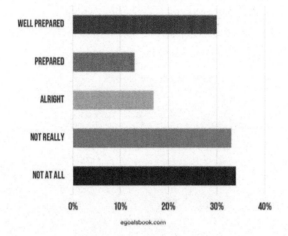

DEALING WITH EGOS: HOW PREPARED WERE OUR CONTRIBUTORS WHEN THEY STARTED IN ELITE SPORT?

egoalsbook.com

ACHIEVING "SUCCESS" BEFORE YOU KNOW WHAT SUCCESS IS

Absolutely! Especially starting out in the field, I had a lot of early "success." I put that in quotation marks because it was how I perceived success back then. Having already worked with the world #1 tennis and squash players, as well as an Olympic Champion, before the of age 28, I thought I knew it all! I didn't feel I needed to learn from those who hadn't achieved such a status.

Early success can derail you, as I learned. I realized how little I really knew.

Ashamedly, I learned that my success was attached to my ego. I viewed success back then by the level of athlete I worked with - in a way, they were my "trophies." This is where I believed my success really f***ed me up. I decided to humble myself and change my perception of what success should look like.

Today, I view success as being a humble servant to others and having a greater purpose, something far bigger and more meaningful than myself. (Allistair McCaw)

VOLUME CONTROL, PART I: TURN IT UP!

Javi Garcia, goalkeeping coach, FC Valencia: I have been in a couple of situations where a bigger ego could have helped me have an easier path on my work, or not waste energy and time to achieve the same goal.

Colin Lewin, Head of Medical, Arsenal FC: My lack of ego has cost me a few times, as I am reluctant to accept praise as an individual, while the egos around me have been desperate to receive praise or recognition.

I chose to leave a club early in my career because, on reflection, my ego was too low and, in hindsight, I should have confronted my egotistical boss. (Paul Balsom)

Alain Sola Vicente, strength & conditioning coach and physiotherapist: Thinking too much about how the work done by others is perfect and how small and insufficient mine is. Simply comparing too much with others have prevented me to get positions I wished I could have.

I would say it's cool for S&C coaches, sport scientists, etc to say they should always be in the background when athletes are successful. But I don't agree with this. If you help an athlete be successful, you may only be a small part of that success but you are part of their team and great teams should recognize every member. Don't be ashamed of recognizing and feeding your ego in these cases. Just make sure it is not a maladaptive feeding of the ego!! (Joseph Coynes)

Claude Karcher, handball coach and strength & conditioning coach: At times, I was not strong enough to be heard and push for my ideas. Simple examples include trying to convince the head coach not to do a session and reduce its length to avoid injuries... which eventually happened. I then even heard that I was the black cat!

There have been occasions when I have started a new role, with a new team, a new back room staff, in a new country, etc., where I felt and possibly displayed self-doubt. Even though I have worked extremely hard to earn my role on back room staffs throughout my career I feel I genuinely have doubted myself and have put others up on a pedestal. This might have been from their previous successes, large presence on social media, time spent at the club, etc. (Adam Waterson)

I would probably say I have a low ego, but it probably just manifests itself differently than what some would expect. My ego acts to protect my self-esteem by pulling me back from conflict and threats, as opposed to fighting against them. This has meant that at various points in my career I have too easily backed down in a debate or argument, and we ended up not making what I believed was the correct call. (5)

As a handball player, I didn't believe enough in myself. I lacked some ambition and missed some great opportunities, such as enlisting in the army to play for the country. This would have allowed me to train more and better, and in turn reach the international level in club. I've seen players who were initially less skilled than me make it in the long run by doing so. I should have boosted my ego! (Pierre Mangin).

Andrea Scanavino, athletic trainer, Zenit St. Petersburg and Italian National Football Team: During an interview to work with one of the most successful coaches of the moment at the beginning of his career I was realistic and asked him what style of play he had in mind. I did not give convincing answers for someone who wants to be in front of a professional who has the truth about the infallible training method, regardless of context. My "moderate" ego was not enough!

Having a moderate ego, I've always been careful not to show off and not to put myself in the centre of the picture. For example, I don't use social media to develop my personal brand and talk about what I actually do. It's not my thing, but trying to have a low profile in this case prevents people from understanding who I really am and what my expertise is. Not many people are aware of what I really do, and my image has been limited to being "The Infographic Guy." Meanwhile, I have been working with top-five world tennis players, Ligue 1 football, Olympic champions, etc.

People's opinions don't really matter but being discreet has prevented me from getting more opportunities that would have boosted my career. I believe it's a fine line between being humble and showing off: staying true to who you really are (humble and discreet for me) vs. getting enough attention to develop your company. Staying in the background with all my athletes and not divulging much information gives people the opportunity to create their own opinion of what I (can) do... which can be a double-edged sword, too. (Yann Le Meur)

In 2007, I was filling two roles: First Team Fitness Coach with Fulham FC and Australia's National Team fitness coach at the same time. It was almost like a clash of two cultures from a staff perspective. I found it much easier to deal with the Australian NT players as they were very compliant, had a strong standards-based culture and were, to a large degree, self-regulating. The EPL boys, as much as I loved them, were far more challenging with a greater preponderance of self-centred and manipulative behaviours. Keeping such strong individual egos on track and working for the collective goal was a constant daily effort. You had to be a strong and clear leader with them – you could not be their friends. In contrast, I found that some of the Australian staff were a little too close to the players and there was a need to be friends with some of the senior players – a bit like a 'fan' culture. I later saw some of these staff move into European professional leagues and I am told that they struggled to deal effectively with some of the big players because of this approach.

I found that when working in Australia, my ego volume could be low. But in the EPL, I had to turn up the ego volume, otherwise they eat you! (Andrew Young)

VOLUME CONTROL, PART II: YOU CAN'T ALWAYS BE AT 11

ONCE A SUCCESS, FOREVER A SUCCESS... RIGHT?

In 2011, when I was 24 and I became the head fitness coach of AS Rome in Serie A, I felt my ego out of control for some weeks. Fortunately, I realized few weeks later and I was able to correct that. (Rafel Pol)

I had been at a club for a number of seasons, and we had achieved a large amount of unexpected success rather quickly. We had been fortunate enough to keep the same squad together for consecutive seasons and the training techniques / strategies we were prescribing to the players in our weekly periodisation were showing fantastic results.

This continued success allowed for complacency to creep in. You then start believing that you have all the answers and what you are doing on the training pitch and gym is the main reason. The following season we had a larger turn over in player personnel. I just thought because we had achieved so much success with the previous group that the new group would be able to adjust easily and the same successes would follow.

Injuries, poor results, lack of adjustments and nine months later you are at the foot of the table.

Lessons: We are in the background. What we do is important but we are not curing cancer. Don't get caught up in all the hype. Generally, the teams who have the most success are the ones with the most talented playing rosters. (Adam Waterson)

I remember warming up a team before an English Premier League game. I was pretty confident I knew what was needed from a warm-up for these players.

However, instead of considering what the players needed from their pre-game routine, I went a little rogue and started adding some extra drills and methods that I thought would be valuable. It was me trying to demonstrate how much I thought I knew about things.

At that point, a number of players started to question what we were doing and calling out my methods. They weren't happy with me changing things up and got in a pretty shitty mindset. We got beat in the game to a team we should have beat easily. Players called the warm-up out in the press and indicated that it might have been the reason for the loss. Of course, there are way more factors, but the lesson was that at the point of competition, don't let your ego get in the way. The players are the most important factor at that moment. (Duncan French)

I heard David Martin say one day at a conference: "If you are willing to take credit for the wins, you NEED to be accountable for the s**t". I loved it so much… It helped me a lot to stay where I was and respect the team, the others and the processes. (Martin Buchheit)

I (ALREADY) KNOW EVERYTHING

What we do often see, is young practitioners who, on entry to our industry, believe that they have really "made it? and that they are more significant / important than they really are. Fortunately, there are normally enough experienced heads around to slap these kids back into place (Chris Barnes).

For the first decade of my career, I had to work pretty hard. The profession of working with athletes on their physical preparation was not well-established. I compensated for the uncertainty and challenge of this by being very sure of myself. I didn't grow as much as I could have, as a result.

If you think you have all the answers, you stop asking questions! I also didn't show any vulnerability, which is not good when trying to get people to cooperate with you (Jeremy Sheppard)

With the constant will to do things right, and since I believe in constructive criticism and open relationships, I have always attempted to say what I thought was right to my colleagues based on research findings, best practices in other environments, etc. Ego gave me the confidence to speak out. I realize now that most of the time this attitude of saying "the right" things has been interpreted as my need to be right all the time, and has pissed off many of my colleagues. This has unfortunately costed me some important relationships. (Martin Buchheit)

Dave Carolan, sports scientist and app developer, Millwall FC: I have, in the past, as one of the early exponents of sports science in the English football arena, thought that I was "ahead of the game" - a pioneer, and confident that my knowledge and understanding were worthy of recognition. I networked less and less and, when the time came to go back out into the industry, other people and methods had passed me by.

David Dunne, performance nutritionist, European Tour and British Canoe: Being exposed to top athletes made me realize that the Ph.D. letters after your name don't matter. You have to understand both sides of the practice-academic split. My ego got in the way, for sure. Mind the Dunning-Kruger effect: realize you're not that smart. I thought I knew more than I did, and I showed less respect that people deserved. It's more important to listen.

Practice: Know your role and understand your environment. Practice helps you to realize what's really important and keep in check your academic side.

Maurizio Fanchini, Head of Performance, AS Roma: When I was at the beginning of my career as fitness coach of a professional first team, I was sure of all my knowledge about training methodology. During work discussions with a coach, my ego made me so sure about what I was supporting that I was perceived as arrogant. Unfortunately, it happened that subsequent events and training outcomes didn't support my beliefs.

Fergus Connolly, performance coach, former University of Michigan, San Francisco 49ers: Early in my career I felt I had all the answers. Later in my career I have felt I had no answers. Both cases can be detrimental.

Early on, I pissed people off by being so stubborn and absolute about opinions and facts without considering the person. Later in my career, I tried to do too much for too many without looking after myself first.

Many times in my career, tone (or misunderstanding tone) has been my biggest downfall. Within my club people understand that I ask a lot of questions to try to gain insight, but to new members of staff or people outside the group, it may sound condescending or like I am disagreeing. When a new leader gave a presentation to the group, I questioned many of the ideas being presented: some because I wanted more information, but others because I felt that maybe the individual was not aware of current work or philosophies. As the presentation continued, I continued asking questions, which eventually created a large amount of friction with the new leader and caused a difficult relationship for many reasons (Garrison Draper)

Rafa Maldonado, fitness, rehab and injury prevention coach: Since my beginning in the professional world, I was convinced that I had the best innovative method for training, and I tried to "convince" everybody of that. It could be that I sent a message which was arrogant and caused fear, but the aim wasn't that at all.

UNWILLINGNESS TO LISTEN, LET ALONE CHANGE

I believe the biggest f*** up ego can cause to us practitioners in our field is when it causes us to deviate from the biggest mission: make our players / clients better.

I think a lot of times I decided to not hear what others had to say because I would think they would be judging the way I do things. But I should have looked at it the other way around: they just might be more experienced in the field and are offering to help me because they have been there and know other ways that could work better in a specific situation. A lot of times in the past I probably lost the opportunity to learn new things from these people. I thought I had the best answers and solutions for those specific problems, and just decided to not even listen to what they had to say. (Ivi Casagrande)

Being too rigid in my programming. Trying to make players do things they don't want to do. You just spend too much time resolving or being involved in conflict. Almost the Dunning-Kruger effect: having all the answers but no questions. I was too stubborn and opinionated regarding "my way" of doing things. Elite level players need an n=1 approach. They may end up doing the same program. However, how the process evolved to how they got there may be completely different! (Chris Tombs)

Some years ago, I was young but had considerable experience conducting research on athletes' responses to altitude training, and had a lot of experience conducting altitude training camps (2-4 months per year). I believed I knew all about altitude training.

A new member to the team, a Japanese rider, was invited to the early season altitude camp. The rider expressed reservations as he had negative experiences with altitude camps in the past. My attitude was that those experiences were due to inappropriate exposure / load management - that is, the people running those camps did it wrong! - and that under my guidance he would have a good experience. The rider was new to the team and too polite to refuse so he came to the camp, where we discovered that he does respond very negatively to altitude. He seems to lack any kind of hypoxic ventilatory response and, on the bike above 1600 meters, he would not be able to train. He could not sleep at night.

After one week of insisting that he will feel better in a couple of days, I realised that my own ego had interfered. I had not listened to this experienced athlete and had not been open to an alternate possibility. That cost this rider substantial training time at a critical moment of the year. (Marc Quod)

Early in my career I believed that frequent heavy strength training was required to prepare the athlete for the demands of the game. I was heavily fixated that whatever I had previously planned had to be completed, no matter what. I thought it was a sign of weakness and an inability to stick to structure if I adjusted the plan, as I believed the program I had written would prepare the athlete to the best of their ability.

There were a number of times I thought an athlete required greater volumes of strength training, so, instead of taking into account how they were responding to field sessions, I continued to increase volume and intensity as I believed it is what they needed to be a better athlete / performer.

Unfortunately, a few athletes over the years weren't able to adapt to both stimuli, which resulted in non-contact related injuries or modified training sessions.

Understanding that, while strength may play a role in an athlete's development, there are a number of other factors that are important to consider when developing an athletic program, identifying an athlete's strengths and growth areas are important when determining which elements to focus on and prioritise. (Selwyn Griffith)

I experienced some moments when egos couldn't simply work together, which led to unnecessary frustrations and unresolved conflicts.

When I first started with the French National Team in Alpine Ski and downhill, I needed to find my place in the group and obviously work closely with the athletes to prepare them for the upcoming season. During the first training camps, I quickly found myself in an awkward situation. On one side, the coaches wanted the athletes to take it easy outside of the ski context to recover, and on the other side the athletes (and myself) were willing to put more strength & conditioning work in. Being a team player I obviously followed the coaches' decisions, but the athletes then started to think that I wasn't close enough to them and not doing my job properly. I tried to discuss this at length with the coaching staff, hoping that we could find intermediate ways to run the training programs, but they were not willing to listen, and told me that I had to follow their plan, whatever I might think about the program. I was stuck.

From that day, I stopped discussing things with them and focused only on the athletes. While I personally have always been willing to accept criticism and have been happy to reconsider my ideas and positions when needed, here I clearly realized that egos and unwillingness to listen to others were the first limitation to team work. (Sébastien Carrier)

OVERCONFIDENCE: TOO MUCH OF A GOOD THING

There are probably too many to count... I have made judgment errors without really assessing the situation, taking things for granted that have led to injury and wrongly upsetting people's feelings. I assumed I had the right treatment option to improve someone's biomechanical pattern - it did just the opposite, compromising their back and putting them out for some days. I have luckily never been fired as a result, but I have had arguments with friends, family members and colleagues. Later I realized my ego got in the way of my really understanding the context or mental model of the person or circumstance I was involved in. (Darcy Norman)

Alberto Mendez-Villanueva, Performance Manager, Qatar National Team: Several times I have experienced this feeling of being overconfident in suggesting something and realizing afterward that my recommendation was wrong. I guess with age and time working in complex environments you learn to be less confident and more humble.

We came back to coach a club where we previously worked. The team was performing poorly and the economy was terrible. We obviously thought that we would be able to save the situation. But it didn't happen!! (Eric Blahic)

I was coming as a consultant into a new club midseason to save their season, a club at a lower standard than the ones I had worked with before. The previous staff had left and everything was pretty disjointed. We were busy setting up what we believed was appropriate for the club, we worked pretty hard for a week to organize their gym and pitch work, data management etc. Second game, a bad injury occurred for a key player. When an injury happens you always reset everything. This is why, in a sense, injuries are needed - they make you think. In this case, it made me realize that I had spent 85% of my time programming what I thought was best for the team. But I partially neglected what I could have learned from what the previous staff had done. Classic oversight. Knowing this in advance didn't help, because I fell into that trap as well: "it was really poor there, so..." (Martin Buchheit)

In my early days in Columbus, I had a role that required me to wear a lot of hats. It was my first Head of Fitness role. I was young. Some thought too young, and expressed it often.

In the middle of 2008, an important player of ours was in the end stages of rehab for a Grade II MCL tear. We were in between the fifth and sixth week of his rehab, and the volume of work for the week was significant.

We were approaching an important run of fixtures in the coming weeks and I had been told by the technical staff that there was no way I could get him ready in time. In the middle of the week, the player had expressed that his body was feeling pretty bad and that he felt the volume of work was a lot. This player was not a complainer. He was an Argentinian veteran who was a fantastic pro. I should have listened. But I thought, "we just need to get through the next couple of days and he will be ready." What I really meant was, "I'll show them. He will be so fit they won't believe it. Keep pushing. You're almost there. He'll be fine."

We got to Friday of that week, the very last day for him in the training week. I was going to give him the weekend off. He would be training full with the team on Monday. With 20 minutes left in the session, he pulled his hamstring. Grade II. Out for what would be another five weeks.

The stupid thing is, did I really think those two days were going to make a difference? I knew he was ready. He knew he was ready!! All I needed to do was keep him ticking over. When the ego volume is turned up too high, you can't hear anyone but yourself. (Steve Tashjian)

The national team matches are often scheduled at the worst possible time for clubs. These two matches were scheduled for the week before the final of the Cup. One of our top players was playing in La Paz on Wednesday and the final was on Saturday night, giving him about only two days of recovery. That is already a pretty short period, even before you consider the specifics of his situation: the travel, the extra fatigue from playing at 3600 meters of altitude, the fact that he had already played 90 minutes the preceding Sunday. I was starting to think that his participation in the final would be very compromised.

As if all this could not be enough, the match against Bolivia went to extra time – 30 more minutes in the legs!!

When the player came back the next day, he was broken. He hadn't slept, he was jet lagged... he was a mess. I meticulously listed all of the above objections and qualitative elements, and went to see the manager to tell him that, in my opinion, we should not play him on the Saturday. Yes, it was a final, but we had so many other good players in a better condition than him. It was not worth the risk, and we still had Champions League matches to come later in the season. The coach listened to me as he returned to his computer, and said calmly: "Don't worry, he will play. It's the cup final and I can't imagine the team without him. Thanks."

Imagine my reaction. I couldn't breathe. I dug my heels into the ground and went back to my colleagues and told them what had just happened. This player was going to be injured and I didn't want to be held responsible for that. What a weak decision the manager had just taken, and it was such a poor appreciation of all those elements and, obviously, my work as well.

On Saturday, the player delivered one of his best matches of the season. He not only scored and assisted one goal, he also equalled his running and sprinting records of the year in terms of physical performance.

We won, and when the coach came back into the locker after the match, he gave me a high-5 and said with a large and euphoric smile: "I knew I shouldn't listen to you, but thank you for your work." (Martin Buchheit, adapted from [Thiebart, 2020])

Tony Strudwick, Head of Performance, Arsenal Academy: I was once delivering a coaches' education session for independent schools' teachers. I was demonstrating the use of a Swiss ball and the creative ways to build strength and balance. There were about 20 teachers at the session. The session was going really well and I started to get more confidence.

At this time, I was pretty good at balancing on the Swiss ball. I progressed to kneeling on the Swiss ball unaided. The group was really impressed. I then said to the group, "If you get really good, you can do this." I then proceeded to stand on the Swiss Ball. I managed to get up on two feet and was feeling really good. Then, suddenly, I lost my balance. There was a split moment where I thought "F***, I am falling." I then slipped spectacularly and landed heavily on my shoulder. It really hurt. There was a moment of shock on the spectators' faces. I was in agony. The rest of the session was a complete scrub. I ended up popping my AC joint! I am told people still talk about the guy who fell off the Swiss ball 10 years later.

Following my damaged AC joint, I went with the English National Team to the World Cup 2014. Trying to bench press with the players landed me with another popped AC joint. Moral of the story: Let the players work and don't try to compete with them. I spent the whole tournament in pain!

I've had many, but one situation that springs to mind where it definitely messed me up was in a post-knee surgery rehabilitation of a very important athlete. I had given them a return to play program which involved some treadmill running that I had used many times before, was based on the athlete's current speed and "should" have been safe.

However, this athlete only had a Woodway curve available and I thought it would be fine, despite the whole self-powered bit.

Anyway, the athlete's knee got quite aggravated and it set them back a number of weeks and severely impacted a World Championship preparation. In a debrief with athletes and coaches, I couldn't admit that maybe - just maybe - the Woodway treadmill was not appropriate for them, as I had used the program many times before, albeit on belt-style treadmills. I really got my "back up."

I should have just swallowed my ego immediately and said "you know what, maybe that was a mistake." That is what I ended up doing, but because it took a couple of days for me to come around, it really hurt my relationship with the athlete and altered my long-term relationship with the coach (Joseph Coyne)

WHEN YOU'RE LOOKING IN THE MIRROR YOU LOSE SIGHT OF THE MISSION

I was in between my fourth and fifth season at Everton Football Club. Up to that point I shared the lead sport science position with another colleague who had been at the club for over a decade. David Moyes had been appointed manager at Manchester United and Roberto Martinez became manager at Everton.

In the transition, I was retained but my colleague was let go. With the restructuring of the department, I was promoted to Head of Sport Science and End Stage Rehab. With all the excitement, I immediately began updating my profiles on social media and other platforms. What I did not know was that my colleague had not been formally released yet. He had no clue. I basically told our whole community that he was being fired, albeit indirectly. Our entire network of friends and colleagues saw it immediately.

Naturally, once my colleague was informed of his release, he was upset with my carelessness. It was a stupid thing to do that was totally driven by a high volume of ego. I was an American named as Head of Sport Science in England. I was proud. I was excited. I was only thinking of myself. It effected my relationship with my colleague significantly. To this day, we have not been on speaking terms.

It is my deepest professional regret. Sometimes we learn lessons the hard way. (Steve Tashjian)

As a physiotherapist in modern football, agents and players often want a second opinion or prefer long-term rehab by their own preferred "therapist." This annoyed me in my early career and I wouldn't treat players who went on their own path. I isolated them and preferred to have little or no contact.

Over 2-3 years, I reflected on how my ego prevented me from asking why the players requested this, and how I could have gone along to see what this other rehab service looked like. It opened my mind to alternative ways of treatment, that we are all unique and the best place for long-term rehab may not be the club environment. I learned there are so many ways to treat injuries. But most importantly, treat and work with the person / player and get them to own the rehab process. You hold them accountable, and if they go down their own pathway, watch and care with interest: you may learn something new. I learned and reflected that my ego can never be bigger than player well-being or the good of the brand we represent. (Grant Downie)

An international player signed at the club, but came with his personal coach. When I heard this, I turned the guy down and said that it wasn't the best practice. I lost the player immediately, since it was obvious that if he had to choose between his long-term trusted partner and me… I realized only after that I should have accepted the situation that I couldn't change anyway, gain the trust of the player and work around that later on. (Pierre Lassus)

At one club, I experienced two fantastic head coaches with whom I developed great working relationships and was able to influence. When the new (third) head coach came in I was quick to point out how we do things around here and how successful we were! I never listened to his journey or side, as we had success and we had a formula. After 18 months, he sacked me from my position. He was right, and I am now truly grateful as I learned so much from that experience, about myself and how to form meaning and trusted relationships! And, most importantly, how to contain my ego and how every new head coach is a learning opportunity for me. (Grant Downie)

After moving to a new club and looking to rapidly change the training culture, I put my performance goals for the group well above anything else, even the self-esteem of some players. If I had been more considerate of the mental well-being of my players and compromised somewhat, the outcome that season may have been better. (Andrew Gray)

After a bad loss, I organized a team debrief during which I basically put all the blame on the players, so it wasn't my fault. I realized only after that this wouldn't help at all - the players were already looking for help and to regain confidence. So rather than me saving face, it was counterproductive for the team. (Sebastien Gardillou)

COLLABORATION IS FOR THE WEAK

As I get older and progress in my career, the more I try to realize that collaboration is more important than what I (my ego) think is best. I look back on my past experiences and now know that there were much better ways to deal with things. (Adam Douglas)

As I have gained more experience, and reflected on my practice, I would like to think I have become better at working within teams, understanding that what is most important for athletes does not necessarily always have to involve me. I don't have to have control, for example. I have seen better results from trusting colleagues and allowing them to do their jobs. (8)

In my last year coaching England, I gave my assistant coach - who I have known for a long time - total control over coaching defence for the team. One week he was away, I spotted something in a practice that made me want to ask the players about defensive coaching and practices. I should have waited to speak to my assistant but my ego started to take hold. By the end of the week I had changed all the defensive systems, totally undermining him and showing the team we were not united as a coaching group, all because my ego had got involved and took over everything. My relationship with my assistant was never the same again, and whilst I apologised later it was too late. (Ben Ryan)

An elite female cyclist was struggling with fatigue. I met with the cyclist, showed her some data and told her how we could resurrect her form by modifying her training program. I did not include the coach in these discussions, and he found out later that I had advised the cyclist to participate in a modified program. The coach was very upset with me and my ego got in the way as I responded to the coach in an arrogant way that was not helpful. My relationship with the coach was not good for more than a month because he thought I had a big ego and didn't respect his authority and leadership. (Dave Martin)

There's no specific occasion where it has significantly impacted my career, but certainly in my early days my ego meant I had to feel like I was doing everything. I was protective of my work. I needed to be in control, and I would become defensive if I felt others were encroaching on my domain.

As I have gained more experience and reflected on my practice, I would like to think I have become better at working within teams, understanding that what is most important for athletes does not necessarily always have to involve me (i.e., I don't have to have control). I have seen better results from trusting colleagues and allowing them to do their jobs. (8)

In my earlier years working within elite sport I used to be quite reactive and confrontational. I have many examples where I would take a coach's decision about a player personally. With experience I learned that, at whatever level you work at, this doesn't work.

Speak to people how you like to be spoken to. One of the best pieces of advice that I still stick to is to never react in a working environment on emotion. There may be times (very infrequently) where you might feel that you need to do this to create a reaction or confront an ongoing situation. However, I believe that when I did this and when other do it, it tended to be followed by regret. As sports medicine has evolved and multi-disciplinary teams have developed it has become so important to create relationships, respect each other's specialities and know each other's boundaries.

Delegate, empower people to provide them responsibility, which also brings accountability. Finally, communicate. I have found that a lot of issues arise when colleagues are not kept well informed. This tends to breed paranoia and potential disconnection that often leads to confrontation. (Lee Nobes)

A new manager came in and wanted to bring his previous staff to do my job - as is often the norm in football - but the players and the chairman supported me to stay. Shortly after joining, he came into a busy staff room and loudly started to criticise me for one of our players being overweight (which he was). I reacted strongly to this public degrading and we were quickly nose-to-nose saying god knows what. A month later I had moved on. (Thomas Little)

My first example goes back to the period of time where it was beginning to become clear through both data and rationale (to me) that sugar, in many contexts, was, in fact, more often harmful than helpful to the physiology of our athletes. Of course, sugar is still used today in sports drinks and in other products, and has its place in sport, but most of us realize now that you can get too much of a good thing. That was the case at my place of work.

I led the physiology team in an Olympic program, and others led the nutrition team. Both teams tended to work more or less in silos, despite the call for collaboration.

So here we had a physiology team that was seeing physiological data suggesting that too much sugar / carbohydrate could impair metabolism and health, while we had a nutrition team that at the time had more or less a philosophy to push sugar-laden sports nutrition products to their athletes. Additionally, our physiology team was early to the party on our new anti-sugar philosophy, and there was no shortage of other experts in the field willing to cite the evidence of the importance of high sugar / carbohydrate for athletes. On top of that, the government entity had industry relationships with the sugar-producing product manufacturers; and, to make matters worse, the athletes loved getting their sugar fixes from the nutrition team! It was an uphill battle.

Ego f***ed me up from that point on in my position. Despite the consistent harm that was evident from the practice, and despite having round table discussions and debates, my team and I could never convince a change in practice otherwise.

Then, of course, when you care about athletes and their performance, opportunities present themselves to work behind the scenes - under the table, so to speak. This work, and the ability to have full control with athletes, ultimately led me to where I am now, as a coach.

So, while I went through many uncomfortable challenges, and with my own ego also to blame, of course, at times, I am happy with where it has landed me today. (Paul Laursen)

I think back to working at the AIS, and I think we all had strong egos. I know for sure that I did things to protect myself, to "armour up."

At times, it felt almost unsafe to not have an ego going. You know there were a lot of amazing professionals there, and a lot of really good people, too, but we didn't always act like good people. It was a high-performing sector for sure, and it wasn't always about the team. We were separated into disciplines and sports in a way that felt divisive. There was real competition for resources. I learned a lot from that period. I have some great friends, but I also have a few apologies to make! (Jeremy Sheppard)

OVERLOOKING CONTEXT

I can be very strong in my views, and at times am not sensitive to the culture, the background and the environment I am in. For example, telling someone who has been in that environment for 30+ years they are wrong (a little too strongly). I have gotten better at this over the years, but it was a particular challenge for me at the start of the career. (7)

I received a phone call from a professional football club in Thailand. They wanted me to come in and take their preseason program and get their players fit. 48 hours later, I was addressing the playing group before our first training session. I spoke about working with the best players in Europe and how it was important that they worked really hard, be accountable and tried to emulate these professional standards, etc. The Thai players were very quiet and respectful as I spoke but did not say anything. It was only later that day when the captain of the playing group came to see me, that I realized I had completely fucked up! In Asia, and particularly Thailand, players have a great sense of national pride and the concept of face is central. My talk, as well intentioned as it may have seemed, had embarrassed them and they had lost face. From their perspective, I had inferred that they did NOT have high standards and that were not hard working like their European counterparts. I had arrogantly assumed things about them that I did not know.

I did not withdraw my ego enough to put myself in their shoes. It was a clear cultural oversight on my behalf. I think that in my ego-driven need to impress them all, I had actually disenfranchised and belittled them. A very good learning experience for me, and I am forever indebted to the captain who came to speak to me – otherwise I might never have known. (Andrew Young)

I think there was a real danger of being ego-driven when I was brought in by an organisation from another league, another team, another continent, even.

Was it my responsibility to bring what I thought I knew and what I'd done elsewhere and implement it in this team / league? Was this environment "behind," and I was here to impart my sports science knowledge?

Well... ABSOLUTELY NOT!

Thankfully, I quickly realised that I had a lot to learn about that environment and also a lot of people there to learn from. While I had experience in football, I had a beginner's mind in relation to this sport (ice hockey) and so I needed to be a sponge to learn from other people's experiences. Had I been egocentric in my approach, I would have put more value on my prior experience and dismissed the thoughts and lessons from those around me. I'm sure there were moments when my ego reared its head - for example, when introducing interventions or technologies that I felt strongly about - but hopefully awareness of the situation along with the emphasis I placed on trying to build relationships with my new colleagues and peers helped us work together to find the best approach for the environment at the time. (Jo Clubb)

Confronting a league MVP two minutes before practice about something he said he was going to do and he didn't do. I needed to wait until two minutes before practice to make sure he wasn't going to do it last minute. He proceeded to yell at me and tell me to f*** off and he would never be doing that again. Similar to my other stories, I still feel like I was right - just not culturally sensitive. (7)

I made a decision without consulting the manager. It was not my decision to make without consultation. I was not in possession of all the facts. Not all my fault, as I should have been told things, but I should have known this might not be the case. I made the decision, and it turned out to be wrong. (Ian Beasley)

Challenging a head coach and key decision maker in the organization I used to work for. We always used to have discussions about training philosophy. I always thought it was valid and constructive debate with provision of evidence to back my argument. He saw it as challenge that he was not prepared to accept. Ultimately it cost me other opportunities when he moved clubs!! (Chris Tombs)

Early in my career, during an interaction with a well-respected and highly successful coach, I started to lay down the law about what I would and wouldn't do based on the science and my experience - of which I had about four weeks! The coach pretty quickly enlightened me on how things were actually going to work and what the consequences for me would be if they didn't pan out how he wanted them to! (Nick Grantham)

I faced difficult soccer seasons when I wanted to change head coaches' opinions or representations about strength & conditioning. As a specialist, my ego claimed my legitimacy and my knowledge in this area. I had to show the right way to get the players fitter, stronger and injury-free.

Unfortunately, when this way does not fit with coaches' perceptions, it's a waste of time and possibly counter-productive. Ultimately, it was only a lack of ability to explain our way of thinking in simple and, most importantly, clear words. (Karim Hader)

Many years ago, I was communicating test results to a young athlete. I found the individual and told them about their excellent jump test, choosing to frame their results within a comparison compared to more senior players on the team, which showed them in a good light. Their coach overheard and we had a constructive conversation afterwards about my communication with the player.

First, with them being a young player and I being new to this situation, I should have communicated with the coach before informing the player. Second, the coach said they were having issues with the individual's perception of their performance compared to others' (i.e., ego!). Therefore, how I chose to frame the results was probably not in this individual athlete's best interests at that moment.

On reflection, I think my ego drove me to be the one to deliver the results to the player and also, in turn, try to fan the player's ego by boosting them up with a comparison, rather than being more objective with the results. I've never forgotten this incident as an example of the importance of communication and the power of the words you choose to use with a player. (Jo Clubb)

At the start of my career as a new graduate, brimming with confidence, I stated that no athlete that I worked with would suffer from a non-contact soft tissue injury, because my programmes would ensure they were ready to deal with the demands of their chosen sport. The first sport I worked with was gymnastics! Good luck avoiding all non-contact soft tissue injuries in that sport! (Nick Grantham)

I would say it is one of the hardest things on your ego in going from a practitioner position to a management position as you move up the ladder, e.g., S&C / technical coach or physio to performance manager / director. Especially if you have a lot of staff and you may not have much direct contact with athletes as you take on more and more senior roles, sitting back and letting others work with and develop the relationships with athletes is difficult. To do this, you have to put ego aside to some degree. I also think you need to have had sustained previous success with athletes that lets you absorb this "blow to your ego," as you have something in the bank. So beware of going into these type of management roles too early!! (Joseph Coynes)

ONCE YOU OPEN YOUR MOUTH (OR HIT SEND), THERE'S NO GOING BACK

I am sure there have been occasions, especially earlier in my career, where I have conducted myself in an inappropriate and unhelpful way with colleagues. I am sure this stemmed from my own insecurities or lack of knowledge / experience. I would hope that I have learnt from this, and will deal with those situations better in the future. (8)

In one of my former clubs, we were discussing a lot with the head physio and the assistant coach about how much strength training we should be doing or not. The communication had never been great between us, and I often had arguments with the head physio. But this time it was too much. They started to implement things without letting me know. I felt that the physio was overstepping his role and making calls that should have been my responsibility. I got really p***ed off. While my colleague was next door in the hotel we were staying at for an away match, instead of knocking at his door to have a constructive discussion, I overreacted and sent an email to the GM (cc'd the coach) to tell everyone that I wasn't happy with what was happening. At the exact moment I clicked on the "Send" button, I realized than it was only my ego sending the email, not someone willing to solve the overall problem!! (Benjamin Kugel)

I remember an email I sent to a colleague once as I left work. I deliberately didn't go and have a face-to-face conversation because I wanted to make a point. I was very clear that I felt that they were wrong and I was right. I walked in the next day to their office and was verbally threatened. The hairs on the back of my neck were standing up ready for a fight, my heart was racing but I somehow managed to calmly point out that I never wanted to be spoken to like that ever again and left.

The high stakes world of elite sport and the egos often found there within individuals trying to mark out their territory can create clashes and tensions that are completely out of proportion. We both apologised to each other later, and nothing more was said. Our working relationship after this was much better. It wasn't right for either of us to end up ready to fight, but that was what happened when a conflict situation wasn't handled well. Time spent together prior to that incident, better understanding of each other's perspectives and philosophies, plus an opportunity to respectfully disagree behind closed doors would have gone a long way to preventing this escalation.

I'm not proud of my email and was wrong to send it. I wanted to provoke a response but perhaps not the one I got! I was fighting for my beliefs and protecting some of my colleagues and the athletes I worked with. (Ben Ashworth)

Working with an Olympic program preparing for the Games, I was the head of strength & conditioning. I had a real issue with the way the program director was trying to influence our prioritization and programming strategy. I felt that I was the technical expert and he was merely an administrator poking his nose in. Every time he questioned or challenged what I was doing my ego bit at him and I challenged him. I was consequently fired from my position just as the team set out to the holding camp five weeks before the Games.

Don't let your ego become so great you fail to acknowledge that opinions are necessary, as from that tension comes growth. Instead of your swagger and ego taking over, shut them down before they lead to bad situations.

Watching the Games with a bad taste in my mouth was not pleasant. (Duncan French)

I was requested by the management to stop rehabbing a player, so he could train with another staff member on the pitch. I felt my job was incomplete, and I felt offended. The player came to me to ask why we were stopping, and instead of giving him a corporate response (i.e., we all believed that he should train with the other staff), I told him the truth and that I wasn't happy with the others' decision. (David Utrera)

The specific example I can think of was when I (foolishly) went toe-to-toe with a recently retired long-time-player-turned-assistant-coach regarding how the team was training / preparing.

The team was in the middle of a losing streak (one of many), so there was this real funk in the room. I dug in my heels surrounding my plan for the off-ice training without even listening to his opinion. Mind you, he had played over 900 NHL games and would have had a very good opinion on the subject matter. That was the start of a rough few weeks and months for me as I had to do a lot of damage control (something I was vastly inexperienced in doing) with staff and players, because surely word got out after our tête-a-tête.

My ego got in the way of my ability to critically listen and evaluate the other person's point of view. I thought that because I was the team "expert" and had gone to school and had experience training athletes that other viewpoints were not correct. I guess years of experience has now taught me how wrong I was 11 years ago. (Adam Douglas)

Once I had an argument with a colleague who was challenging my work, and reacted violently. This obviously didn't solve the problem, and after that I was perceived as someone with aggressive behaviour, unable to control his emotions. Not the way you want people to look at you. (Franck Kuhn)

At the end of the junior World Cup, I spent a lot of time preparing strength sessions for the players. They came into the gym at D-2 before a big game with joy and happiness... but they didn't want to listen to my session explanation carefully. It hurt my ego, so I ended-up throwing out the session and telling them to f*** off. I should have listened to their mindset and reframed my session at the last minute. Instead, I made a fool of myself in front of everyone! (Mathieu Lacome)

I once got into a verbal argument with an experienced player about his attitude towards the gym sessions. This player was in his early 30s and had decades of European playing experience. I was 25 years old at the time and my ego got the best of me. I argued with the player to a point that I could not get him to comply with any gym sessions for the remainder of the season. Putting my perception of "knowledge" before the player's needs definitely f***ed me up in terms of that individual's buy-in. (Alex Calder)

I've had numerous toe-to-toe arguments with individual players that got a little heated, but my most embarrassing one was when I fell out with all the players and just walked off during a session because I was DISGUSTED with the lack of effort. A staff member cajoled me to come out but I refused and fell out with him. The result: players and staff impersonating me with a bit of extra dramatic flair for a good month or two. (Thomas Little)

I reacted poorly when a player told me he didn't want to work with me anymore, while there were probably a myriad of reasons why he took the decision, not all related to my actual work. (Paul Quetin)

Early in my career I would often get into arguments and heated debates with coaches and team management as I couldn't understand how they could be so uninformed, or lack the thought process to understand the points I was trying to make. I would get so upset at their lack of understanding of what, to me, was a basic idea or approach, that I could not see past it and move on - or recognize that I was the one who needed to figure out how to get my message or idea across in a way they could understand.

I sometimes allowed this frustration to get the better of me. In one such instance, an athlete was rehabbing an injury with me (mind you, one of the hardest working athletes I have ever worked with) and we were finishing up our training. He was drenched in sweat. Our general manager came into the weight room to work out while practice was going on, as our weight room was open to the practice court. The GM made a very flippant remark about us not working hard and not taking things seriously. Again, he had just come in, while we had just finished an hour-long training session. My ego took it as a direct attack on my ability and role with the team. Rather than calmly have a conversation or let the comment roll off my back, I immediately engaged with him and got into a heated argument. It became so heated that practice - again, happening right there in the open - stopped, with our players and coaches watching us get into this argument. The player who was rehabbing with me stepped in and physically picked me up and walked me into my office, the whole time telling me to stop arguing and let it go.

I remained quite heated about this interaction for some time. But when I was able to really sit back and look at things it caused me to reassess how I go about interacting with people and how I need to do a better job of communicating, as opposed to thinking whoever I am speaking with should just "get it." So, while in some ways I look at that example as a low point in my career, I feel as though it allowed me to grow and advance significantly more than had it not happen. (Keith D'Amelio)

My first year in the NBA, I made a decision based on ego and unfortunately was too interested in proving to other people that I was capable of making the decision. It f***ed me up because it clouded my judgment of the situation in front of me. The situation definitely turned out alright, but I had to look in the mirror and recognize it was my ego that was driving the decision-making process. (Maggie Bryant)

After 10 years of being the National Sport Science Coordinator for Cycling Australia and publishing 10 papers describing the benefits of altitude training and working with elite cyclists who had won gold medals at the Olympics, I had a junior elite cyclist tell me he didn't think altitude training worked. His comment was given to me just before a big research altitude camp we were conducting in Italy and my response was arrogant; my ego got in the way. It took me a couple of weeks of supporting this athlete with respect and empathy before he started to trust me and agreed to participate in all the testing. (Dave Martin)

I used to be bad with officials (refs). I'd go beyond what is acceptable when I thought the official got a decision wrong. It was never about the decision but my ego. I wanted to be proven right. For me more than the team. It meant that referees who I had argued with wouldn't have had a great opinion of me, and that can spread quickly and be of detriment to you and the teams you coach. (Ben Ryan)

Having travelled 300 miles to attend, I once turned up a few minutes late to a CPD seminar with a certain high profile coach / fitness consultant. I was very apologetic, but in a quickly escalating turn of events, ended up in a heated discussion as to whether or not it was acceptable to be late, where I was questioned if I would accept these standards in my daily workplace. Knowing the personality traits of the individual I was conversing with, I should have backed down, but my ego got the better of me. I pressed on with (in my opinion) a well-justified and fairly reasonable account for being late, whilst remaining apologetic. However, this only antagonised the speaker more and ended up in my being asked to leave the seminar!

Lesson learnt: When working with big characters, pick your battles and get good at eating humble pie! (Charles Vallejo)

WILLING TO BE WRONG IN ORDER TO LOOK "RIGHT"

Early in my career, an influential player who I had some degree of conflict with retired and moved into a staff role at a parallel level to my own. This created additional conflict, some healthy, some unhealthy. Later, he moved into a senior executive role at the club, which eventually led to me deciding to leave. In hindsight, I could have done more to address the issues relating to our conflict, but neither of us were prepared to budge. (Andrew Gray)

Keir Wenham-Flatt, strength & conditioning specialist: When I was working in Japan I had a poor relationship with the team's captain, Michael Leitch. From the first day, it was clear we would not work well together. He tended to disagree with everything I would say and suggest to him in the gym. We were in permanent conflict. One night at the end of the season at a team dinner as I was leaving the club, we finally sat down together and I took some time to talk openly about our relationship and admitted some of the errors I made, etc. This allowed us to finally connect, and start a (remote) relationship in the following years. He kept messaging me and even started to admit that he was now realizing the value of my work. As we say, "when the student is ready, the teacher will appear." But definitely, if we both had lower egos, we could have saved time and had this discussion earlier.

I resigned from my position of strength & conditioning coach when I was asked to step down (i.e., become #2) after the arrival of a new staff. In fact, they didn't have anything against me, they just wanted to be in charge at all levels, which is clearly understandable. But I didn't want to understand and accept the situation.

Thankfully, the president didn't accept my resignation letter. I stayed as a #2 and, to be honest, now I realize it's been a great experience. I thank the president for this: without him I would be somewhere else, maybe without a job and I wouldn't have learnt what I did since. (2)

I once gave an opinion that was contrary to what I truly believe, just to contradict people for the sake of it. (4)

During a compensation session on match day for substitute players, we were doing some intense HIIT runs. I was starting to feel that the players were tired and I probably needed to cut the session short. At that moment, one of my assistants watching the live GPS came to me and told me that I should stop the session, given the load already accumulated. While what he was saying was, in fact, just confirming my earlier thoughts, I dismissed him and kept on with the session, just to not give him credit. Right after our chat one of the players stopped by himself, complaining about his calf. Thankfully it didn't turn into a proper injury, but I realized that my ego could have cost us one important player. (Pierre Lassus)

I had been working with an injured goalkeeper and managed the load for him to rest on a day that the whole team had as a day off. He requested to train because he feels bored at home. The session he wanted to do made no sense for him. I suggested he rest, but he got angry, saying I was paid for that. I felt offended and argued with him about load management. The next day we both came to train. (David Utrera)

I felt offended too often in coaches' meetings when my opinion was not judged as the holy grail – when there shouldn't be any problem in simply discussing things! (Andreas Beck)

Early in my coaching career I got caught so much on the drama of a coworker not letting me do my job because of his ego that I, unfortunately, let my own ego get in the way. I decided to distance myself from my players, thinking that would be the way for the leadership and management to see my value. I kind of wanted my co-worker to f*** up to a point that would be so bad the leadership would rethink and use my services instead (since the players openly communicated to me they preferred what I programmed and saw the value way more than management did).

Thinking back at it, I feel embarrassed by what I did because I lost so much time that I would rather have spent making my athletes better and doing what I could to prove my value otherwise. (Charles Vallejo)

Mostly it's been times when I've pushed myself or others too hard to achieve an outcome in order to prove to others my competence. (David Joyce)

My ego has gotten in the way of my learning when I'm challenged and put on the defensive. When I've had to defend what and why I'm doing something, I have more difficulty taking on new ideas that could be valuable. I find it much easier to take on new ideas when they are presented in a constructive way. If combined with non-constructive criticism, or criticism that's valuable but not presented well, I am still working on taking the valuable information and not taking the criticism personally. I try to be as open as I can, but I recognize that I have shortfalls as a young practitioner and can be very sensitive at times to criticism, particularly from people who I don't trust. (Amelia Arundale)

It happened too often that I put myself into intense discussions with colleagues who didn't want to see things as I did. Because my views were systematically based on scientific evidence and facts, I simply didn't understand how they could have a divergent opinion – mine was the only possible truth!! Having this attitude cost me a lot of relationships and I have been perceived as someone highly opinionated and pretty closed-minded! In fact, that's completely the opposite of how I am.

With time, I learnt that even if those people had opinions that were probably not as valid or coherent as mine (my ego again?), debating those ideas was not worth it in 80% of the cases: most of the time we would argue on details, e.g., running with one or two changes of directions; eating a yogurt with 15% or 20% fat.

On a larger scale, it doesn't really matter for the program and the athletes, so why fight? Allowing those people to keep doing and thinking what they believed would have allowed me to better maintain those relationships and change the way I was perceived, which in the long run was obviously highly beneficial at all points, including the other 20% - those important points that really needed to be addressed for the health and benefit of the athletes (Martin Buchheit)

SEEKING ATTENTION OVER ACCOMPLISHMENT

In between some pretty good jobs in Champions League clubs, I once found myself working in a second division club. I didn't have a club at the moment and the head coach was a great friend of mine. I went there to help. But because the club was not at "my usual standards," I wasn't happy. I didn't enjoy it. As if my ego wouldn't admit or accept the situation. I was trying to justify the job, find excuses for being there. And this is what I kept repeating to every person asking me why I was in this "small club." "I am just here to help a friend," was my go-to response. It took me a lot of time to reverse this mental model, until I finally realized that it was rather a ridiculous attitude. I then felt much better and thoroughly enjoyed working there, until I got another phone call... (1)

After many years working in a big Champions League club and being exposed to all sorts of uncontrolled egos and the associated challenges, I took a job in a much smaller club. People there knew where I was coming from and they were all pretty respectful of what I was saying and willing to do. I had nothing to prove there. Players and staff also had less to prove because they were in a less prestigious club. Smaller logo, smaller egos. I realized that that this situation had completely but unconsciously killed most of those old needs and daily habits that I used to do just to ensure I would be recognized for my work. No more need to justify my working hours, to advertise my decisions, chase the status with my colleagues, etc. I was now in control, just focusing on the work. It was a great feeling. This taught me a lot about myself, and I wish I had been more like that in my previous role(s). Things would have been easier at all levels. (Antonio David Sánchez)

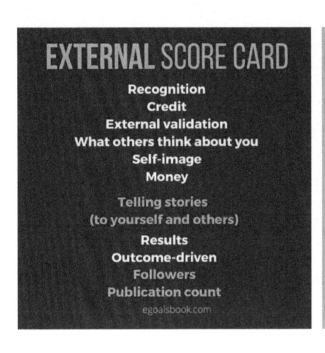

We buy things we don't need with money we don't have to impress people we don't like.

— *"Tyler Durden," Fight Club*

It took me too long to realize that chasing more accomplishments, more papers, more conferences, and constantly looking for more boxes to be ticked in the name of professional and social recognition is an endless quest. There is simply always more that can be done. It's infinite. It's impossible, in fact, to do everything you would like to do, what you think you should do, or - even worse - what you think the others would like you to do!!

The reality is that you better step off the hamster wheel, understand that this bulimia is rather dangerous, and fix some smaller, qualitative and impactful targets. Those can bring personal satisfaction when you hit them (assuming this is still what you are after). Reassess, and only then get back on the treadmill for another well-defined project. (Martin Buchheit)

David Howart, Head of Athletic Performance, Connacht Rugby: I had a boss that used to say to me "comparison is a punk." At the time, I didn't know what he meant by it in a real sense, but on reflection I have realised what he saw: I was constantly trying really hard to be better than the people around me, trying to match or top their contributions... instead of focusing on the job I was there to do and doing it well! I would convince myself that I was doing this from a humble place, striving to be as good as the people around me. But in reality, I was trying to boost my own ego.

Instead of being a "yes man," I complained out loud about the lack of periodisation in training and testing within my former club, starting to be quite negative about what we were doing, always seeing the bad points of the training. This was - likely - mainly because my ego was hurt by not being involved in the design or discussion about the periodisation, which I believe is one of my strong suits, or the testing setup.

This ended up with me not being asked anything AT ALL, and removed from all things related to this area. I should have managed my ego and tried to be a problem solver rather than a grumpy cat. (Mathieu Lacome)

I was three years into one of my roles, and feeling like I lacked influence. So instead of working together with the right people to help them understand my frustrations, I looked outside my job for what I felt I needed. I applied for some other positions and started to develop my own business. The extra work and the energy this required was exhausting. I felt like I deserved to be more valued and respected within my job, both financially and in terms of level of influence, but I initially avoided addressing this until a stage where I had a wobble in my own health.

When I look back on this time in my career, I can see how my ego blurred my perspective of the value that others felt I added to the role. Now I try to reflect on what I have achieved and recognize that I am not trying to tackle the world on my own. I have reached out to people for help with work and life, and have found this hugely rewarding and important for a greater sense of calm. This has been life changing. (Ben Ashworth)

Martin: "Ahhhhh, Martin the superhero is back."

"You have something to say about everything!!"

"But you really think you can do everything?"

"And why are you doing all this (stuff)? You just want to exist!!?"

I have heard this too often from colleagues and people who I thought were my true friends. It's a long story about someone really willing to help and give the best of himself to the team and the players. But I realized later that an unclear job description - at least to others - and both my profound interest for performance and somewhat large knowledge in a broad range of topics have sometimes pushed me to "do too much." Those actions created jealousy and my being perceived somewhat negatively by some of those around me.

I have never been a big fan of superhero books or movies. But then I had to have a reflection about superheroes: if I had to be one, which one would I like to be?

I thought that to avoid such critics but keep doing what I like, I should turn myself into Batman. Serve the cause in a more anonymous way, stay behind the team and keep doing the thankless jobs in the shadow, and distinguish myself from the Ironman's and Black Condor's that pollute elite sports.

The difference between Batman and those two superheroes? Black Condor made himself into a superhero, without having an actual super power.

And Ironman ended up revealing his identity, chasing the spotlight in the quest for recognition.

George: After a year of working with Martin, I can assure you: he may be a polymath scientist like Bruce Wayne, but he is no Dark Knight.

With greater fame and recognition comes increased scrutiny of one's motives, methods and the consequences of one's actions. Those are what Batman sought to keep in the shadows, because he knew that, as the Dark Knight, he was deep into some moral shadows. Yes, Tony Stark wanted the fame and adulation, but he knew deserved it and knew it would be forthcoming as he flamboyantly saved the world. Did Batman reject fame because he didn't want it? Or was it because he knew he would never get it? Or, darker yet, because he knew he was unworthy of it?

Stark may have gone too far in his personal #brand promotion, but he never compromised himself or his mission to do it. Batman, on the other hand, is one moral compromise after another.

The difficulty with this industry is that many people think of themselves as Superman, act like Ironman and suspect everyone around them of being a fellow gray-area Batman, an evil genius like Lex Luthor or an agent of chaos like the Joker. Self-promotion can be as much about playing defence as playing offence.

We should be proud of what we do and willing to "open the books" like Tony Stark / Ironman. We should be willing to accomplish our aims anonymously and without ever being recognized, like Bruce Wayne / Batman.

Basically, be Clark Kent / Superman.

EGO SANA IN CORPORE SANO

In 2013, I was with a team and the coach got fired. The new regime that came in hated sport science. I got increasingly depressed and, after an accident in the gym by lifting too much weight, I had a coronary artery dissection that led to multiple heart attacks and near death - all because my ego was hurt because I wasn't being listened to. (Craig Duncan)

It was a fantastic opportunity. The money is good and you live incredible things, but after a moment you just realize that you don't want that anymore. I made unbelievable sacrifices to be there. It's been the hardest two years in my life. When I was working in the NBA I think I didn't sleep more than 0-4 hours per night. I think there was one year where I had dinner with my family four days in the month! I realized it was a fantastic opportunity but left zero time for the most important people: my wife and two boys! You want to be home and kiss your kids in bed. Also, I dropped 9 kg of muscle with a poor lifestyle (Johann Bilsborough).

I have been asking myself for many years what was waking me up at night and causing me stomach problems. The fact that some practices I was observing weren't optimal (at least not in my assessment), or the fact that I wasn't listened to and my work was not considered as I thought it should be? I am sure that with less ego I would have managed to let things go a bit more and get over it. And, eventually, sleep much better. (Martin Buchheit)

I, too often, was not prepared to deal with some personalities and the role-sharing among the coaches or medical staff. This often created anxiety and was difficult to handle. (Antonio Gómez)

I don't have a specific moment in my mind, but when I began my career I was afraid of failure. Failing meant for me "be inferior to the other" or "be weak." So, when I had less experience, I was more stressed and anxious when important competitions came around because I was scared not to have a good result. I think it's the main problem for professionals who have a big ego: the anxiety that you can have when you lose. It was quite contradictory because I think I am being self-confident. (Julien Robineau)

In regards to my family and where to draw the line between how much work is enough when working with your hobby and interest, where hours and days don't really matter because it's so much fun… it's a thin line, since your ego tells you that there's always something more you can do, to learn, analyse, etc., which is then taking time away from the people you love the most. (Johan Swensson)

Many years ago, when I was an athlete at the Australian Institute of Sport, it was a given that you had to be quite self-centered and driven as a person to achieve sporting success. This was an accepted part of the deal, to fully focus on your sport and yourself: spend less time with family, with friends, relationships, exploring outside interests, caring for others. But I was a single person then with no family, no wife, no children, no older parents to care for.

When I retired from football and became a staff professional, this dynamic had changed.

During my 30 years working in professional sports with clubs and touring teams, I have lost count of the number of staff relationship breakdowns, divorces, unhappy children and regular family relocation due to work opportunities. I found professional sport as a staff member even more selfish because NOW there was collateral damage with family, spouses, children and elderly parents who were directly affected. Guys who were constantly touring, attending conferences, etc. We have all been there to some degree.

In my experiences, I came across a number of fellow professionals who were quite obsessive about their work and the time that they dedicated to it – with little thought to the effect that it was having on their family or personal life. Even when they were at home with their children, their attention was not really focussed on their family – they were planning their next training session or jumping on Twitter or organising their next conference presentation. The cognitive dissonance in their behaviour was actually sad to observe.

When I am at home with my family, my children, I really try to make a conscious effort to authentically be with them. I am definitely no saint in this regard and far from perfect. I personally do not do any social media or networking except with close trusted colleagues. Of course, to be an effective professional in elite sport, you must dedicate enough time to fulfil your role to a high standard. But sometimes you need to have boundaries and say no to outside demands. I have worked with a number of professionals who have spent inordinate amounts of time on social media, doing mainstream media, chasing contacts, excessive networking, etc – in addition to dedicating a large number of hours to their club role – all at the expense of their personal / family life. Balance is the key here – but it is not always observed in my experience.

There is no doubt that to work successfully in professional sport you need to be a hardworking, driven individual. But I do often wonder if sometimes there is a deeper underlying anxiety driven by the need to CONTROL everything, which I think is somewhat of a fool's errand given just how inherently unpredictable many professional sports, such as football, are on match day. The best match-winning players that I worked with always had a strong streak of unpredictable creativity, independent decision-making and risk taking in their DNA. I always tried to embrace such characters (within reason) and try not to be claustrophobic or dictatorial in placing MY program demands upon them. I think that sometimes we forget that these are the guys who win matches for us but, more importantly, make sport so beautiful to watch. (Andrew Young)

It happened to me a few times, and a lot of friends or colleagues told me the same. You get a super sexy job offer, good money, lots of responsibilities, the job title you have been chasing… and then, thankfully, your wife reminds you that given the location, the working conditions, etc., it's in fact a super poor choice for the family and work / life balance overall. It's so important to have the support of the family to stay grounded. Don't make all the decisions based on the job and the conditions that would directly feed your own ego. (Martin Buchheit)

It's also very important to have a good and healthy life - family, friends, physical and mental health, etc. - which clearly helps balance your overall mental load. It makes you stronger and more resilient when up against toxic battles and others' malignancy. (Yann Le Meur)

VOLUME CONTROL, PART III: LEARNING FROM GETTING IT RIGHT

It is important to be confident in your ability, but know what you are good at and don't bullshit people. I think there is a difference between self-confidence and an over-inflated ego. Self-confidence allows you to perform in front of a group within a certain context. Ego, if left unchecked, can create a false sense of security and provide your peers with a negative image. Always be honest. It is important. (Tony Strudwick)

Early on in my academic career I had a major conflict with the director of my academic institution. After a few years of successful lecturing (as rated by the students) and research (as shown by my publication record) in a temporary position, I was offered another temporary position lecturing on topics I was not interested in. I thought I deserved better, and instead of looking for some kind of middle-ground compromise, I left the institution without any alternative source of income. It felt like the right decision at the time, and it still feels like it was the right decision today, but it was a decision made on pride and ego, rather than logic.

Maybe my ego is still as big as it was back then and it does not allow me to recognise any serious conflict or f*** up in my career to be a consequence of my own ego. (Iñigo Mujika)

I refused a very poor offer from a very important club to restructure a part-time role into a full-time role with an exclusivity contract. When I refer to "very poor," I mean one-fifth of what I consider the minimum conditions to accept that high responsibility. A number of people told me that my ego f**ed me up and that I would never will have another opportunity like that.

I never regretted that decision, but it was several years until I got a similar position. However, from that point, I was honoured with what I consider fair offers and contracts. (Julio Tous-Fajardo)

It was my first day at an EPL Club as an Assistant Fitness Coach. The players were undertaking a 3 kilometer running time trial on an out-and-back course. My job was to man the pole at the halfway mark and make sure every player ran around that pole. The trial was almost finished when the last player approached the halfway pole. He was an older player, fast-twitch striker and clearly overweight. He was also one of the leading goal scorers in EPL history. He approached the pole, looked me in the eye and stopped well short of the pole and turned around to continue running.

What should I do in this moment? If I did not treat him the same as every other player, my integrity and reputation was gone on my first day. So I called out to him and told him that he had not gone around the pole as he was supposed to. He continued to jog away and politely told me where I could stick my pole. Half an hour later over lunch he apologised to me and we had a laugh about it. He respected the fact that I had challenged him on my first day and we went to have a really good working relationship. (Andrew Young)

I was in the locker when players were (again) playing football tennis, the net being the table in the middle of the room, where we used to put a bunch of supplements and other important stuff for the day. A millionaire player lost the ball and, in a gesture of both despair and rage, smashed all the supplements and mixed every single pill and drinks, totally ruining the nutritionist's work that had taken her about 30 minutes to set up earlier in the morning.

Being witness to this, and with all of the players seeing me there, I had about 0.01 seconds to decide what to say and what to do.

Without saying a single word, I turned the ego volume up and picked up a few pills on the ground and went straight to the offending player, giving him the list of players' supplements so that he had all the necessary info to put everything back in order. The other players started to laugh at him, realizing the amount of work he had to do. The player slowly started his work, but was soon rescued from his duties when the coach called them for the start of the training. This wasn't the most important part: my integrity was safe, and I think I kept the respect of the players. I still spent 20 minutes tidying up everything while they were training outside, at least to make sure they could get their supplements after training. The program was safe, as well. And my ego was back in check. (Martin Buchheit)

A highly-committed player entered the gym very early and asked me while I was reading "Do you think we may have a mandatory strength training session later on, since otherwise I would like to train in half an hour with you individually?" I responded to him, "I don´t think so, so let´s train anyway."

In a subdued tone, one of the rock´n´roll stars of the team told me: "Hey, here you don´t think anything." I stood up like a spring and replied "This is the only human ability that sets me apart from you."

He insisted by saying: "Why do you think? Because you read?" I immediately replied: "Reading is an intellectual ability that may promote critical thinking, but I think because if I lose this job I would immediately find another way of living. In your case, if you break your leg and a bad rehab does not allow you to return to play ball, you just go home to play 'sitting ball.'" He was mute and put his head down and suddenly I felt so bad since I tend to behave in a calm and respectful way.

However, the real leader of the team (a true legend) approached me and whispered: "Don´t feel bad. He deserved this lesson. You had the courage, we respect that." (Julio Tous-Fajardo)

With time, I became less aggressive but more assertive. This is because I was worn out, and maybe getting angry was not very productive in a professional environment. Basically, I had to re-invent and redirect this anger and frustration, as it becomes very draining mentally. (Johann Bilsborough)

TAKE AWAY

Venture capitalists don't hand a founder a check and walk away. The money is only a small part of what investors bring to a company, particularly a new one. Young innovators ready to up-end the world are going to make a lot of mistakes along the way - "fail early and often," "move fast and break things" - and investors understand this, accept it, recognize the importance of it. But they obviously want to tame those mistakes and mitigate the outcome. They're there to make money, after all, so they appoint managers and executives to make sure their investment grows into a return.

They do this because they know that being an executive is not an entry-level job. But it is for one executive: the ego.

Like anything else, you can read countless books and articles, listen to lectures and podcasts, sit through conferences and webinars about developing your ego and still not have any actual ego aptitude. The only way you can truly learn, the only way you can bridge that gap between knowledge and competence, is through experience, which entails informed experimentation. That is to say, fail early and often, not just because it's a catchy slogan, but because people are more forgiving of mistakes when they come early.

We expect people just starting out - whether they are old or young when they decide to start something new - to make mistakes. Good friends, colleagues and mentors welcome those early mistakes precisely because they show the desire to learn for oneself and improve by doing.

Later on, people rightly expect more. As long as any mistakes are in the service of growth, they are still a net positive. But entry level mistakes by an experienced executive - or an executive who should, by this point, be more experienced than *that* - reveal something went wrong.

At some point, we might direct the question "Why should I listen to you?" to our own executive, the ego. The ego's answer to the internal question should be the same as when it comes from the outside: "Because I've earned it. Here are the receipts, and I'm ready to continue earning it."

5 | CALIBRATE YOUR EGO TO REALITY

In communication terms, ego is a transponder. It receives information from the external world and transmits information from the internal world of the self. Ego also includes the middle step: processing what it takes in to produce whatever it puts out. These are the functions behind the relationships with the external world, which lead to the self's differentiation from others or the world.

The ego errors of the previous two chapters reflect a breakdown in one of these steps. In some way, the ego is not consistent with reality.

George: We have a section in Chapter 3 titled "Legends in their own minds." That phrase came from my first captain in the US Navy. He responded to one of my routine high-volume ego moments by saying "George, you're a legend in your own mind!" He was right about all of it! Whatever I was going off about, it was only in my own mind that I was achieving legendary status. The facts of my tale were surely more mundane, and my role was certainly less than legendary. Only in my mind, not in reality, was I that awesome. Fortunately, it was all in good fun, and he was there to provide the necessary reality check, one that provided a solid laugh to the rest of the officers in the room, further bringing me back to reality.

Part of what made us a well-functioning unit is that we knew each other's strengths and weaknesses (George's strength: Confidence! George's weaknesses: Too much confidence at times, and engineering maintenance). We could then address each other's weaknesses to keep the team strong. In that case, and many like it, it meant the occasional reality check in front of my fellow officers.

We can't rely on others to be that reality check. Having leaders, family members and colleagues like that is, sadly, the exception and not the rule. The rule is, we have to be our first line of defence to keep the ego oriented to reality, both in its processing and its projection.

> Ego can be bad because sometimes the person or the athlete loses touch with reality, stops having his "feet on the ground and his heart in its place" and imagines himself above others, leaving aside some key factors in the analysis and evaluation of his own performance. It can even lead to justifying absurd or difficult situations, or seeking apologies if things are not as one would like them to be. It opens a void and a crack in the self, where achieving fulfillment becomes more complicated every day. (Juan Carlos Álvarez Campillo)

Ego calibration should be a continuous process. We're always interacting with reality, and small uncorrected errors can become major ego miscues down the road. "Garbage in, garbage out" is bad enough as a linear function. Imagine some chaos theory "butterfly flaps its wings" chain of events.

Sometimes, though, people overlook ego calibration when they need it most: after a dramatic impact on the ego, such as a crowning win or devastating loss.

Coming off a success - whether that is winning a championship or reducing man-games lost to injury for the third consecutive year - your ego deserves a slight raise (as do you). However, too much and you risk losing the will that propelled you to this level. Perhaps you always saw yourself as a scrappy underdog who had to fight for everything. Now you realize those exhausting days are behind you - you've made it. For the first time in years, you let your guard down because you have that most delusional of thoughts in high-performance sport: you think you're secure. Too good to fail, too vital to sack. Worse still, you might feel entitled to ego flare ups - and we now know where those lead.

> Pushing the ego up can be beneficial if it's done in adequate doses, because by having an extra level of self-esteem, self-confidence or valuation over others, a person then trusts that he/she can achieve more things than others. And that also activates brain mechanisms that generate chemicals that can give more energy. Neuroscience explains it perfectly.
>
> On the other side, the excess of ego moves people away from reality and produces such a high pressure and demand that it can cause the opposite effect: tension, stress, isolation, etc. By wanting to demonstrate so much, one then makes more mistakes due to nervousness, pressure, blockages or excessive ambition. The ego can be the opposite of plenitude and balance because it needs more and more, but this path is not sustainable in the long run, nor is it possible to stand out and always do everything well. So the ego, in the end, generates permanent conflicts. (Juan Carlos Álvarez Campillo)

Or you have the opposite reaction to success. While the younger guys jet off to Dubai or Ibiza and your colleague rereads *Ego is the Enemy* for the 12th time, you pick up one of your guideposts: *Only the Paranoid Survive*. If you don't reduce man-games lost for a fourth season, you're done. If your team can't defend that title, it's over. Some group in another country launched a brand that looks suspiciously like yours, and you're seriously planning to take a week off?

The old advice "Don't rest on your laurels" is a bit misplaced. The people who earn laurels rarely are the type to rest comfortably. They should. They've earned it, and it is necessary.

When we don't take time to process the success and put it in the broader context of our goals, our ego can develop a bit of near-sightedness. We see only the trophies, the bonuses and the KPIs - not the ambitions and values we set out to attain. We started our "career marathon" by running through cities and from one vista to the next, but somehow ended up on a treadmill, chasing numbers and whatever trinket is within arm's reach.

There is a need for modulating one's ego. While a high ego is, without doubt, required to survive in this highly competitive world, if you don't control it, you can't grow, which in the long run means you won't last. (Sebastien Gardillou)

I think that some of what makes elite performers good holds them back in other areas. I am talking some of the world's elite best: guys with multiple Olympic gold medals, league MVP's. They believe they are invincible, which is great in the heat of the battle. But they believe they are invincible, not so great in the middle of practice, when you are trying to help them get better. (7)

Don't let an inflated ego derail you from becoming your best self. (Allistair McCaw)

Defeat, failure or some other significant setback can have a similar effect on the ego's reality-orientation and, from there, on the individual's drive and ambition. High-performance environments rarely set the conditions to do anything productive with those setbacks. All the more reason to use your post-win periods to refresh and refuel. Without the fuel provided by rewards in both the mental and neurochemical sense, people may lose the drive, the energy, the "edge" they need to function and thrive in these environments.

CAN YOU RISK...

1 Being creative rather than powerful and central sometimes?

2 Playing your role for the team if it means you are not the hero?

3 Being faceless if it gets us the result?

4 Failing and looking foolish, and not reacting emotionally?

5 Being a learner, not a master, every day on the pitch?

6 Making someone else on the team look good?

egoalsbook.com

I really see ego as an oversensitivity. Let's look at it from the perspective of risk. What kind of risk to agree on?

For people with oversensitive egos, their appetite for risk can be skewed. On one side, chasing the amazing, they can try some risky but spectacular tricks on the pitch, like very difficult passes or shots that look spectacular. But on the other hand, there are many aspects for which they may not be willing to expose themselves or accept a certain level of risk.

This is where it becomes interesting to drill in further, and uncover some important aspects of their own I-dentity. It's about asking them to acknowledge what they can accept, whether they accept not looking perfect all the time, if they can learn from their mistakes, and what they are happy to risk to be successful on your common terms.

The end goal is for the players to stay mindful enough about WHEN to do their tricks, and not do them automatically. There may be better risks to be taken at some moments. This is maturity. The ability to be fearless when taking a risk. (Pippa Grange)

WHY IS IT IMPORTANT TO CALIBRATE YOUR EGO?

I genuinely believe that if you can keep egos away from elite performance staff then you have a great chance of moulding a brilliant team. (Colin Lewin)

I believe that, in the long term, for a practitioner working in team sports, a modest ego will always progress further than a big ego or being egotistical. (Paul Balsom)

The high-performance environment is stressful. But the high-performance model is grounded in selflessness. It flourishes when all voices are heard and everyone on the team is allowed to influence the environment with the fullness of their talents. Ego volume should be low during collaborative times, and turned up just enough when it is time to make a critical decision. Not so much that you can't hear anyone, but just enough so that you make the final decision with confidence. (Steve Tashjian)

I think elite sport can't exist without egos. You put that many Type A personalities in the room there is bound to be an ego clash. Often times, the success of the team is dependent on the successful cohesion of the coaching staff and support staff. The best outcomes occur when everyone involved, from the top down, are able to check their egos at the door and work towards the team's goals. (Adam Douglas)

We have to manage all that so that it doesn't become a distraction! We have to find ways to utilize ego to challenge athletes to strive to be better, we have to navigate around ego so that it isn't disruptive, and we have to find the triggers in someone's ego that makes for positive interactions rather than negative ones. (Duncan French)

A big ego can stand in the way of learning, honest communication and challenge. It can also stand in the way of genuine relationships and teamwork. It can be important for athletes, though, as the best hate to lose and need to be self-centred to keep winning and be the best. You don't want to take away this competitiveness. (Tom Vandenbogaerde)

I think when the ego is controlled, and that is twinned with being successful, then it can elevate the respect others have around you and lead to greater opportunities both for the team and for you. That's happened a lot in last few years for me, and it reinforces the point that if you control your ego, the team achieves the goals you have set out. Then it can elevate your status as a leader, without you having to say anything. (Ben Ryan)

Keeping ego in check? I think the key word is "try." In all my stops in the sporting world, nothing is more valuable in a team setting than communication. Ego can be a barrier to strong communication, and, as such, needs to be something that is minded and kept in check (as difficult as that can be). (Adam Douglas)

Where I see it most is in the "ownership" of knowledge. Knowledge is the currency, communication the way we do the transaction. I often see ego become the block to communication - be it someone forcing their own point of view from a senior position and stifling others, or people clamming up and siloing themselves so they feel "important" for what they know. These things happen every single day and it is important to recognise them... particularly in yourself! (David Howart)

I now see my ego as combination of confidence and arrogance. I love the confidence perspective but try to avoid the arrogance. There are many times when it is important for me to present myself like I know what I am doing, but at the same time I need to recognize that I am interacting with extremely bright and accomplished individuals that can bring unique and important perspectives to the projects and challenges I am working with. If I think I know all the answers, I will miss out on the potential benefits of collaboration and shared ideation. (Dave Martin)

I think having a healthy ego keeps you in balance between arrogance and confidence, low self-esteem yet not inferior. (Fergus Conolly)

If you feel humiliated or can't tolerate failure, it's becomes impossible to do your job properly as a coach. Oversized egos have difficulties managing failure, while balanced and moderated egos (true champions) manage to handle the situation and learn from it. The problems slide off them like drops of water, and they move on to the next challenge. (Frederic Bougeant)

Ego, one could argue, may occasionally be tied up with "self-belief." In order to progress in sport, one must have a deeply ingrained sense of self-belief. The crucial difference here is that those with "big egos" may be viewed to exude a sense of insecurity, so their self-belief is misguided or is actually disguised hubris. I believe it is possible to have humility and self-belief, and to keep the ego in check. Achieving this is likely to lead to longevity in sport, good relationships with colleagues and better outcomes for athletes. (8)

Everyone is the star of his own movie. It's easy to think that you are the center of attention, that people are following what you do because you are in this big club. The problem is that ego needs people to recognize who you are, and chasing external recognition has serious limitations because as soon as you leave one club you're forgotten almost instantaneously. So what's next then? You need to control this ego, so that eventually, you realize "I know how good I am and I don't need others' opinions." (Keir Wenham-Flatt)

Gregory Dupont, performance manager and researcher, formerly Real Madrid, French National Team: I think the need to discover the best way to perform, to live new experiences, to learn about people can help to progress, but not the ego. Well-being and happiness require you to reduce the ego.

It took me a while to realize that to be happy it is important to know the difference between what is good for your ego, and what is good for you. If both can be aligned, then great - but it's very often not the case, so choose wisely. (Martin Buchheit)

MASTERCLASSES IN EGO MANAGEMENT

EDINSON CAVANI: EARNINGS OVER ENTITLEMENT

Edinson Cavani, the Uruguayan striker, became another icon in Italy, especially in Napoli. He scored 33 goals in each of his first two seasons (2010-2012), followed by 38 goals in his third season, where he also finished as Serie A's top scorer with 29 league goals.

On 16 July 2013, Cavani transferred to Paris Saint-Germain for a reported €64 million, at the time the most expensive signing in French football history. He also was on the front line of fame playing for his country at the World Cup and Copa America.

We can easily imagine the sort of competition and the special relationship that existed between Edinson Cavani and Zlatan Ibrahimovic at PSG, after everything we know about the latter's ego and eagerness to keep the spotlight on himself. While there were some obvious frustrations for Cavani coming with his new role in Paris - not always playing in his favorite position as a true No. 9 on the pitch, not being the center of attention anymore - Cavani managed to maintain his focus on his role on the pitch, scoring 25, 31 and 25 goals during his three first seasons alongside Ibrahimovic's 41, 30 and 50 goals, respectively.

Photo: Christian Gavelle

Martin: During their two seasons together, Cavani always kept a professional attitude and, despite the obvious frustrations, never said or did anything that could be counterproductive for his teammates or the club. He maintained his ego in check and put himself at the service of the team.

One night, coming back from a very a poor and disappointing defeat in the Champions League, instead of simply collecting his stuff and heading back home to try to sleep, Edinson stayed for a moment in the locker room at the training ground. The defeat we are talking about is one of the more famous defeats in the history of the club, even in the history of the Champions League. After having won against Barcelona 4-0 at home (which gave us an incredible advantage and almost qualified us for the next round), we had managed to lose 6-1 at Camp Nou. We were out. Beyond the indescribable frustration and disappointment with the defeat, what left a bitter taste for many of us, including Edinson, was that many of us had thought too early that we would make the next round, even before the game started. The details and stories of players' and staff attitudes in the weeks between the matches have been told elsewhere [Molina, 2017]. But this night, Edinson did one of the things I will always remember the most from him. Without saying a word, he went to take some blue tape from the physio's office, and he added the missing word "HUMILITY" on the wall of the locker room, where some motivational quotes and words were already displayed.

Image via Oh My Goal

The flipside of ego is humility. While pride is concerned with being right, humility is concerned with doing the right things. It's about the importance we give to others vs. being self-centred on oneself. Humility moves you away from the I-dentity.

The central distinction between healthy and unhealthy egos is willing to be part of something and a community vs. being all about you. (Pippa Grange)

Once Ibrahimovic left, Cavani became Ligue 1's top scorer, scoring 49 and 40 goals during the 2016/17 and 2017/18 seasons.

Martin: This ability to put his own fame and objectives on the side and work for the team in all circumstances always impressed me. He came with a lot of humility and resilience, but also had the way he would never discount his efforts on the pitch. He was able to run the full length of the pitch to defend balls in the box to help his teammates, which is pretty uncommon among strikers, who tend to restrict the majority of their effort to attacking sequences.

The situation when he had to play and share goals and fame with Ibrahimovic is not unique.

More recently, the combination of injury and Mauro Icardi relegated Cavani to the bench. Icardi signed with PSG in the summer of 2019 and started playing incredibly well, scoring 17 goals in 19 matches.

Cavani didn't play at all for several matches. But he stayed humble and showed an incredible team attitude, encouraging his teammates and working even harder, until the situation swayed back to his favor. Icardi became less efficient and the coach started to give Cavani more minutes, until he was again back as the team's top striker for the Champions League against Borussia Dortmund. This match was played just before the COVID-19 shutdown, and was, in fact, Cavani's last match with the club. He never came back to Paris before signing for Manchester United (ironically, one of Ibrahimovic's former clubs) in October 2020.

While the lockdown and his transfer during the post-COVID-19 preseason denied him the opportunity for a proper goodbye to PSG's fans, he remains one of the most adored and respected players to have worn the jersey. His humility and attitude have touched more hearts and souls than the spectacular goals and COVID-vanquishing tweets of Zlatan.

Cavani's combination of humility, stillness and resilience represent a successful character shared by many top professionals.

THIERRY OMEYER: BUILD *DIE MAUER* AGAINST *LE BOULARD*

Ego: There is a very fine margin. To be and remain the best you need to have high levels of self-confidence, while not having - as we say in French - le boulard: roughly, someone with a big head behaving like a d**k.

Some people may say that I have always been highly centered on myself, my own performance, which may sound egocentric. Fair enough, but as a goalkeeper, this is the only way you can help the team.

Being the goalie, you can easily be the hero: you save the last opponent's final shot and your team wins, for example. It's easy to think you made the difference. But if you miss too many shots during another match, you can definitely be held responsible for the team's defeat. So after each match I reset completely. It takes time to build confidence, but if you don't reset, you can lose everything very quickly, especially when playing at this position. It's like playing golf or tennis. You NEED to be focused ALL the time. You need to control your attention more than at other positions. I do the same with my ego. I control it. Every day.

Similar to this overall attitude, I don't display my trophies. I don't have a room for that. I don't need to look at them to know what I have achieved. I keep that for me.

A NOTE ON HUMILITY

George: The word humility traces back to the Latin word "humilis," meaning "on the ground." "Humilis," in turn, derives from "humus," meaning "earth." It's easy to see how these roots gave rise to the idea of humility as prostration and grovelling, lowering one's face or body to the earth.

Does that sound like something a professional athlete would do, or call on his teammates to follow him in doing? Would that be a winning strategy?

"Humility" does not mean degradation or self-abasement any more than "pride" means boastfulness or self-puffery.

In sporting terms, a call to humility is a call to be "on the ground," a reminder to the players to keep their focus on the 110 x 60 meter patch of *humus* on which they do battle. Wherever the players' minds were during that Champions League game - maybe they were thinking of the trophies at the end of the season or their post-season holidays, maybe they were on autopilot or simply letting their minds wander - their heads were in the clouds, and Cavani needed them back on the ground - *humilis* - where they play their sport, do their work and succeed or fail.

This calls to mind Raphael's *The School of Athens*. At the center are Plato, pointing up to the world of Forms and Logos, and Aristotle, palm down, orienting his teacher and his students to the reality of life on earth. Aristotle, who called pride "the crown of the virtues," was making his own call for a life lived *humilis* - on the ground. Not in self-abasement, but in reality and in purpose.

BEN RYAN AND FIJI RUGBY: YOU CAN ONLY PURSUE THE VALUES YOU KNOW YOU HOLD

Ego boosts can be part of the compensation package for working in high-performance sport. The prestige of working for a top tier club, the opportunity to work with some of the world's finest athletes, the kid-in-a-toy-store feeling of having a training center full of the most innovative equipment and technology with acres of manicured pitches, and the feeling that you - among hundreds of your peers - were selected for the position can make up for the small number that results when you divide your salary by the hours you work. Wages and perks are just a small part of what motivates you to sign your contract.

None of that applied to Ben Ryan in 2013. Over the previous six years he had amassed more games - 378 - than anyone else as England's Rugby Sevens coach. He led England at two Commonwealth Games and took them to 28 semifinals or finals, including the finals of the Rugby World Cup 7's, the first time in 20 years England had made it that far.

He didn't need an ego boost, a posh training environment or any experience to pad his CV when he decided on his next job. The one thing he needed most was a salary - and that was the one thing not in the contract he signed with Fiji's national team in September 2013.

Ryan coached Fiji for several months before the team was in a financial position to negotiate his wages. For all he knew at the time, it could have been six months or a year. Meanwhile, he was working on a substandard training pitch with minimal gym equipment.

He had the only thing he needed and wanted: a strong, cohesive team in a country that simply loves rugby.

Those previous stories and others made me change my whole outlook, and that was reinforced by my next job, working in Fiji.

We had nothing in Fiji: no money, no resources. But valuing those around you and putting others first cost nothing and I immediately felt a change in my outlook. I was always a good coach, and 90% of my time I kept my ego in check. But that 10% spoilt me really becoming a great coach. Leaving England and going to Fiji got rid of nearly all the ego and allowed me to be a lot more mindful, and coach and live with a lot more clarity. I left Fiji and I got a tattoo on my wrist which, in Fijian, says "vei lomani."

It was the Fijian 7s team's one and only value we came up with. It means work together and love each other, and it was first in any decisions we made. The team made history and won world titles and then the Olympic gold medal in Rio. Whenever I feel like my ego is about to pop up then I look at my tattoo, take a breath and tell the ego to f*%# off! (Ben Ryan)

FRENCH FED CUP: FORGIVENESS, REDEMPTION AND TRIUMPH

France's success against Australia at the 2019 Fed Cup - the World Cup of women's tennis - shows the power of ego management.

On the third day of the competition, Kristina Mladenovic upset No. 1 Ashleigh Barty, and then teamed with Caroline Garcia to win the decisive doubles match.

Mladenovic and Garcia, former French Open doubles champions, powered France to their third Fed Cup title and first since 2003. It was redemption for Mladenovic and Garcia, who lost the decisive doubles match against the Czech Republic in the 2016 final.

The headlines could tell of the triumph, but could not capture the work that Julien Benneteau's team invested to win the trophy.

Following the 2016 defeat, Garcia left the team to give priority to her singles career, apparently just sending a text to her doubles partner, Mladenovic. Unsurprisingly, this did not go over well with her teammates and the federation. In April 2017, Garcia said her back was injured and she would not play in France's match against Spain. Her three teammates reacted with identical tweets: "LOL," because they didn't believe she was actually injured.

Le forfait de Caroline Garcia provoque le LOL des autres joueuses françaises

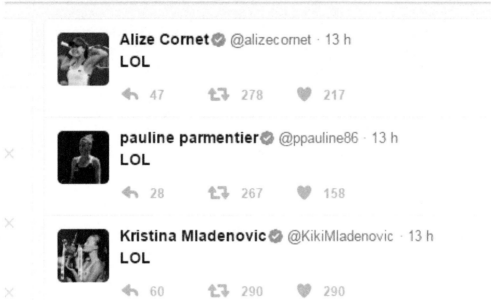

The relationship was over. For the next two years, Garcia had no contact with the others. Away from the team, Caroline Garcia reached world #4 in singles, while Kristina Mladenovic - who was in the top 10 - lost 15 matches in a row and exited the top 60.

The emotions, fights and Mladenovic's loss of confidence made it seem impossible to reunite her with Garcia as a doubles team, not that anyone wanted bring that negativity into the French national team's camp. Yet everyone knew they were still the best players in France, and their doubles team was one of the best in the world.

This is what Julien Benneteau, a French retired professional tennis player, came into. His career-high singles ranking was the world #25 in November 2014. He never won a singles title, but he had success in doubles and reached his career-high doubles ranking of world #5, also in November 2014. He won the 2017 Davis Cup with France.

On 23 June 2018, he was appointed captain of the Women's National Team. He managed to convince Garcia to come back, and put the team project above all of the personal fights and differences. No one really knows how amiable players' relationship was. But they found a way to come together and win the Fed Cup, finishing the match with an embrace.

Benneteau said afterwards: "I was new to the team so I started from a blank slate. I asked them to put the team above their personal interests. They must be proud of what they did, not only as athletes but especially as women. They kept their ego on the side." [Blondet, 2019]

If the team wins, you win. Your ego will be rewarded anyway!!

HAVING THE RIGHT EGO FOR THE JOB

I have been fortunate enough to work with some of the world's best coaches. I have forged some excellent relationships with these people and I would like to think that my personality and levelled ego has allowed me to do this. I would consider having to build relationships and prove myself as an individual and as a clinician to these high-level coaches as the biggest challenges I have faced in my career. I consider being able to provide an informed opinion, being calm under pressure, not being afraid of having difficult conversations and being a big personality with a little ego has helped me along the way. (Lee Nobes)

Working abroad, the ability to question, understand and respect other people's habits has helped me a lot. The world is very complex and we hardly have enough elements to judge the other without making a few mistakes. (Andrea Scanavino)

When a new head coach arrived at the club I was working at, I was the High Performance Manager. The new head coach brought in someone he had worked with in the past to take my position, but asked me to remain on the staff in a supporting role. I could see that there would be benefits for me in the areas of self-development and improved working hours in the new job, so I accepted and thrived.

Taking a back-seat allowed me the freedom and mental "space" to develop my software / analytics business, which has since been a wonderful part of my career. Had I not been prepared to "get in line," I may have missed out on this opportunity to build the other layer to my career that has been so rewarding. (Andrew Gray)

I don't think it's personally a particular issue for me. I've tended to have "imposter syndrome" pretty much throughout my whole career. I always feel that I'm hanging out with all the clever kids in class, so I guess that prevents my ego getting out of control! (Nick Grantham)

Certainly, in recruitment for jobs, being less egocentric or egotistical has proven valuable, as later on you find that others who had applied for the job were ruled out because of their ego. Some of my most recent opportunities were because of a perceived "lack" of ego compared to others. (Dave Carolan)

My low externally-facing ego means that I am seen as a calm and steady member of the staff, one who is willing to share in successes and credit. This has helped me move around various countries and cultures and build successful working relationships wherever I have gone. (5)

I think my "moderate" ego overall helped me a lot. During my career I have worked with coaches, fitness coaches and players who have made the history of European and world football for the past 20 years. If my ego had constantly contrasted with theirs, I would have stopped working long ago. (Andrea Scanavino)

In my present position, I deal with National Technical Directors, National Team coaches, coaches of international level athletes and also athletes of five different sports (under the umbrella of the same national federation). Almost everyone in this list comes equipped with a rather large ego, and I feel that without some healthy degree of ego, it would be extremely difficult, if not impossible, to carry out the job. However, I am making a conscious effort to leave my own ego at the door to avoid the usual clash of egos that is so detrimental to the success of a high-performance sport organization. (Iñigo Mujika)

It's a difficult question, but the willingness not to consistently dominate others and to show vulnerability has helped me a lot to show my competence, gain the trust of my peers and the players that I coached and, in turn, to be successful. (Pierre Mangin)

Building relationships of real value. Having humility, but also the confidence to be a man of integrity. Northants Cricket was a real challenge, but I put my ego aside for the betterment of the playing group. Initially, I had limited engagement in the training process. However, my ego allowed for the barrier to entry to be broken down, and players bought in. (Chris Tombs)

When I first found out that Usain Bolt was coming to the club, I wanted to make sure that our performance and monitoring methodologies would be best practice. Especially because he was essentially an unadapted athlete who was about to be exposed to the physical demands of a new and unfamiliar sport: deceleration loads, change of direction, aerobic requirements, etc. The potential for excessive neuromuscular fatigue and soft tissue injury was high. That would be compounded by worldwide media attention on Usain and our management of him.

With immense assistance from my good friend and colleague Nick Poulos, I sat down and designed a best practice program for Usain including 30:15 testing, aerobic testing, strength testing, NordBord testing, ForceDeck monitoring, wellness monitoring, a strength and injury prevention program.

However, that all changed in my mind when I had my first meeting – an informal dinner – with Usain and his really knowledgeable and supportive manager, Ricky Simms. Immediately it became clear that Usain was taking a great reputational risk of failure in attempting to transition to being a professional footballer under the glare of the world media. He had a lot to lose, and there were anxiety and trust issues associated with this. Historically, his athletic training program had really been quite organic, without high tech daily monitoring and repeated interventions from sports scientists on a daily basis.

At that point, I decided to put my ego aside and modify our program so it was less intrusive and more organic in terms of what Usain was used to in Jamaica. Ricky helped me enormously in this regard. We still included non-negotiables such as wearing a GPS unit in training sessions and trial matches, regular force plate neuromuscular jump monitoring and heart rate monitoring as well as some basic verbal wellness questions (sleep quality, etc). We also modified his program to limit his running on harder grass pitches surfaces in the Australian summer.

I also made contact with Usain's personal sports physician, Hans Mueller Wohlfart, to get a deeper understanding of Usain's medical and injury history. This gave Usain further confidence that we were well prepared and leaving no stone unturned in terms of designing his program.

Nicko and myself still did a lot of back room data analysis and program modification but we greatly reduced the time each day that we "got in Usain's face" with sports science data collection.

Quite rightly, Usain wanted to integrate socially with our playing group and not be treated as a special case too much. You could see that he genuinely loved being part of a playing group dynamic and this was a very important factor in why wanted to pursue this opportunity.

This modified approach worked really well, as Usain seemed a lot more relaxed. We even got him to do a sub-maximal heart rate running test with the squad once he was comfortable!

Most importantly, Usain participated in all training sessions and matches during his time at the club. His neuromuscular force production metrics were surprisingly resilient to fatigue and he did not suffer any soft tissue injury at all, despite having had a history of hamstring injury in the latter parts of his athletics career.

This situational compromise of my ego, to modify my initial program, was very effective in gaining Usain's trust and compliance. It minimised any training anxiety without compromising our standards or putting Usain at an increased risk of injury. (Andrew Young)

STRATEGIES FOR KEEPING YOUR EGO IN CHECK WITH REALITY

Few things are more obnoxious to sports fans than fair-weather fans and bandwagons, the ones who emerge decked out in team colors and proclaim their lifelong support when a title or cup is within reach, but vanish when a season ends midtable or worse. As supporters of George's favorite football club like to chant: Where were you when we were s**t?

You should ask your ego the same question every once in a while.

We encountered plenty of fair-weathered egos in Chapter 3: they're front and center for the trophy lift, on the fringes during the preseason grind and nowhere to be found during the midseason winless streak.

People like Thierry Omeyer are successes in handball, ego and life because they commit to one ego, in good times and in bad, for richer or for poorer. The same ego that punches the air and stares down an opponent after blocking a shot is the same one that is torn apart by the shot that goes past him into the net. The same ego that drives home from a track meet or match thinking "That was incredible! You did it!" is the one that arrives home thinking "Alright, better spend an hour reading before bed, because, really, a lot of things could have been so much better out there and next time won't go as well."

YOU'RE STILL JENNY FROM THE BLOCK

A lot of stats matter at a professional sports team. Here's one that doesn't: number of peer-reviewed publications.

Martin: I arrived at Paris Saint-Germain two months after they won their second of what would be four consecutive Ligue 1 titles. In the previous season, Zlatan Ibrahimovic scored 41 goals and Edinson Cavani scored 25 - the same amount the defense conceded that season. The players had worked collectively with thousands of coaches and training room practitioners. They were currently under the guidance of Laurent Blanc, a man with extensive experience as a professional player and manager for clubs and France's national team, and who was dubbed "Le President" for his leadership abilities.

And here I am, a "retired" semi-pro handball player with a Ph.D.

You might not be surprised to hear that the players had little interest in what I had to say at first, but I was. My ego certainly was not prepared for it.

Only when I was able to step back from myself and look at the situation from their eyes - their titles, their international careers, their years of experience in making themselves the best - did I understand who I was in that training room.

If I wanted to do the job I believed I could do to help them and the team, I had to earn my right to do it. I had to gain their trust by proving to them every day that I could be a useful part of their performance team. I could draw on my degree, my research and my experiences to date, but the only thing that would matter to them - the only thing that ever matters to a player - is what I brought to the training ground every morning.

Much easier said than done. I try to take the time to really understand the context of a situation before I respond. That is why I find social media challenging. I am amazed at how people can respond to things without knowing the full context of a situation. There are also many people in the industry who are much brighter than I on all topics in performance and rehab, therefore I know I don't have all the answers. For me it is about assessing the situation and then trying to apply the right response, not the other way around. (Darcy Norman)

I also make it a point to embrace being able to say "I don't know" or "I'm not sure." While I like to know things (and show off this knowledge sometimes), I enjoy opportunities to say that I don't know or ask for help and allow someone else to teach me. I think this really helps to keep my ego in check. I feel like most people are so afraid to say that they do not know something or ask for help that it gets in the way of them learning and being able to put their egos aside. (Keith D'Amelio)

Philosophy: listen more, talk less. Realize that 50% of what we think we know is wrong - it's up to us to figure out which 50% is more likely right or wrong. (Paul Laursen)

I have always tried to learn from the different nationalities I have worked with. Just because somebody from a different country does something differently doesn't mean it is wrong. Can I learn anything from the way they do things?? (Lee Nobes)

KNOW HOW AND WHEN TO LET GO

George: One of the maxims of the US Navy is "Always train your relief." We had two reasons for preaching this. First, if there wasn't someone ready to replace you, you could never move up or out to a better job. Second, given the line of work, there was always the chance that you might suddenly not be around, and no individual's absence could ever risk the mission or the crew.

I needed several years as a coach to understand how that perspective applies to the sports world.

Starting out with my crisp graduate degree and big ideas, I thought I knew and could teach things better than what my athletes already knew from their years of training. At the same time, the twists of fate that landed me coaching a semi-pro track club left me terrified of losing my athletes to more experienced coaches or more popular training partners.

Superficial knowledge plus professional paranoia (not the kind necessary to survive) is classic "garbage in" for the ego.

After the first two years, I realized that I was giving the same instructions, the same cues, the same notes. That meant I wasn't progressing. The runners were getting faster (a good thing, to be sure), but they weren't progressing. If I was travelling with one athlete, I would freak out about how the others would be training that weekend in my absence. When they would fill me in on how it went, I'd question their decision-making even though I never gave them a basis for making the "right" decisions.

I violated both reasons for always training your relief. I didn't put them or myself in a situation where we could progress together into being better coach and athletes, and I made their training (or at least my perception of it) dependent on me.

Conflating "control" with "effect" is the sort of error that lands you on the treadmill we talked about earlier in the chapter. In the end, you have neither, and your ego is left asking "WTF just happened?"

Napoleon said "Men of great ambition have sought happiness, and found fame." Ralph Waldo Emerson took the measure of the man and described Napoleon's life and career as "an experiment, under the most favorable conditions, of the powers of intellect without conscience." From Napoleon's "vast talent and power... immense armies, burned cities, squandered treasures," of this general who "immolated millions of men [leaving a] demoralized Europe," Emerson asks, what did Napoleon achieve? What were the results not of the moment, but for history?

"No result. All passed away like the smoke of his artillery, and left no trace."

Martin: I can relate to this when it comes to players and staff in big teams. While they make a big fuss when there are in, it's actually astonishing how quickly the team and the locker room operates without them once they are transferred or leave for another job. I witnessed this many time, and every time it struck me to see how quickly a player or a colleague is "forgotten."

I remember especially a staff member who was in charge of a few particular players in terms of a bit everything: treatment, strength, nutrition, etc. He was "their" man, and operated as if the players would break if they were not working with him.

When he left, it took two days for the players to find their new routine, and I never heard anyone asking about him.

"Nature abhors a vacuum!" so others fill his or her space immediately, and it's fine!! We are all replaceable!

We should embrace this. We should want our institutions to be strong enough survive the normal comings and goings of life (and the accelerated comings and goings of high performance sport). If a club, clinic or athlete is weaker without us, then we failed it. Our ego should want things to thrive after we leave - our legacy is what keeps going.

Aside from the hopeful benefits for the athletes and teams, sports performance work is more enjoyable and fulfilling as you take those steps back. Training sessions are less stressful for all involved, and the athletes come to you with increasingly interesting and "advanced" questions. Because you're not holding them down at the lowest current level, they push you with the graduate and doctorate level questions you came into the field to answer.

TAKE PRIDE IN WHAT YOU'VE DONE - AND NO MORE

If you really want to know a person's heart, watch him behave with people who can't bring him anything.

— Indian proverb

Martin: I've been lucky to spend a bit of time with Zinedine Zidane in 2011, when he was taking classes for his coaching diploma with the French federation. I was among some of the "professors" who visited him in Madrid as he was coaching La Castilla, the B Team of Real Madrid. At that time, he hadn't yet won three consecutive Champions Leagues as a coach. He was "just" one of the greatest players of all time: FIFA World Player of the Year in 1998, 2000 and 2003; the 1998 Ballon d'Or winner; and winner of both the 1998 FIFA World Cup and 2000 UEFA European Championships.

In addition to the profound stillness of the person, it's his humility and friendliness with the "least important" people around us that struck me the most. He would shake everyone's hand entering a restaurant, for example, and take the time to enquire about people's health, their family and well-being, with a smile and a lot of empathy. Likewise, instead of sending us a driver at the hotel as almost every other person would have done, he came in person to pick us up and drove us to the training ground in one of the club's service cars. No fancy Ferrari.

There are a lot of people way less famous and important than him who don't give a f*** about others, and even less about "small" people. You obviously build a career and a name first with performances on the pitch, but the way you behave and the respect you show to those "small" people elevates you at far higher levels.

I've witnessed this attitude in other top players, too, including Maxwell, who I worked with for a few years at Paris-Saint Germain. Maxwell is a Brazilian player whose 33 trophies put him in among the top five footballers in history. Many remember him as one of the best defenders in the world. Calm and gentle on the pitch, the perfect incarnation of a team player, he would always have a nice word for every staff member at the training ground, and would never put himself in the centre of a conversation. A true gentleman.

Laurent Blanc is another exceptional character. As a player, he won the World Cup in 1998 and the UEFA European Championship two years later. He played for many prestigious teams, including FC Barcelona, Inter Milan, Manchester United and Marseille. He was one of the best central defenders of his generation. He always publicly supported his teammates and later, as a coach, his players. He never once showed any negativity when talking about others to the media. He always respected the opponents and the players he would not select in the team. Further than that, when fans asked for a selfie, he does more than just pose with them: he asks about them, what they do in their lives and what makes them strive.

When I would watch him talk to superstars in the locker room, I was always amazed by the calm and confidence he showed around them. There was never a single bit of overconfidence or arrogance. Just by being there, saying what he had to say, he does good for the team. No extra words, no attempts to say anything in his favour and never offering excuses. A master of simplicity.

For Zidane, Maxwell and Blanc, this peace of mind and simplicity comes from a mix of a few things. One, they have been such reference points for generations of fans. They have so much in their lives that they don't have anything to prove anymore to anyone. This instantaneously kills the need to turn the ego volume up where many others keep theirs. Second, their high level of recognition and achievements provide them an incredible level self-confidence. That helps them navigate through any situation and into any headwinds. They possess healthy and mature egos, pitched to the right volume, that they keep inside for themselves.

Working in football makes you special, but it's because football is special, not you. (Grant Downie)

I think because it is so competitive to get into elite sport, that once someone has a position it's easy to see oneself as "above" other practitioners, or gain recognition and think there is clout that comes from working with particular athletes. I think ego can be fed by other practitioners thinking "Oh, because they have made it into elite sport, they must have X, Y, Z qualities, or be better than me at X, Y, or Z." Even though this is not necessarily the case, it's easy to feed an ego. Positions and titles lead to benefits, like being asked to speak at conferences or lines to speak with you at conferences, and these could easily be taken for granted and feed ego. I always feel humbled and not worthy of being asked to do things or talking to people, but I've definitely seen the opposite (Amelia Arundale).

Beware of letting working in elite football feed your ego. This is a foundation on sand. Former athletes do not change personality just because they change jobs (Ian Beasley).

One of the biggest issues I see now is that few practitioners know anything else other than the "sports world." It's an artificial world. It leads you believe what you do is life-saving. We teach guys and girls to run around a field and make money for billionaires in what is now an entertainment industry. We don't save lives. Keep your ego in check. The true role of sport is to help young people prepare for the challenges of life - not sport as an end in itself. (Fergus Conolly)

People easily believe that you are the best strength coach in the world when you are with the German National Team and winning the World Cup. It's both easy and pleasant to think they are right!! You also need a good level of ego to stand in front the players. The job, in fact, encourages your ego to grow. But the reality is that you need to work on yourself to keep your feet on the ground! It's the only way to move forward. (Benjamin Kugel)

I do, I honestly remind myself every day to not get too high or too low with the results of the team. I also remind myself that there are thousands of other S&C coaches around the world who do what I do with varying levels of success, so keep it all in check. I try not to let the role I am in define me. Balance in life is crucial. (Adam Waterson)

I reflect on myself! Am I really capable of doing this, or am I lying to myself or pretending that I can? Ego is often manipulated to pretend to be someone you are not. (Eric Blahic)

I never take myself too seriously. Be serious with your work but don't try anything that your body cannot cope with. I manage to laugh at myself, which keeps my ego in check. (Tony Strudwick)

If I feel that I have said something that did not come across well, I will reflect on that conversation and maybe revisit the conversation with the person to try to leave the discussion on a more positive note than the first time. (Adam Johnson)

I make sure to remind myself of moments when I have looked back and thought "oh my god, what a dick, Joseph!!" on a regular basis!! (Joseph Coyne)

I try to control my ego every day. If a player doesn't work as I wished, I try not to take it personally but relate it to the overall context we work in, then find strategies to reach my goal with him. Acting with authority is not a good option, since its shows a lack of adaptability. (Franck Kuhn)

I keep my ego in check by always thinking how my comments and responses affect others. If I am in disagreement with someone, I will try to anticipate how they will receive my response. I remind myself that some things are certainly more important than pleasing my own mindset. (Alex Calder)

Many practitioners today think they are bigger than players which is not the case! We are and need to be in the background!! (Grant Downie)

PAUSE, READ AND LOOK OUTSIDE YOURSELF

I try to avoid any response or decision too fast. Stop and breathe. I enlarge my perspective to the full context: usually the team, and not just myself. (David Utrera)

Every morning I try to take a few minutes before going to work to organize my day and repeat to myself a few important things about how to control my ego. (Alain Sola Vincente)

Creating time to ensure I have an opportunity to check my internal biases and be aware of the external factors influencing decisions / performance help avoid the personalisation of success (and failure, which is more common). (Marc Quod)

I am constantly reading different types of leadership or self-help books. I try to learn from other sports, the military and business executives to see how they deal with high pressure / stressful events. I welcome different courses, separate to sports medicine, that might provide me with something different to help me develop as a person. This will inevitably help to keep my ego in check. I have also developed some close relationships with professionals in leadership, life coaching, psychology that I often bounce ideas off / get advice from to provide me with a different opinion on certain situation. This helps me to think before reacting. (Lee Nobes)

I strongly reject being ego-driven. I´ve found that extensive reading from different knowledge areas keeps your feet on the ground because you realize how scarce your background is. (Julio Tous-Fajardo)

By constantly questioning my decisions and evaluating alternative scenarios, not to a level that creates anxiety, but actively seeking possible flaws in my solutions and looking for possible alternatives. I read and/ study a lot about failure, especially in the business world, as there is a lot written about this. A quote from What I Learned Losing a Million Dollars (Paul & Moynihan) that helps this process is to remember that "Success can be built on repeated failures, when those failures are not taken personally. Likewise, failure can be built on repeated success, when the successes are taken personally." I have tried to think proactively and recognise when my ego gets in the way of progress. I have also tried reading around the subject, and purposefully tried to push my development in this area through reading books on debating, negotiating and crucial conversations. (Marc Quod)

I have a few strategies in place to help my ego from having a negative impact on me. One is trying to be a constant learner. While this might seem like a really basic idea, I think constantly seeking out information or skills, from a variety of fields and not just my domain, allows me to try to always have an open and growth-based mindset. (Keith D'Amelio)

I try to keep a journal (daily or weekly) to note the things I am grateful for and those things I need to improve. It allows me again to understand that I don't know much (but sometimes more than others) and that it is important to accept all kind of feedback. (Mathieu Lacome)

I think the sign of a good practitioner is his or her ability to allow new methods and others to challenge his or her current or past methods and philosophies. I try to remind myself every day that what I believe in can, in fact, be completely wrong. Too often people's egos get in their way. They just don't learn and would die for their own version of their truth. (Martin Buchheit)

These thoughts are best done by running! Then we have to go back to reality to continue observing, studying, reasoning about the "progress" of the world in which I work to continue to be part of it in a proactive way. (Andrea Scanavino)

REALITY: ACCEPT NO SUBSTITUTES, NOT EVEN THE FEEL-GOOD ONES

There are some really convincing substitutes for reality out there. Emotions, stories and heuristics all have their place in making sense of a situation. As situations get more complex and doing our reality check becomes more challenging, the temptation to fall back on one of these stand-ins increases. "Well, I don't know, but my gut says… this convenient narrative says… this framework says…"

Emotions give us a useful snapshot of what we feel about something. But they don't tell us what we know about something, and they exemplify "garbage in, garbage out" as much as the ego. Heuristics offer a useful way of thinking about things, but they do not tell us what to think. At best, they help us organize what we know.

And stories? Stories are great! Humans string together events into narratives to make sense of things, resulting in everything from epic poetry to the latest conspiracy theory on Reddit. Stories based on facts do not replace the facts themselves, no matter how much we like the plot or the outcome.

Fact: He was late. Story: He is ALWAYS late because he NEVER cares about others.

Fact: We had a successful year this season. Story: It's only because of my coaching strategy and because we were doing my drills.

Fact: There have been leaks in the media about the preparation plan for the match. Story: It must be Steve who talks to the media, because I often see him talking to the TV reporters on game day. He does that on purpose because he wants the rest of us to be sacked.

Fact: A few of the players have their skinfolds slightly higher this year compared with last year at the same time. Story: It must be the supplements this new nutritionist prescribes once a month, since last year she wasn't with us and players were skinnier (and, oh by the way, I personally don't like supplements).

Reality checks need reporters and analysts, not imaginative writers or ones who know how they want the story to end.

I am also not sure if it is just ego but it is also about our heuristics and biases that drive our ego. For me it would have been more beneficial to learn about the heuristics and biases first, and then more about ego. (Darcy Norman)

We all look at the world through our own subjective lenses, and, at its essence, this is inherently an ego-driven process, driven through selfish means. (Stu McMillan)

Not now, I have grey hair!!!! I would like to think I have learned with time and mistakes to listen, watch body language and reflect. This allows me to check myself and control my feelings and emotions before "seeing through the lens of others." (Grant Downie)

I do try every morning before I face my staff and players. Our emotions affect our behaviours and we are not always at the same and right state. (3)

I shut the fuck up!! In a meeting, sometimes I really need to manage myself not engaging the discussion for not being too rude and open. (Andrea Azzalin)

I endeavour not to react to situations when emotions are charged. I try to take time to consider decisions, and to do what is best for people (and not necessarily me!). (8)

I try to step back and look at situations, look at how I'm reacting and what is emotion, ego and fact; as well as what is my perception. In the heat of the moment, this can be difficult, as well as when stressed or tired. (Amelia Arundale)

Balance, openness and communication. Developing high levels of emotional intelligence and understanding situations from every level helps to keep egos at bay. At the higher end of this business I often remind myself that I am here for a reason. I always keep calm in confrontational situations without backing down if feel strongly about a particular topic. I have learned to pick my battles with certain situations, but always try to understand a discussion from everyone's point of view. It is important to consider cultural differences and how this might affect people's opinions. (Lee Nobes)

As I've gotten older, I try to give myself a day before responding if something has annoyed me. This is especially so if my response is written, as I think we can be far harsher on email / text. (Tom Little)

Yes. By applying more patience, parking something that's triggered me or going out for a cycle. (Steve Ingham)

LEARN FROM OTHERS' SUCCESSES, UNDERSTAND THEIR FAILURES

I remember the many great mentors and colleagues I have had who are extremely humble and supportive and kind and giving. I try to remember how they treated me early in my career and remind myself to treat others in the profession the same way. I also like to reflect on situations with colleagues: How did I come across? Did I sound arrogant or dismissive? During meetings, am I holding my ego in check and ensuring all points of view are provided before we make a decision? Strong leadership does not mean a big ego. I try to get feedback from the groups I work with on whether they feel comfortable with the leadership and the "egos" in the room. (Dave Martin)

Having outlets, mentors, and people outside the organization to help debrief and strategize. I've found it helpful to have people who are objective and not part of the situation to give me an honest opinion and help me talk through my own emotions and issues, and then develop a way to approach the situation. (Amelia Arundale)

Yes, I have certain mentors (Kelvin Giles) and family members (dad, wife) who would let me know if I am becoming an egomaniac. (Paul Delvin)

I tried to have a network of high achievers around me to be mentors. People that I trust a lot so I can always remind myself that the journey is very long and I'm far from being the best! My wife is here every day to remind me to clean the shit and to keep my ego as low as I can! (Yann Le Meur)

I have a few people I work with that I now have a relationship with that allows me to have open and honest debate about the best possible program for the athlete / team, and I encourage them to challenge me daily. (Selwyn Griffith)

Yes, I do. I think that this comes from all of the experiences to date in my adult life and a better understanding of my personality. I think my upbringing and mainly my schooling created a hugely competitive mentality, which, whilst important for achievement in the world that we are working in, could appear at times to be less in touch with the human side and the softer skills that are necessary for making others feel comfortable. I constantly reach out to the people in my life who will give me an honest answer and are prepared to challenge me. I value the opinions of others to help bring balance to the way that I go about my business. I have spoken to a sports psychologist to help me be a better person and to better understand myself so I can bring that to the people within the organisations that I work with. (Ben Ashworth)

I am seeking other opinions as often as I can, especially from people outside the sport industry. It helps a lot to put things in perspective. (Pierre Lassus)

The best lessons usually come from people with no academic background but high wisdom of life. I love to talk with these unique individuals since they are able to challenge all your preconceptions with one small sentence or concept. I consider myself fortunate for having the ability to unlearn or change my point of view when someone shows me either strong scientific or practical evidence. (Julio Tous-Fajardo)

Every year I seek out information about myself from those that know me and interact with me in various capacities. I try to rotate people each year so that I am getting different perspectives. It is a type of year-end review or planning ahead exercise, and provides feedback on myself from these people. It helps me to understand areas of opportunities that I can work to improve myself. It also sometimes helps to highlight areas that are strengths that I might not see in myself but others do. This allows me to be more aware of not only areas I can work to improve, but be aware of things that I do that people view as positive - and maybe I should do more of. (Keith D'Amelio)

Dylan Mernagh, First Team Sport Scientist, Queens Park Rangers FC: By taking a step back and understanding in my quest for knowledge how little I actually know. I try to understand that everyone has something I can learn from. Even when I may disagree with others, I try and see things from their point of view to help my understanding.

I quickly realized that we are only isolated experts in small areas and need to collaborate to have an impact. Nutrition without behavioural change experts - nothing happens. So, from this point of view, my ego is in check! (David Dunne)

It's important to be aware of how our behaviour affects others. I know I can trust my wife on that regard… and for sure she'll tell me immediately if my ego starts to fire up! (Yann Le Meur)

I try to work with as many smart people as possible. I quickly recognise my limitations. I have some pretty smart mentors who highlight areas I need to work on, also. (Andrew Murray)

I don't think you can work in many elite level organisations if you are unable to reflect and adapt your own ego accordingly. Reflection and communication with colleagues and running regular needs analysis has helped me take note of where my ego might be. Understanding the needs of "clients" I am providing a service to is important. Whether that be athletes, coaches or even colleagues within the performance / medical environments you have to continually reflect, not just by yourself, but also by discussing with those around you who are willing to have honest conversations.

Honest conversations and not taking offence are definitely ways I have tried to ensure the level of my ego doesn't affect too many situations within my professional career (or even my personal one!). (Steve Barrett)

I believe that when working with someone who has a large ego for a prolonged period of time, there is a strong desire not to let them impart their personality to you. (Adam Johnson)

I learn from the people I interact with. I write down at the end of the day all the poor ego-driven attitudes and actions I have seen from them. This constitutes the base and the reference of things that need to be avoided for me. It's a constant learning process, not a "leading by the example" strategy, but just the contrary. I say this with humility now, but I think it's been incredibly valuable so far. (Martin Buchheit)

It's actually quite easy. I look at others around me who have huge egos, how they are perceived by others, and the number of occasions they make a total prick of themselves, and it reminds me to wind it in. (Chris Barnes)

The biggest (and easiest) way to understand the need to control your ego is watching others fail because of the unawareness they have about the devastating effect of their uncontrolled ego. (Charles Vallejo)

Watching others in great jobs has made me learn from how others act in front of people in their jobs. I had several high-performance managers as bosses, and you learn what you like and reflect on how you would do it given a job like theirs. From observation, I have kept a very low to no profile and tried to do my job. This has helped any thought of being egotistical in check. Doing my Ph.D. was an eye opener, and learning to write was a nice reminder of how far I needed to develop. It was humbling. (Johann Bilsborough)

I think the phrase "A little bit of knowledge is more harmful than no knowledge" seems to be the main source of this. I have loved all my jobs and couldn't be more blessed with the personal and career trajectory I have experienced prior to saying this! Watching someone of a high position dig themselves into a hole, thinking their little bit of knowledge was the equivalent of the Queen's speech at Christmas, by inaccurately interpreting simple data points and contradicting my interactions with that person was astounding and eye opening to me. A clear example of the potential pitfalls of ego in elite sport.

However, I ask myself and, on reflection, despite that experience of watching someone crash and burn, they are still in a high position, so how have they managed that, and is that a potential positive from having a high ego level? We should ask similar questions of ourselves: Are you the right person for that organisation? If you have been at an organisation for five years, are you still improving the service you are offering? (Steve Barrett)

Focus on your own path and story. Dedicate your time and effort to those who are worth having them. Silence the noise. Know how to listen and take it in, and when to listen and throw it all away. Surround yourself with good mentors that will always be there to guide you through situations that you might not be comfortable going on your own. (Ivi Casagrande)

SET THE RIGHT VOLUME

Don't let anyone tell you otherwise: when you come into a team environment, you do not "check your ego at the door." If that's the expectation, you should be wondering what they want of you if not, you know, you.

Once you're through the door, remember that you're not the only one with brought their ego in with them. In these environments, everybody does because everybody has to. That's part of the reality of being in a high-performance workplace: your ego has to coexist with everyone else's. Calibrate accordingly.

We all have ego. Nobody will be out there without a decent and strong ego. All the big dawgs. Coaches, comedians, CEOs, locker room staff all have a more robust self-esteem and a bigger drive. All have a strong one. None of us could have done what we have done without it, to be able to give these talks in front of large audiences, lead sessions with top players, etc. But it's about how sensitive it is. It's about channelling the ego. Keeping room for humility alongside. Can you see the team and the others beyond the I?

I have seen people on both sides of the spectrum: some have a very sensitive ego and they can be successful with that. But since they close so many doors, are they really happy in their professional life? Are they able to develop and reach their potential?

On the other hand, I have seen others much more humble. People say "they have no ego." That's wrong. If they didn't, they wouldn't be there. It's just that they excel when it comes to managing this trigger. They keep their own hand on the dial. They have the maturity and have learned how to channel their ego.

Turn the volume down to allow your heart to feel successful. When you are caught in fear with the volume high, like in a defensive mode, constantly on guard, you can't even hear or feel the success. With the right volume, you can enjoy the journey. This is the most important, no? Otherwise, why bother? It's about finding the right volume. Find your very best. (Pippa Grange)

Being a practitioner: reset your emotional state to ZERO. Too high, you can regret afterward. Too low, no confidence. (David Dunne)

I reflect upon my motivations and my actions, and try to ensure they remain consistent with my purpose. I look at ego as a dial: sometimes I need to dial it all the way up, and other times, it needs to be dialled all the way down, dependent upon the situation. (Stu McMillan)

Adaptability - knowing when to step forward (lead) and when to step back (follow). (Keith D'Amelio)

Absolutely. As stated in my definition, ego is a balance of self-worth, confidence and humility. I try and recognize situations where I need to tread carefully and others when I can push harder. I guess it's a reflective process and constantly seeking to learn about myself and get better about managing personalities and situations. (Chris Tombs)

It's important to find the right balance. I know it can be dangerous, but I also make sure not to turn it off completely, since it helps me to stand up during difficult moments and be stronger. It's all about being aware of it and using it wisely for the best. Ego is not an on / off switch. It is there for everyone and exists on a dynamic continuum. Therefore, I think keeping it in check is an ongoing process. (Sébastien Carrier)

Like with anything, awareness is the first step, and so it is important to remind yourself of what you don't know. This is arguably even more important when working in science because our knowledge and understanding is constantly evolving. As the Dunning-Kruger effect teaches us, our confidence is inflated in our early career years despite a lack of knowledge, but as we progress from fresh-faced know-it-all's we experience an inverted U-shape relationship between our knowledge and confidence. Although acknowledging we don't know it all is important to unlock learning and keep our ego in check, it can also push us to the other end of the spectrum, which can present itself as Imposter Syndrome.

Striving for an accurate understanding of ourselves can help keep us away from the extreme ends of the spectrum of ego and imposter. In Ryan Holiday's book The Daily Stoic, he quotes Epicetetus as saying "It is impossible for a person to begin to learn what he thinks he already knows." The philosophy of stoicism, centered around our lack of control outside of anything other than our "reasoned choice," is a useful way of thinking, both in terms of keeping our own ego in check as well as dealing with those around us. (Jo Clubb)

REMIND YOURSELF WHY YOU ARE IN A TEAM ENVIRONMENT

> Try to ask someone with a high ego volume: "Would you risk being faithless?" or "How much of your life is oriented toward others vs. yourself?"
>
> This connectivity and orientation toward others is a central thing. If you want the very best you for the communal benefit, for others, then your ego is unlikely to be inflated.
>
> If you want to be seen as the very best so that everybody can see you on the throne with the crown on your head, your ego is likely inflated.
>
> Orientation to other people - to the greater good and the team - is central to the volume you play your ego on. Inflated ego and being grounded don't go well together. (Pippa Grange)

I always try to ask myself why am I doing the thing I am doing: a behaviour, an action, a conversation. I also push myself to go three "why's" deep. If the answer to any of them is something in the vein of "self-centered ambition," I put it in check - that is, stop immediately. My aspiration in exploring human potential is to help make others better. If it only serves me and my personal circumstances, then I am not living in alignment with that aspiration. (David Howart)

I find reflection - journaling, debriefing situations with colleagues or mental performance coaches - is important. It's a form of being more mindful, so that seems to help "awareness of self." If success is when my behaviours match my values, then it seems like a good idea to reflect on my behaviours to see where I was aligned, and where I was out of alignment. (Jeremy Sheppards)

Life should be simple - solutions to sporting problems should be simple - when everyone is engaged and aligned. If I feel my ego is taking over - the "I'm right" approach and I'm not listening - I reflect and put myself in the position of the other person and align myself to the purpose of what WE are trying to achieve. (Stuart Yule)

One of the most important questions to ask oneself daily is the following: "Am I satisfying myself and my ego, or does it benefit the program and the athlete? [Blanchard, 2019]" How many practitioners have the humility to ask themselves this question? How many can actually respond with the second alternative? (Martin Buchheit)

Is everyone running the boat in the same direction? There are too often too many people more interested in themselves rather in the big picture of the club. I constantly remind myself that personal agenda should never be the drive for any type of decision. Easier said than done though. (Antonio David Sánchez)

I like this challenge that I often tell myself: when I sit on the additional bench for a Champions League match (which is right on the touchline), is it because I can better see the match or is it because this is where I can be better seen? (Martin Buchheit)

Is what I am going to say for me, or for the group? (David Dunne)

MISSION FIRST. MISSION FIRST. MISSION FIRST.

Martin: Five minutes after coming off the bench in his first appearance back from injury, a top player I helped rehab scored a goal. He ran towards the bench to celebrate with me, knowing how much I did to bring him back to the pitch and back to goal-scoring form. That goal and the celebratory hug made all of our hours together and my many other hours of effort worthwhile. Those hugs are the moments players and coaches live for.

Except the hug never happened. I stood there as he ran right past me to hug two of his best friends on the team.

I never felt as alone and as stupid as that day. And it was entirely my fault.

I clearly wasn't in it for him to score or return to full fitness. I wanted the recognition, the praise from my colleagues, the hug in front of the entire stadium and TV audience. A thank you would have been nice.

That incident sums up the difference between doing and being. I was being, when I should have been doing.

Ryan Holiday writes "Purpose helps you answer the question: To be or to do? quite easily... If your purpose is something larger than you–to accomplish something, to prove something to yourself–then suddenly everything becomes both easier and more difficult."

Since then, my focus is on my job. I know what I need to do, so I do it well and make sure I enjoy doing it. By doing my job instead of trying to be some guy with the job, I'm no longer dependent on someone else's approval. I get confidence from my work, which feeds my ego in a good way, as opposed to the cheap ego high I wanted so desperately on the touchline that one day.

> *Ego is a massive problem in our field. People started to lift weights to be noticed. And they can't get away from that in their coaching life as well. But the goal of the coach is to eliminate the coach. When you do a really good job you don't really need to be present anymore. People may sometimes not even know what my role is. This is want I want: I want the guys to see me as my staff's assistant. I don't have ego anymore.*
>
> *I still worry if people like my book or if they enjoyed my talk, but I don't need to be the front man anymore. It's like being in a band, I am happy to play the bass, not the lead guitar. This allows me to live the life I live now and that I enjoy.*

– Michael Boyle, strength & conditioning pioneer

Too many people like the idea of being the performance director. They love the title, tweet it, put pics with the team on Instagram. But doing the job and having the job title is not the same thing. You need people who are on the same page (Johann Bilsborough).

Always keep in mind it's not about you: it is about the greater picture. In football, most people's actions are usually driven by a personal agenda. (9)

The more experienced I become, the more I am focused on creating an environment that is about others, not myself. (Andrew Gray)

I had a colleague share that we, as the health and performance team, are the invisible framework that supports the players' and the coaches' success. So you have to be OK being invisible. And as I get older, the more invisible I am, the better I can do my job behind the scenes. (6)

If, as a coach, we start to compete with athletes who are often already superstars, the battle is lost in advance – and it's the wrong battle, anyway. Coaches need to leave their ego at the door when they enter the club to support the other egos to perform! (Martin Buchheit)

I would say that no matter how "important" you might think you are, you are never above anyone else. For me, that means giving my time to those who ask questions or send Twitter messages or e-mails asking for advice. Honestly, 10 years or so back, and ashamedly I say this, I would not have done that-- I felt I was too important. Giving back and having time for others has helped me in my career more than anything. (Allistair McCaw)

I don't have to check my ego now because I learnt that the best way to achieve a goal is teamwork. All the time, I'm careful that it's always about the player, not self-interest or because I am chasing numbers. It's my job to sometimes have difficult conversations, but those are only in others' interests. I'm always conscious of it. (Andrew Wiseman)

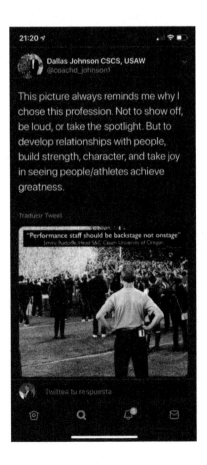

I'm fortunate enough to have worked in my career with some of the best players and networked with some of the best practitioners. There is NO shortcut for experience and no substitute for being open-minded. A clear understanding that my role is essentially to support the players that I work with to perform at the highest level possible level on a regular basis is something that never leaves me. I'm not fond of clichés, but to be able to look at yourself in the mirror at the end of every working day knowing that you have done your best is something I find comforting. (Paul Balsom)

We, as applied practitioners, must always focus on putting the athlete first. Every decision we make must have the athlete at the top of the "pyramid." Is this the optimal activity? How much coaching does the athlete need to be successful? Do I need to be here right now? Each of these questions is one I have asked myself multiple times throughout my career to ensure that my decision-making process is coming from the right place. When I could answer NO or MAYBE to one of these questions, then I had to assess if my desire to apply such an action was because of me or other factors.

We must always protect the athletes from selfish individuals (sometimes ourselves) who seek to be in the spotlight more than the athletes they serve.

While it goes against our industry, Andrea Pirlo has the quote, "Warm-ups are masturbation for fitness coaches." Sometimes when you watch some pre-match warm-ups or even some training sessions you can understand why he might have been driven to say something like that. Does the fitness coach really need to be yelling like that? Is the fitness coach warming up to play, too?

Pirlo's quote has always been stuck in my head, and is something I think about when working publicly with an athlete. The term "minimum effective dose" is an important topic in our field currently. Maybe this is also something we need to apply in the way we coach and interact with our athletes, to ensure we are not wearing out our welcome. (Garrison Draper)

Working with top tennis players, I know that I have to deal with large egos. I start by trying to listen to them and understand them, so that my own ego doesn't get in the way of what we should achieve together. (Paul Quetin)

As a coach, if you don't adapt, you die, so in the end the need for adaptability is a good antidote to ego. It forces you to look outside for assistance from others. (Frederic Bougeant)

I've always tried to look for advice and feedback from peers to improve our overall training process, with the athlete performance as the target. Where do I personally stand here doesn't matter. (Sebastien Gardillou)

As a coach, I tend to be as objective as possible, foster divergent opinions and admit that there are always different ways to reach our goals. While casting doubts on one's ideas and strategies is warranted to progress, it's important to put all your energy into one plan to push it through, while still keeping the opportunity to re-evaluate and modify / adjust on the fly if required. It's kind of an art! But it's the overall process and keeping the focus toward our goal that drives the process, not what we want and wish to do personally. (Pierre Mangin)

It's far from being easy given the amounts of ego here, but honest and clear reasoning about reaching our goal should always come first over any individual agendas when it comes to making decisions. (2)

USING MENTAL TECHNIQUES

Yes, I think it's essential, in work and in life equally, to keep your ego in check. Meditation has been really helpful, for me to sit quietly and observe the craziness of my mind, my ego, jumping around from plan to plan, unable to be quiet for 10 minutes. When I was younger, I was very quick to dismiss the ideas of other people, quietly in my mind saying that they were wrong and I was right. I think that comes from being good at school as a kid, where there was a right and a wrong answer and I mostly was right. But that is entirely the ego. And in real life situations, there is rarely a 100% right or wrong choice. Now I am far more open to actually HEARING the suggestions of others, and thinking of them as equally as possible as my own. (6)

I do everything I can to avoid excessive ego and better control my emotions. Practicing sophrology and mediation has helped me a lot. (Alexandre Dellal)

I seek challenges that I know will humble me. I meditate and aim to role model gratitude and compassion on a daily basis. These seem to be an effective antidote to ego excess. (David Joyce)

I've been aware for a long time that I don't know everything and the wealth of knowledge is in the regular exchanges of information. For this reason, I've tried to read about human behaviour and the emotional aspect to have more tools in discussions with my colleagues. It's very important to listen and discuss with empathy and assertiveness to reach an agreement. (Rafa Maldonado)

With more experience, I learnt to manage better my emotions. I try to be more relaxed and not to be upset by the fear of failure. I thought that at first it had a negative impact on my personal life and, therefore, on my work. Because I can't imagine that you can have a good flow in your job if your mind is disturbed. To keep my ego in check and not to feel this anxiety about defeat, I used to meet a psychologist. I think it's a shame that psychology is not thought of more highly in elite sport in France (Julien Robineau)

Scott Guyett, assistant manager, Brisbane Roar: By constantly reminding myself of where I started out in my football journey and appreciating how privileged I am to do the job I do.

#TOOMUCHINFORMATION

Competitive sport feeds ego, it builds heroes, not necessarily on the pitch, but through the fanfare outside as well. If you buy into this image, fear comes quickly into that because you don't want to lose this. (Pippa Grange)

The way other people from the outside look at you and the fact you may be on TV at every moment leads your ego to become the first motivator of your actions. Many people then live for this... and the reason why they are in their job can get lost as their career progresses. To know yourself better, it is very important to ask yourself where do you stand in relation to (social) media. (Antonio David Sánchez)

You always have to be aware of it. When an offer is made to you or a media interview is taking place, it's easy to want to elevate your ego to centre stage. You always have to be aware, and I think I've done that well now but it's taken over a decade of working in elite professional sport to achieve. (Ben Ryan)

Elite sport gives you access to fame (social status, social network, TV) and money. But while this can easily can make you think you are good in what you do, the truth is that this "reward" isn't necessarily related to your actual and true value. You could do exactly the same job in another sport with less media saturation. Would that mean you would be worth less as a player / practitioner?) (Martin Buchheit)

The modern-day athlete has become more defined by extrinsic factors such as social media and, as such, their egos are inflated with other influences outside of the changing room. Identity is becoming more important than being defined by hard work and excellence. Elite athletes need self-confidence. This should be built through intrinsic hard work and challenge, not defined by the outside world. (Tony Strudwick)

When I look at some people on social media, I can't stop laughing at those idiots making up their profile. What for? It's not meant to be about us. It's about players, coaches and owners. After that, we want the good scientists to put out their work - not the opinion-based BS that we have to stomach from practitioners with their new sexy titles. There are so many titles: Executive Vice President of Health, blah blah blah (Johann Bilsborough).

Sharing articles and achievements on social media has helped extend my network and spread my contributions to a wider network. I have had opportunities to write blogs, articles and book chapters, as well as speak at multiple events through my career, supported through social media. Is it ego that is driving these projects? Even this very project: was my agreement to take part driven by the egotistical appeal of being involved in such a book with such other leading names...?

I think it is human nature to want more publications, more citations, more likes, more retweets etc. But making this our driving motivation is placing our self-worth outside of our control in external validation. This has the potential to inflate our ego but also to hinder our own self-worth. So there is a balance to strive for with our use of social media. Rather than seeking more interactions, I try to reframe my motivation for using social media and similar opportunities as a means to try to help others via education, as well as helping to develop my own learning, writing, speaking etc. It is much healthier for your motivation to be driven by helping a wider cause than seeking to boost your ego through validation from external sources. (Jo Clubb)

I still spend too much time checking how popular my social posts have been. It's interesting to gauge the interest of our community in some topics, of course, but you probably don't need to check that multiple times a day! And, more importantly, getting satisfaction from this kind of external validation is pretty dangerous: what if tomorrow your account breaks down? Who is going to like you and where is this "love" going to come from? (Martin Buchheit)

I personally never post something for the sake of it, and will always add a link to full text or content to make sure the tweet brings some level of information. This means the tweet is more for the others now, it becomes less self-centered - even though you still hope to be recognized for what you bring to the others, of course!! (Martin Buchheit)

H.I.P. : Helpful / Inspiring / Positive. If it's not all three, don't post! (Allistair McCaw)

Don't be a d**k. Don't be confrontational. Don't drink and tweet.

Give, give and give. Create good content

Good social media growth is about organic growth, it's and about giving people content that help them. They come back to you if it helps them. They will be your best ambassadors.

— *Michael Boyle*

MARTIN BUCHHEIT
@mart1buch   ...

👋 🎙 We all have listened to someone presenting at a conference, and every 2nd slide there is a picture of him/her either running on the side of a top player or looking like in charge of everything, right?
What does that mean to you?
🙏RT

It gives him/her credit	18.1%
ok need 2 see more slides	5%
I can't be bothered	23.8%
Is this necessary?	**53.1%**

160 votes · Final results

While most people go to conferences to tell to everyone how good they are, I usually take off my accreditation or say I am a graduate student so they leave me in peace and I can enjoy the talks and catching up with friends.

Amazing that people will look at my credentials, see who I am affiliated with and then ignore me when I've put "student" on my tag. I deliberately do it to see what people are about.

Some people that never would speak to me when I was working in cricket, suddenly I get this new job in soccer and Rugby 7 and now these same people start calling and emailing me. I am the same person they didn't want to talk to or snubbed, but now they want to contact me. I just don't answer any more. If you weren't there when I was a student working my butt off, then I don't want to talk to you now (Johann Bilsborough).

CENTER YOUR EGO ON THE BEST OF YOUR HUMAN NATURE

One thing that jumped out at us from the reference definitions of ego is the lack of conditionals and caveats. They don't say ego exists if, when and unless; exercises its "executive agency" only under the following circumstances; is experienced as the "self or I" among people who meet (or suffer from) certain conditions. Ego is, if not a primary, a universal consequence of having a self, that is, of each individual's existence.

But listening to some people talk about their ego, you get the impression they consider the ego a vestigial organ of the psyche. The appendix of the mind, you could say. It's there because we haven't managed to evolve it away, and sometimes it gets really inflamed, causing pain and requiring surgery.

Psychologist and author Steven Taylor [Taylor, 2005] posits that an "ego explosion" launched humanity out of an "earlier, healthier state." In this prehistoric and pre-egoistic era, according to Taylor, humans lived peacefully amidst plenty. There was no violence, no status, no plagues. Humans spent less than 20 hours a week foraging for food. For this "original affluent society," in the words of anthropologist Marshall Sahlins, whom Taylor approvingly quotes, perhaps the most difficult thing was that "half the time the people do not seem to know what to do with themselves."

Life became "nasty, brutish and short" only after an environmental catastrophe forced early humans to give up their hunter-gatherer ways. Survival and selection pressures caused humans to "[develop] a stronger and sharper sense of identity, or of individuality."

If this all sounds familiar, it's because it's the Garden of Eden story with archaeological and anthropological footnotes. Taylor calls this turning point in history "The Fall of Man" and speaks of other cultures and peoples who are "unfallen." Ego, in this reboot, plays the role of original sin.

Since our interest is high-performance work environments, let's consider how Taylor leaves hanging the question of what those early humans did with the "half the time" when they did "not seem to know what to do with themselves." His reconstructions of that era are based on circumstantial evidence. He does not reference ruins or writings. He alludes to "prehistoric art galleries" only to note the absence of depictions of warfare, not to tell us what they show about the individuals and societies who made the paintings.

Affluent societies leave a mark on the land and on history, from Parthenons to skyscrapers, philosophers to scientists. The "original" one, in Taylor's telling, left little more than bones. They had millennia of free time on their hands from having to spend no more than half a work week on their subsistence, and yet… nothing. Within a few hundred years of the "ego explosion," though, history takes off.

Taylor is making a powerful point about ego. Without ego, we eat and reproduce. That was the to-do list in the Garden of Eden. That was the extent of what it meant to be a human.

Then Adam and Eve took a bite of knowledge or, if you prefer, the environment selected for stronger egos. The external world presented an existential crisis to those early humans. Some of them had components of their personalities that engaged in a relationship with the external world that enabled them to survive. Despite his pseudo-evolutionary cast, Taylor does not marvel at how those early humans adapted their minds to confronting the challenge of survival in a hostile environment. He does not credit the ego with helping mankind overcome the zero-sum resource competition of that primitive era to bring us to a point where we have more people enjoying a higher standard of living than ever before, even if it comes with downsides.

He, instead, condemns the adaptation - the ego - knowing it brought us to the world of today.

Those early high-performance cavemen brought about the "Fall of Man" only for those who would rather be in the cave than in the "arena for admiration." Where will you direct your ego to take you?

FROM THE PLAYBOOK: "SET PLAYS" FOR EGO MANAGEMENT

Karim Hader

When needed, I try to keep my ego in check and go through the following points:

1) Try not to react immediately when a situation itches my ego.

2) Take a big breath.

3) Then, step back to analyse the situation to get the answer to the following questions:

- Is this situation worth involving my ego? If yes, why?

- If yes, how? Wording, ways of communication, etc.

The objective is to bring a rationale to these sensitive (for my ego) situations.

Jonny King

I like to read and listen to podcasts to help develop my interpersonal skills, mainly about those working in different high performance environments, from a variety of backgrounds and industries: business, sport or the arts. I take inspiration from those with more experience than myself and from various conceptual models. From these experiences, I have developed three really simple rules of engagement, that help to keep my ego at bay when interacting with my peers, colleagues and athletes on a daily basis:

1) Do not interrupt others.

2) Do not be judgmental.

3) Gain a real appreciation of others' points of view.

Ivi Casagrande

I try to go through my checklist at least once a week:

1) Did I listen to what others have to say and considered what they had to say without letting the noise of "I know better" get in the way?!

2) Dedicating time during my week to talk to younger coaches and not only mentor them but, most importantly, ask how they do things and what I can learn from them. Sometimes I think in this industry we think because we have more years of experience we don't get to learn anything from the young coaches who are just starting. You can always learn something from everybody.

3) Constantly talking to people and coaches who are so much ahead of where I am and have so much wisdom and experience. Always helps us to understand that there is SO MUCH that we still don't know.

4) Keep learning. Never allowing myself to settle and continuing learning from others are great ways to keep our ego in check and know that we never know ALL the answers.

5) Have the humility to listen to criticism and know which ones are worth considering and changing behavior, and the ones that are just noise.

Pause, put emotions down and act.

Allistair McCaw

Every day, I want to be known as a better person than what my career title is. One of the tools I like to use to keep my ego in check is by self-reflecting each evening. I go through my day and ask myself these three questions:

1) Reflecting on my strengths: What did I do well today?

2) What could I have done better? This particular question is the one that takes me to how I behaved, how I approached conversations or how I handled things that day - all very much to do with ego.

3) Who did I make better today, serving my purpose and being of service to others?

TAKE AWAY

"How do you balance having shoes and pants? You don't! You want both!"

— Michael Malice, author (Fridman 2021)

As the coaches among us know, balance is a tricky thing. Even the best athletes will wobble and fall when they're standing blindfolded on one foot on an unstable surface with people bumping into them as they walk past (which is a better analogy for some of our jobs than a worthwhile balance test in the gym).

As the managers among us know, you don't give the balance task to the elephant - you give it to the monkey. And you don't try to "balance" the elephant's lack of balance with the monkey's lack of strength. Give the elephant the strength task and the monkey the balance task. That's why you keep both on the team.

Questions about balance often assume a zero-sum situation. There's only so much… whatever… to go around, so you're trying to dial in just the right amount to give to this, that and the other, to him, him, her, the rest of them and yourself. Balance my ego against his, my goals with the team's, my career and my family (more on that in Chapters 9 and 10). Much like while doing a balancing task in the gym, "finding the balance" only gets you so far. You have to continuously, endlessly, maintain your balance. You don't find a solution - you just buy yourself some time.

A better way of dealing with these situations is to drop the zero-sum approach, consider context and complementarity and then calibrate. What does your ego deserve in a given situation? Know it and enforce it. What does someone else's ego deserve in that same situation? Know it and respect it.

That's ultimately how Martin and Zlatan came to have a productive working relationship. No amount of balancing could have led to these two sharing an ego-space: Martin can't dial his up that high, and Zlatan won't dial his down that low. But they could co-exist as neighbors in the crowded ego-space that was Paris Saint-Germain football club.

Over time, Martin used his knowledge, experience and professionalism to build his ego to a level that Zlatan could relate to and recognize the benefit for himself. Zlatan didn't "balance" his perspective on sports nutrition with Martin's persistence to drink the protein shake he prepared. He definitely didn't sacrifice his recovery and pre-game preparations to make "Genius" feel smart. In the shared domain that mattered most to them - human high performance for the good of the players and the team - they both came to recognize that Martin's ego was a benefit. Martin had to venture into new, slightly uncomfortable territory to build and project his ego to that level, but it was necessary for him to achieve his goal: helping Zlatan achieve his own goals.

Martin earned the outcome he desired and Zlatan gave Martin's ego what it was due because doing so was good for his own. He drank the damn shake! And, yes, we understand how ridiculous this must sound for non-sports people.

We don't "balance" shoes and pants because we know they are two different things. We want them both and we want them to complement each other. Same for egos. Recognize that each person's ego is different, and find creative ways to give each their due. Starting with your own.

6 | EGO: DO

> "Between..
> What I think
> What I want to say
> What I believe I say
> What I say
> What you want to hear
> What you think you hear
> What you hear
> What you want to understand
> What you understand
> There are 10 possibilities that we may
> have difficulties to communicate...
> But let's try"
> — EDMOND WELLS (BERNARD WERBER)
>
> egoalsbook.com

No matter what you specialize in, no matter how well-defined your job is, no matter how effectively you have socially distanced yourself so that you have no interactions outside of Zoom and Slack, you're going to have to deal with people. Maybe that makes you uncomfortable. Maybe that's the part of the job you dread, or, at the very least, shy away from.

Take a moment to step back and ask yourself what people think when they have to deal with you.

At some point, we all have to engage with people in a situation we didn't ask for and would rather avoid. Very often, this happens when someone's ego gets between us and the mission, whether it's the long-term mission of a large corporation or your mission as a one-on-one freelance consultant.

We need to have as many tools for dealing with ego as we do for our actual job, and be just as judicious in applying them. Remember the prayer about having the serenity to accept the things you cannot change? Other people are high on the list of those unchangeable-so-you-better-accept-them things. No matter how thoughtful your techniques or coherent and rational your persuasion, serenity may entail simply walking away - but that has to be a conscious choice, not a default evasion.

For the other times, those that require the courage and wisdom to change the things you can, we all need to have at least a generalist's acumen in handling our peers' egos. We will all encounter an ego-laden situation and will have to deal with it ourselves. Given the personal nature of these situations, we can't just refer ego conflicts to the person in the next office.

Most of us chose to be a specialist in something other than dealing with other people's egos, but having some skill in handling them could at least prevent us from being a specialist in ego failure.

CONFLICT IS INEVITABLE, RESOLUTION IS A CHOICE

Olivier Krumbholz, Head Coach, Women's French National Team: If you can't handle conflict, change job. There is so much that can't be put on an Excel spreadsheet, so much information that needs to be processed that, at the end, you have to make a lot of subjective decisions. And subjectivity means that many highly confident and opinionated people around you (players, staff, people on the outside) will have different views, and will likely disagree with you all the time. You need to be prepared.

One of the most critical capacities in this world is to able to stay on track with your ideas when other people question you work (since this happens daily), and to manage to discuss and disagree with them without creating conflict. (Alexandre Dellal)

DON'T POUR GASOLINE ON THE FIRE

Those battles can take a very long time. They are never won, and you can lose within minutes if you say something wrong. A bit like you are walking on eggs or defusing a bomb. You need to fake it and use strategies not to be perceived as a threat. Make sure you don't question their ideas in public. Flatter them. Open the door and gain trust, give them the impression that you are willing to follow their views and, above all, that you're not going to do anything that could go against their power and magnificence. Eventually you'll start, micro-step by micro-step, discussing very gently the things that are important for you and may need a change. Obviously, this strategy goes completely against my vision of relationships and my personal ethic but, unfortunately, this is often the only way to be heard in this context. (Yann Le Meur)

A storm will normally blow out. Rather than argue and interrupt someone who is in full flow, let the other person finish and then pick apart the flaws. Once the energy has dissipated, there's more chance of getting agreement. First and foremost, when they have finished, highlight something that they will agree with you on - perhaps using their words back - so you set the foundation to move on. (Dave Carolan)

Again, remember: ego is valuable, but when it's overstretched, that's when it is unhealthy.

How can we help this player find a way that his ego is not triggered so easily? You often hear "he has too much ego." But it's not about controlling the ego itself, it's about controlling the triggers. This starts by making him understand that he is safe.

Then, what is sure, is that a very sensitive ego doesn't like to be told what to do. And the central part of an over-sensitive ego is wanting to be seen as amazing.

Don't let the player define himself by what the amazing is and what success looks like. Together, you need to shape what is amazing - aligning expectations - your common vision of success. Express what matters to both of you and find a way to work together.

Tell him "This is how I see you as successful. Doing this, you will be amazing, with you willing to play your role in the team."

Overall, it's about shifting behaviours. Not expending so much energy on looking good but putting it into performance and doing things to unleash their full potential. Why would you not look good if we win? Do it because you want to achieve more!!

The language you use around ego is so important. Ego has such negativity around it. If you are easily moved into a state where you care too much about what people think, if you are easily moved to a defensive state, how are we going to manage this together? Wherever the discussion ends up, the coach needs to reward the behaviours that are aligned to what they talked about. (Pippa Grange)

I have learned that one the best ways to get your message across to someone who has a very high opinion of himself is to use the indirect route and never expose him publicly.

For example, if you want one of your players to understand that what he does on the pitch is not right or not optimal for his health, don't just tell him what he should or should not do. It's wiser and comes across better to talk to him about what one of his teammates is doing right or not, and even to blame the teammate in confidence with him. He may, therefore, be left with the responsibility of changing his behaviour with regards to our discussion, but with this approach he would not feel offended at any point. It could even reinforce your relationship with him since he now feels he is in your confidence. (Martin Buchheit)

PRESERVE THE RELATIONSHIP

When you put a player on the bench, explaining your choice is important, but you don't need to justify yourself. It's a way to show that you know what you are doing while preserving your role and, in turn, the relationship. (Olivier Krumbholz)

"You catch more flies with sugar than s**t." When you are constantly focused on being right, you start to have bad feelings with people you disagree with. That is everything but the right way to develop a maintain a relationship, which you need to get things moving forward. (Keir Wenham-Flatt)

Telling people their ego is too big doesn't work in my experience. You sometimes can't be that direct about it because it can rattle that person's entire identity. You need to show them. You can do this by modelling the way, and using champions. By all means, say what you mean, mean what you say, but you don't have to destroy someone in the process. The ego is probably too big due to insecurity, so be kind. Help them. I did not understand that well enough. (Jeremy Sheppards)

Connection. Getting to know players and staff through a common denominator. Over the last 7-10 years of my career, I have had a passion for coffee and conversation. Invite players / staff for coffee. Engage with their passion, ask questions, listen intently. Know their wife's or girlfriend's name, their kids' birthdays. Where do they like to go to eat out? (Chris Tombs)

Being modest and leaving your own ego at the door, even when you know that they know that you know more than them and you have accomplished more than them. (Iñigo Mujika)

I don't try to combat it if I like them - sometimes I indulge it for entertainment! If I don't like them, I ignore them completely and avoid interaction, which is probably not the right thing to do, either, but it works.

Once you know someone is driven by ego then it's a lot easier to navigate them. Don't ever try to go against ego head-to-head. Even if you win, the scars of battle will last a long time in that particular relationship. Avoid making anything personal, and look for middle ground and keep things about the bigger picture. Stay in the present and avoid confrontation, but be firm in whatever you are trying to achieve. (Ben Ryan)

I think a more formal 1 v 1 meeting highlights the importance and sends the message that this is affecting the whole department and not just one person. (Scott Guyett)

A point that I would see as very important is how you chose to challenge this type of individual - challenging someone in front of a group will often bring out the worst in people. Sometimes it is needed, but it's a skill to recognise when.

Unfortunately, I don't think this can be learnt in textbooks. This comes from experience. Even if you disagree with points in meetings, you can challenge those points in a variety of ways. I know many people who only know how to challenge people in a very direct, accusatory way and this is useless.

Learn how to challenge in the right way. Sometimes it might be by following the person immediately after the meeting and making your point one-on-one. In my experience, when I have done this (a) the person appreciates that you've not tried to make them look an idiot in front of peers; (b) they listen to your point and consider it in a much better way; (c) the department will start to see changes and they will know you are having a good effect in the right way. (Lee Nobes)

DISTANCE YOURSELF: IT'S NOT ABOUT YOU

Bottom line: don't take the big ego personally. I always stay in touch with the purpose, and ask the big ego individual questions relating to the context of the situation. I always try to see the bigger picture and where this person fits within that picture. If they are an important individual that I have to work with daily, I aim to form a good and trusting relationship to ensure the big ego does not affect the productivity of what we are trying to achieve. If it is a moment in time where I have a one-off encounter with a big ego individual, I just move on very quickly. (Stuart Yule)

I don't think there are good or bad strategies. It only depends on who you are talking to. It has to be tailored to the person and the context. I believe you need to remain yourself first and take time to reflect. Always. It's crucial to centre the debate around the (common) objective. (2)

The position that the person has in your organisation will, to a large degree, dictate the best strategy that you can employ to deal with any potential conflicts. However, the focus must always remain on supporting the players. (Paul Balsom)

Forgive the small things, see the best in people where you can and try to find common ground on which you can bond. Hopefully this will help to build respect to a point where they will trust your opinion, even if you disagree with them. (5)

Instead of wasting time clashing with big ego people, I started to realize they were not deserving of me losing sleep over them. I decided to silence the noise and kind of playing their game sometimes. So that would mean, sometimes, even though I did not agree with them, knowing when to speak up and knowing when to just listen to them and let them talk. I would be mature enough to self-reflect on the things they would say, take the good parts, the constructive criticism, the good ideas and just completely ignore or let the other things that bother me go. (Ivi Casagrande)

> *Bring objectivity. A lot of coaches are ex-players who put their subjective opinion first: "we always did it like this." Bring objectivity rather than opinions to the table. Understand that many interpretations are wrong - we make meanings subjectively. Objective conversations based on facts, data, etc. If you don't create meaning you open the doors for others to create them.*

— *Jay Hedley*, high performance coach [Hedley, 2019]

Typically leading into conversations, specifically ones that could become emotionally charged, I remind myself to ignore tone and focus on what is being said. Many times, experts have large egos, but they have the knowledge that you want, so finding ways to take that information out of the tone is always important. (Garrison Draper)

UNDERSTAND WHAT'S BEHIND THEIR EGO

It's important to know how to actively listen to others to understand and gain context without feeling the need to reply or give your opinion to influence them. Also, being able to afford time for others is a priceless trait. (Grant Downie)

First you have to recognize the person has what is perceived to be a big ego. Then you have to figure out what has driven that ego - their past, present and future - and in what situation the ego comes to the fore. Listen to them, play back what they're saying, find out what makes them tick. (Steve Ingham)

For every ego that we have battled with, there is still a person attached to it that we are trying to help. And sometimes we're that person! It's worth remembering that when we are navigating the frustration. (David Howart)

Easier said than done, but try to put yourself in their shoes to see the situation from their perspective. This should allow you to understand better their reaction and the things they may be afraid of, and maybe even uncover some of their biases – this gives you a base to work on. (Martin Buchheit)

You have to understand what drives people, what is their WHY. What motivates them, why are they doing the job and why they want to be part of the project. Then you need to come at the bottom of things, and understand what perception they have of you. This depends clearly on how and when you arrived at the club, who hired you, etc. But the most important thing is to clarify your role and intentions from the first day, so that you can be seen as an ally, not a threat or a spy. (9)

Find their triggers!! All egos are triggered by something. What are the key things that causes someone's ego to come out? Use those triggers for your advantage to create a win-win situation. (Duncan French)

Understand the person. I have worked with players who appear to be egotistical or difficult, but they have grown up in war zones, so try to see what makes them the way they are. (Andrew Wiseman)

Understanding their philosophy and their non-negotiables, and make sure, when dealing with them, you always address those first. (Selwyn Griffith)

If you apply epistemology (the theory of knowledge) to an individual, and really dig into their theories and evidence for what they believe, their personal epistemology, you can uncover why they are acting the way they are or why they have built up their arrogance. Asking to genuinely understand is the key, but it seems to always reduce the ego. (David Howart)

Challenge yourself to find the method of communication to interact with them. An external perception of ego can actually be driven internally by insecurity, so building trust can help. (Jo Clubb)

I consistently create opportunities for us to better understand each other, and often not in the typical environment that we work in. The more chances you have for interaction, the more you can lessen the impact of ego. You reach a place of understanding where you are trying to reach the same goal, and that it is OK to disagree. If the person is above you in the organizational structure, then you let them know that you respect that they have the final say. (Ben Ashworth)

You have to try to understand what is fuelling the ego and why the behaviour / decisions are occurring. As I said, I am not confrontational, so if it is completely irrational I tend to back down. However, I will try at another time to talk to the person more generally to find out more about them and perhaps what causes them to behave like that. If you can understand the reasons you can look to construct your arguments in a way that will help you succeed in the future. (5)

If I'm not in that management position, I always try to play a long game with these big ego people. Learn what they actually want to get out of whatever role they are in and how they operate. Then I figure out how I can help them and interact with them. (Joseph Coynes)

I run a personality needs analysis on them and try to see the better parts of them. What is the individual like in front of me? What is their background? How can I help them? What personality type are they and what is the best way I can interact with them, if at all? Being a compassionate and caring human being costs nothing. Even these so-called "big ego's" acknowledge this, and this can help develop those relationships. (Steve Barrett)

It is important to understand the mental models of all you interact with. I have found that often we are arguing about the same thing but maybe using different words. Think of the vision that you are both looking at a stick in the ground across from each other looking at each other. The background of that stick as well as the surrounding area is different to each other. It is important to stand in their shoes for you to really see the perspective and biases in which they make their decisions. (Darcy Norman)

Understanding the culture that you are working in is extremely important when dealing with big egos. Understanding how the players perceive such colleagues is key, and failing to do so can be harmful for group dynamics. (Paul Balsom)

How to change people (players) who have ego getting into their way? Listen. Find out why. Because they've always done that? Understand what motivates them. Start with motivation first, and then shape the process to reduce resistance. "Need to lose weight? I don't need to do that! I am the best ever!" Okay... but... Compare approaches. Using another intervention - back to behavioural change. Take them through beliefs in a guided conversation. They need to see the situation differently. (David Dunne)

As I have said - and hopefully as I have matured - I feel I have done a better job of understanding others' points of view. If there is a genuine attempt on others' parts to do the right thing, and I simply disagree with it, then I feel it is important to have an honest conversation. If the attempt is not honest or if it is self-serving (which happens far too often in sport), then I do all I can to not let myself be affected by this person, or to remove myself from such situations. (Stu McMillan)

If I have learned one thing, it is that we all have an ego. It's good to realise the framework where it works well for you, and when it becomes the danger for you and others! Therefore, realise its qualities on a good day but the down side of it on a bad day. Tell others about yours and get them to share their good and bad day egos. We all have them!!! (Grant Downie)

STROKE THE EGO, FEED THE EGO... AND LET THEM TAKE CREDIT

A great option is to act like in many martial arts: take advantage of its energy to manage it in your favor. (Rafel Pol)

Play to it and then use it to your advantage. Just like judo! (Dave Joyce)

Most players give the impression that they are here for the team. But the reality is that as soon as they don't get what they want, they start to be very painful. Isn't this the proof of a poorly managed ego? As coaches, we need to feed these egos and find the strategies to share the recognition at all levels. (Olivier Krumbholz)

Warren Buffett said: "Praise the person, criticize the behaviour." Sometimes praise in specific, criticize in general. (Keir Wenham-Flatt)

I have found that you need to stroke their ego just a little bit, while trying to figure out how to plant the idea from their perspective, so they are under the assumption that it was their idea in the first place. When dealing with head coaches, I have figured out how to massage the message so, ultimately. they think it is their idea. (Adam Douglas)

Stroke it, but don't promote it!! Essentially, you have to use their ego to get them engaged. But you don't want to do it so much that it grows larger and ultimately gets in the way of productivity. (Duncan French)

If you give up claiming relevance, I think you've started off on the right foot. I have no problem making him feel important and, when necessary, I try to manage to make it look like he's the one with the last word. And if you are able to convince him the work you propose is not the best for you, but for him, your goals suddenly converge, and his ego will become your best ally. (Rafel Pol)

Big egos love being praised, so engage them in the process and they will open many doors for you. Play with them, tell them how good they are and, finally, do what you really want to do. (Mathieu Lacome)

Keep in mind our larger goal, at the institutional level. With coaches and directors, I have no problem suggesting things so they end up thinking the decision comes from them. Happy to leave my ego at the door and, at the end, my ideas are executed. (2)

Make sure they believe your idea is theirs! Have informal discussions about how he would perceive these actions you propose so the idea germinates in his mind. If it's a great player, he may feel invested with an important mission and perform well, which, overall, is highly beneficial for the team in terms of performance. If it's a moderate player, he may not deliver as expected, and the problem will end up being his problem, not yours anymore. Then you can get back on your feet. (Eric Blahic)

Play and accept a secondary role (in social environments) in exchange for developing your proposals. (Rafa Maldonado)

First, if I'm in the position to, I always try to give people ownership of roles and have their own flavour to what they want to do. This lets the people with big ego) hopefully get the positive feedback they need for their ego. I might set a framework that I want achieved (e.g. bake a cake), then they can choose how to fit their input into it (e.g. for a chocolate cake, what type of flour, cocoa, etc.). (Joseph Coynes)

Recognise their strengths (they will definitely have some) and play their game a little - if someone has a raging ego, they like that. Then you have the opportunity to influence them a little. Sometimes. (7)

Players who believe they have "made it," even if playing in sub-elite professional leagues, often showcase the greatest levels of egotism. In a role that requires you to demand these players do things, often against their liking, strategies must be in place to proceed with a desired outcome. If needed, I will often feed into their ego in order to develop a healthy relationship. For example, players have often asked me if I thought they played well. Even if I don't think they have, knowing the negative effects that would follow, I chose not to tell them that. My biggest solution is to take a breath and think about how my words will affect that individual's emotions, i.e., demonstrate a level of emotional intelligence. (Alex Calder)

Feed his / her ego when appropriate to maintain the relationship and when the goal is higher. Sometimes feeding the ego can help get an outcome you want. If it is a player that you are testing, feeding their ego may help to motivate them, for example, by using a leaderboard for an outcome measure of the test.

Feeding their ego also stops them needing to seek other opportunities to appear the "big man" elsewhere, so we can just move on.

Ask for their opinion on matters you would like to contribute to, as a means of starting a conversation.

People with big egos want to share their opinion. Getting their feedback builds up their ego. Utilizing their expertise through direct questions gives both the sharer and yourself the opportunity to get what you want. (Garrison Draper)

Make sure to include them as much as you can in meetings and other decisions, even though they are not required there or you already know the responses to your questions. (Alexandre Dellal)

EMPATHY, VULNERABILITY AND WILLINGNESS TO ENGAGE

Like humility, vulnerability is often presented as self-abasing. It's not just admitting you have weaknesses or short-comings, but proclaiming them and, many times, internalizing them as a permanent characteristic. Vulnerability becomes an attribute in itself rather than describing the relative state of some skill.

But you can't be "just" vulnerable. You're vulnerable *to something*: to criticism, to faster players, to a competitor offering the same functionalities at a lower price.

Vulnerability, properly understood, can be ego reinforcing. It starts with recognizing reality: your weaknesses and short-comings exist whether you acknowledge them or not. By recognizing reality, we can act on it.

We should welcome this vulnerability in the workplace because we should welcome any form of honesty that leads to productive action. When we see in someone else the willingness to recognize the entirety of their reality, including the less fun "I kinda suck at these things" parts, we believe we can trust them because they are demonstrating their honesty. We can further trust them because someone who acknowledges their shortcomings is unlikely to bluff and bluster the team into a situation that someone else (maybe you) has to salvage. And, if the vulnerable person takes the maximally pro-ego approach of setting their next ambition for self-improvement to overcoming that short-coming, we can respect and admire them.

Reality, honesty, trust, respect, admiration. Sounds like a great person to work with...

If you think that vulnerability is a weakness you don't know where my strength comes from. (Jeremy Sheppards)

A lot of people in the industry struggle with this, but personally I have no problem at all with it. You need to understand the mechanism to let it go. Vulnerability is consciously choosing to not hide your emotions or desires from others. It automatically drives humility, which often leads to growth and development – if this is what you really want, then you don't have the choice. Be vulnerable!! (Martin Buchheit)

Being vulnerable and philosophical with your fellow staff - but not with athletes, unless they are very experienced or over 30 years old!! (Jospeh Coynes)

The ability to admit you are wrong is a very endearing attribute. It's not a weakness. The cheats and the idiots are ALWAYS found out. Narcissism is a very lonely place. (Colin Lewin)

Be empathetic. Often, we need to utilise skills of emotional intelligence and empathy to relate to others and understand their viewpoint. Simon Sinek expands on this approach in his book "Start with Why," which is important for communicating with anyone, but may be especially pertinent for those with a bigger ego. (Jo Clubb)

Damian Roden, Director of Performance, RSC Anderlecht: Try to empathise with them and then demonstrate your knowledge and understanding - and always stick to the facts.

Kill them with kindness and seek to understand all their reasons for their choices. Then use their words back at them to see the other side of whatever it is they have an ego about. For example, "I know this decision is really important to you and you mentioned XX, and I thought I had heard some alternative reasoning around it, so I went to look it up and thought you might be interested to hear / read what I found." (Darcy Norman)

Positivity, almost to an extreme. Show a problem-solving, positive mindset / attitude / actions, even if you meet egos who carry suspicion, a narrow collaborative vision or a frame of reference that is not consistent and who consider you a possible threat. (Johan Swensson)

I have learned to try to get through to them in a way that is about inclusion and education, not being combative or trying to highlight their lack of understanding. (Keith D'Amelio)

To face oversized ego, you need a strong confidence and relate to the values that you have defined together with the ego-centric person. That way you have a common starting point. (Pierre Mangin)

I believe that the key to working with top athletes is to first show them "love." Show them that you authentically care for them and that they can trust you, based on the premise that many of these guys are inherently quite insecure, despite the alpha male, macho mask they project outwardly. Once these athletes understand that you genuinely care for them, I find that they will do anything for you in terms of the work that you ask them to.

Giving them "love" does not mean that you are a soft touch. Once this relationship is established, I feel that it is then critical that you as a staff member – a leader, a teacher – draw very clear boundaries in terms of what is expected from these players in terms of professional standards and behaviour. You must be very fair and consistent with the playing group and always be prepared to apply sanctions if an individual challenges the group standards or rules. If you do not, from my experience, you lose the respect of the whole group. (Andrew Young)

It depends on the relationship you have with them. I always believe in being kind, no matter what. It's not easy, I tell you. I don't take it personally unless it's disrespectful. However, with people I have a closer relationship with, I would - in a good way - point these things out. They need to know it's coming from a good place. It's how you approach it that matters. With that in mind, having a good level of emotional intelligence is important. (Allistair McCaw)

I believe that humility and patience are the best way to deal in this world. Work hard, learn from others and from your own mistakes and keep studying. This is something I would put in a book. (Andrea Belli)

My approach is generally non-confrontational, and to offer support first and directions second. How can we achieve this together based on what the outcome goals are? Is there anything in what is currently in place that can act as a bridge from where we are to where we need to be? I have a focus on using the group to solve the issue first, before more direct input to change what is done, if needed. (Dave Carolan)

... provided they take the same approach to their strengths.

As we said in Chapter 1 about ego as a whole, if you're going to be forthright about the bad you have to be forthright about the good. That's the difference between being vulnerable to something and "being vulnerable." Chronic, all-encompassing vulnerability is as much an ego f*** up as any of the mutations in Chapter 3. They both start at the same place: ego failing as a reality check. And they both end at the same place: people asking "What's his deal??"

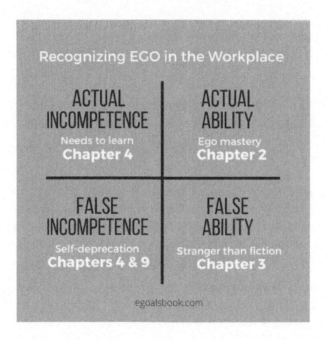

MASTER YOUR CRAFT

Millionaires now want to be treated as millionaires. As a coach you can't ask anymore, you need to convince.

— *Arsene Wenger* [Wenger, 2019]

The right message delivered by the wrong person is still a wrong message.

If you think that I am a d**k, you will never be willing to hear what I have to say. So here it is very clear: you need to frame your actions and behaviors in a way that will get your message across. Develop a relationship and meet others where they are. And then go incrementally. Step by step and take your time. You are not going to change 10, 20, 30 years of beliefs like that. Accept that having things 80% of how you would like them to be is still better than 50%. Don't let perfect be the enemy of the good. And keep in mind that what may look like a big compromise for you may still represent a big change for the others, so it's a big win, in fact. (Keir Wenham-Flatt)

Dan Baker, pro rugby strength & conditioning coach and educator: Learn how to deal with people by watching more successful or experienced coaches deal with athletes. Some elite athletes don't want to be treated differently, some do. Some low-level athletes have much more problematic traits of ego than elite athletes.

I think that is important to play or manipulate your ego volume when dealing with top athletes. You can't be too loud and confrontational or too soft and quiet. It is constantly moving, dynamic, adjusted according to the individual or group that you are dealing with. Overall, I think that it is about mutual respect – showing respect to others and getting respect back in return.

It's a little bit like parenting. If I criticize my children, I try not to criticise the child – just their behaviour. It's the same with players. If you criticise the person, this will only be met by a defensive reaction from the recipient – and quite rightly so. (Andrew Young)

Accept that things won't be perfect. Things can't be perfect. Let go the quest of perfection. Having 70-80% of what you want is already great. Reaching for more is likely unreal since that would probably mean that the others would have to make too many compromises. (Olivier Krumbholz)

I think that building relationships and trust is so important when dealing with people with big egos. Otherwise they could just completely dismiss you. Often, people with big egos are generally surrounded by people who are submissive to their thoughts and opinions. Hearing rebuttals is not always normal to these people, but, if it is reasoned and thoughtful, people with big egos are generally still rational and will understand and come to respect a different opinion. The problem you have is when you encounter big egos who are totally irrational!! Then there might be a problem. Fortunately, these types of people are on the same scale as psychopaths, so they don't come around too often!!!! (Lee Nobes)

Try to build trust, be sympathetic to the insecurities a person might have, take good notes and hold that person accountable. Genuinely try to desire the best for the person even if they are difficult to work with. Celebrate authentic wins when they occur. Have "hard" conversations early, not late, when things are blowing up. (Dave Martin)

A few strategies: 1) Appeal to the ego. 2) Listen, don't talk. Find out lots about them. Be impressed. This builds the trust. 3) Only after trust is established, question any prevailing practice or philosophy. (Paul Laursen)

I give them a lot of responsibilities. This is what they want. It's very good since, in the end, they have to show exemplary behaviour, which overall helps in managing them and is better for the team! (Franck Kuhn)

To maintain someone else's trust, it is easier if they have your trust. Acknowledge their point of view, experience and opinion. Genuinely listen and understand it. Using Rapoport's Rules aids this process. Understanding an opponent's position helps you understand and better communicate your own. (Marc Quod)

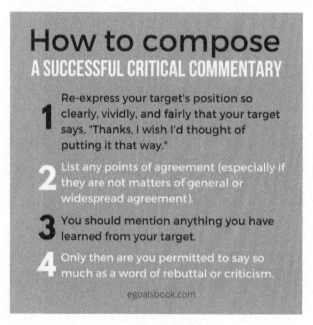

[Dennett, 2014]

With athletes: Genuine care, and practice what you preach. Show them that you really care and that you also are willing to stick to it. To engage with and commit to working with players, go back to coach John Wooden: they don't care how much you know until they know you care.

With staff, I believe that unpretentiousness is key. Actions should focus on: what can be done, even if this means there is a long way to get to an optimal solution; not changing too much at once, as people are skeptical towards change, and too much at once might burn them out; reinforcing, once collaborative decisions are made (regardless of if it's something small). Listen to why the person wants to do things in a certain way without judging, but with a frame of reference of what buttons you can press in order to make this more efficient. Ask open questions to find out how this person thinks we could work together. Ultimately, you reach a point where you realize if you're dealing with a fixed-fixed or fixed but possible growth mindset. (Johan Swensson)

Give them more responsibility so that their ego will be better contained. (Pierre Mangin)

Sometimes that ego can come from a place of high competence. Occasionally, highly talented people need autonomy to feel appreciated and to feel that they can express their art. If they are good teammates, but have a big ego, I tend to lean towards giving them clearly defined responsibility and freedom, so that they can maximize their talents. In the end, sometimes it's not just about having talented people on the bus, but more about whether they are in the right seat on the bus. (Steve Tashjian)

Dialogue, exchange ideas. Put the player in the face of the reality while asking him the right questions. (Pierre Mangin)

Playing back situations, they describe and justify their meaning. Reward with praise when this works, and challenge when it doesn't. Always done privately at first, but I may do so in a multidisciplinary team meeting if I feel it is appropriate. This shows others your actions and how you are dealing with the situation. (Grant Downie)

I listen, don't raise my voice, then put my point of view forward, keep eye contact. They accede or not (maybe not) but if they are the manager / coach, then they will make the decision on what to do. As long as they understand your standpoint, and things are not unsafe, then it has to play out as they requested. I never say "I told you so." I can then use this to guide them better at the next opportunity. (Ian Beasley)

Try to bring them back to reality in terms of the importance they have (or don't have), but ALWAYS with humor. (Miguel Ángel Campos)

I focus on showing them what I do well, knowing it is something out of their scope of practice, so they are not supposed to know. If he is a coach, I talk as physiotherapist. If he is health practitioner, I speak as strength & conditioning coach. (David Utrera)

I try to anticipate what their reactions and decisions could be. By being one step ahead of them, you can adapt your behaviour so that you can be better prepared and handle these people more effectively. (Paul Quetin)

When I do have to have a conversation with a person with a big ego, I always make sure I am as prepared as possible, have my facts straight, and prioritize what I want from the meeting. I also try to smile extra and be as friendly as possible. I also choose WHEN to approach that person, trying to catch them at a "good moment." I think that, as I am new in my job and organization, I have to tip-toe a little as I learn the personalities and power structures of the club. (6)

I try to remove all ego bias, asking for proof of concepts or evidence of their claims. And I strongly stick to it: "It is really interesting, but do you have any evidence confirming your claims?" or "I loved this concept and the complexity surrounding this one, but do you have any proof that this is working, confirming that I can try it on my athletes?" (Mathieu Lacome)

Never easy, but in conversation with these people, "be brief, be bright, be gone, be consistent, be polite and record it!!" And then spend as little time as possible close to them!!! (Grant Downie)

STAY WHO YOU ARE AND KEEP DOING YOUR JOB (VERY WELL)

I try, where possible, to not change who I am with anyone. Whether that is the best thing to do, I'm not sure, but I am staying true to my personal values. (Dylan Mernagh)

I don't deal well with ego people, honestly. But I keep my perspective of things, value what I do and have accomplished, just keep doing my job, control what I can control, breathe a lot and move on when the environment or context doesn't make me happy anymore. (10)

Don't be timid or doubt your actions / responses with this person. Back yourself, and don't necessarily tell them what they want to hear. Be honest and to the point without offending them, as best as possible. (Adam Waterson)

Don't hit them head-on, but show them that you are a strong character and not afraid to give a different opinion / point of view. Pick your battles at times, but when the time is right, stand strong. (Lee Nobes)

Be honest. Trust and transparency are very important. There is no need to fluff up egos or piss up players' legs. If they play well, tell them. If they do not play well, tell them the same. (Tony Strudwick)

Let them know you disagree or think there would be a more optimal way, but don't let their attitude disturb your work. I find this often is uncomfortable for the person who sticks his or her heels into the ground. Slowly they start to get curious, which is the start of change. (Johan Swensson)

I think the biggest thing that I have learned and that has helped me the past few years, especially at the professional level, is focusing on delivering the best for our players, athletes and clients. That is the most important thing in our job. At the end of the day, it is about them and how you, as a coach, impact them in a way that will manifest itself not only in the short term but at any point in their life. That can be in the form of education, resources, confidence or helping them achieve their goals.

I think it makes such a difference when your main focus is on them, not on trying to prove anything for the staff you work with every day or the people with big egos who try to distract you from achieving your own goals and doing your job.

And if you are dealing with ego in players, rather than on the staff you work with, then the same approach should hold true. Are you able to separate things and still guide them to be the best they can be? If they don't take it, then it is on them. You did your job and you were mature enough to not let it affect what you can do best, which is provide good services for your clients / athletes. Also for players with big egos, I have always found it better to meet them halfway and slowly show them the tools that will make them successful, without forcing them in the process. The trust should be developed both ways, and it is a process. (Ivi Casagrande)

Continue to grow within my own skillset and try to limit their ability to influence my self-esteem. Also, being really confident in my skillset and knowledge. Just try to manage others' egos by staying objective in discussions and decision-making. (Maggie Bryant)

Personally, I can't lie or say yes just to maintain a relationship. I can't compromise my ideas and values. Therefore, the more I tend to disagree with people, the more I try to be objective to show them that's it's not me going against them, but rather the evidence, the data or what many others are doing as well. While it looks like a sound approach, to be honest I can't say that I have always been successful with it! It's more complex than that, in fact, and having the trust and buy-in ahead of such conversations is essential if you hope to be listened to. (Martin Buchheit)

Treat everyone equally. There should be no favours for star players. (Tony Strudwick)

Jesus Olmo, Health and Performance Director, Football Science Institute, formerly Real Madrid: Talk to them with the same respect and consideration of any of your patients or the gardener of your house. Not more, not less.

DON'T GIVE UP, BUT KNOW WHEN TO BACK OFF

Try to engage in conversation in areas where their perception of their abilities clearly exceeds actual capacity, in the hope that they will realise that they are not a finished article, and that perhaps a little humility might be useful. (Chris Barnes)

I'll often find someone who is brilliant in their field to speak to them, which tends to show them that they aren't as smart as they thought. (Johann Bilsborough)

Find examples in another context, such as other people or players, to suggest your idea or induce a behavior so that it's not directed at him. (Antonio David Sánchez)

I steer them to an area that they may be less confident in - be that personal or professional - to reduce their self-assuredness. (Dave Carolan)

One-to-one chats with a third person present to witness allows you to touch things deeper. Seeking external help like a mental coach can help, too, when needed. With players, oftentimes ignoring them is a way to show the group that their excessive behaviours are not desired, and that the group should remain bigger than the individual. (Frederic Bougeant)

There is a famous Spanish play from 1654 called "El desdén, con el desdén" by Agustin Moreto that gives you one of the potential solutions. People who are ego-driven tend to disdain and underrate each other. The solution is to "give back the same medicine," and disdain them by showing a subtle disregard. (Julio Tous-Farjardo)

In young or developing people with an ego, show them how much they have to learn. This one can be bumpy, and can take a while to recover from, but can have big upside in the long run. (7)

Wait until things don't turn well for them. People always change when they are in danger or are having difficult times. (Claude Karcher)

Important to let them face the consequences of their choice when they refuse to listen or engage with others. (Andrea Belli)

OK, MAYBE IT'S TIME TO GIVE UP ON THEM

I choose to avoid them largely for as long as you can. I don't concern myself much with others' opinions. I simply focus on my work and values first. (Fergus Conolly)

Just focus on what I can control rather than what I can't. No point fighting the ego as they will lash out and it will become a power struggle (Craig Duncan)

It's very, very difficult for me to work with such people. I learned how to centre myself on my job, my tasks and the things I enjoy doing rather than chasing optimal relations with everyone. But it remains easier said than done. (Fred Demangeon)

If someone clearly has an ego that outweighs their abilities, I tend to not engage at all. If I have to, then how I engage depends totally upon the nature of the current relationship. If it is important that the person feels like the "alpha" - that he is able to display his superiority - then I tend not to do well. I honestly do not have time for such insecurities. I enjoy communicating with smart people, and many of them have healthy egos, i.e., they know they're smart, but do not rub it in anyone's faces. (Stu McMillan)

If they are a staff member, they don't survive at all! (Darren Burgess)

If their ego prevents them from being a good teammate, changes the culture in a negative way, and they do not show the capacity to acclimate, I will let them go. (Steve Tashjian)

If you can't change people, then change people. One of the performance team was clearly a negative influence and had a major ego. We managed him out of the organisation after a number of incidents where he failed to change. (Ben Ashworth)

If the above doesn't work, cut your losses and move on. (Paul Laursen)

As my great friend, Benjamin Boulnois, always told me…. if you can't win… and the ego is higher than you in the hierarchy… smile and say – Yes! (Martin Buchheit)

DEFUSE THE BOMB

1-1 meeting
Phone call

Calm down Be patient Listen Let them speak

Have a low profile

Show vulnerability

Give them their space

egoalsbook.com

SHOW THEM

you want to collaborate

you're just here to help

you're not an enemy

you are not looking for to take away their social status

you are not a threat to them and their position

egoalsbook.com

START BY

Stroking them
Feeding the EGO

Showing them respect

Showing empathy

Understanding what is behind their fear Understanding where their EGO comes from

egoalsbook.com

REMEMBER TO

Stay who you are   Pick your battles
Everyone is different; you may still learn from them

Bring objectivity to the debate

Focus on doing your job well Always act professionally
Give them responsibility Keep them accountable Let them face the consequences of their choice If the above doesn't work, cut your losses and move on

egoalsbook.com

TAKE AWAY

None of these can deliver serenity now, but they can at least give you some ideas and focus when dealing with any wayward egos that make their way into your team.

To work and live with people with big egos, the first thing we can do is to understand why they have that behavior, what need is behind it, what makes them feel good, and why they act like that or in that way. Perhaps it is their environment, their lack of self-esteem or confidence at some point in the past, their desire to prove how good they are, to succeed or feel superior.

There are many reasons and, instead of judging from the outset, it is better to understand. From there, and once one connects and understands the relationship with those people, one can develop a more constructive and productive relationship. This contributes to "understanding" their ego, putting it in the right context and to the right degree. In turn, this can lead them to feel good and then perform at their best.

That should be the goal and the challenge: to give the best that one has, but keeping the essence and authentic values. And knowing that there are always moments when these people can "lose touch with reality" and think they are superior, some kind of gods or above others. We must know how to understand this, for the above reasons, and see it as just another part of the "game" and the relationship. (Juan Carlos Álvarez Campillo)

AVOIDING CONFLICT DOESN'T MEAN COMPROMISING YOURSELF — STAY TRUE TO YOURSELF

egoalsbook.com

7 | EGO: DON'T

Knowing what not to do is sometimes as useful as knowing what you should do. When dealing with someone's maladapted ego, the biggest risk is escalating the situation. Let's face it: if self-awareness and self-control was their thing, you wouldn't be having this problem.

The first step of resolving an ego impasse is capping the damage to what's already been done. Avoiding these pitfalls - some of which may seem very attractive when your ego is inflamed - will put you in a position to resolve things positively.

GETTING EMOTIONAL OR BEING OVERLY DIRECT

I think trying to fight fire with fire is not a good idea, especially if it's not your true personality. I have never had a really bad incident, personally. But when I have had colleagues fall out, generally it is because one of them is too attached to their opinion being a part of themselves, and they get personally offended when their opinion is not followed. (6)

Fight ego with ego. This doesn't make sense since, in this case, you're not trying to solve the problem but rather just trying to be right and winning YOUR fight. (Paul Quetin)

Allow their ego to bring out your ego. Don't ever make it a pissing contest! (Steve Tashjian)

Arguing the point "up front" goes nowhere. You can't win an argument with an idiot. It's a dead end. (Colin Lewin)

Earlier in my career, not having been able to build up a relationship due to distorted, pre-conceived ideas. This just became a daily head-to-head conflict, which is never healthy!! (Lee Nobes)

It can upset players if you are very direct. I once upset a player who joined Manchester United with a big ego. He wasn't prepared to work hard for the team, and I told him. He wasn't happy. However, in this case I say "I tell you when you do well, I also tell you when you don't." (Tony Strudwick)

Direct confrontation. Even when they are wrong, if the ego is large enough, it doesn't matter - they are not arguing the "truth," they are arguing to save face. (Andrew Wiseman)

Being direct or addressing it directly can be a problem. Many of the people with big egos are fragile and insecure and hate confrontation or avoid it at all cost. (Fergus Conolly)

Directly arguing with the person to prove the point. Or using the wrong words to discuss the matter, like saying, for example, "You SHOULD HAVE done this," versus "NEXT TIME, faced with this challenge, it might be worth trying this tactic…" Give a compliment, then use the word "but," then give a negative. (Darcy Norman)

Challenging their opinion on something they are known for their expertise in. Trying to take them down a peg or two - recipe for disaster. (Dave Carolan)

Being aggressive and upset in front of them. We then run away from the argument and logic, and turn it into an ego vs. ego, gut-based discussion. The stronger the ego, the stronger the gut feeling, so you will end up losing the battle. (Mathieu Lacome)

Try to out-ego someone!! Invariably that has never worked for me. If it's an athlete, you have no chance. If it's a staff member, try to find more intelligent ways to influence them and deflate their ego. (Duncan French)

CHOOSING THE WRONG TIME, PLACE OR FORMAT

Communicate via text or email. It opens the door to misperception, which can escalate everything badly; and you can't re-adjust on the fly as you would do in a normal conversation. Need to connect in person, FOR SURE. (Martin Buchheit)

Escalate to line managers without looking to address the conflict face-to-face first. (8)

Getting into a pissing contest! It's very difficult to go head-to-head with someone who has a huge ego. It's even more challenging to do that in public, when surrounded by their contemporaries. The chances are you, they or both of you will end up losing in some shape or form. (Nick Grantham)

Being direct, challenging the beliefs, values and opinion of the problematic ego can cause issues. It can be counter-productive. Problematic egos are not "comfortable being uncomfortable." If challenged in front of an audience, from my experience, they tend to become defensive, and any conversation that follows is usually unproductive and this can create awkward atmospheres. (Jonny King)

Shouting at an elite player across the room / pitch / locker in front of his peers. (Daniel Baker)

Discussing these things outside official meetings has never worked in my experience. (Andrea Scanavino)

TAKING THE DETACHED & DISINTERESTED APPROACH

We all have both rational and more emotional centres in our brains. As a scientist, I feel I naturally relate more to rationality, preferring facts, figures, and science to gut feelings and instincts. However, that doesn't mean everyone works like that. So approaching an egotistical person with the rational evidence as to why an intervention should or shouldn't be used will likely be unsuccessful. (Jo Clubb)

Trying to use rational arguments with someone who doesn't want to hear them. (Claude Karcher)

Giving a presentation and presenting evidence that they really didn't understand. (Paul Laursen)

Trying to speak in scientific terms to make yourself sound smarter. This just pisses people off. (Alex Calder)

PASSIVITY THAT ENCOURAGES THE AGGRESSOR

Instead of putting myself into a confrontational position, I have perhaps been untrue to myself to avoid conflict. Whilst in the short-term this removes the conflict and you feel you have built bridges with the person in question, in the long-term you (or, worse, the team) end up losing out. (5)

Being too compassionate and being taken advantage of. Sometimes within my career, trying to go above and beyond to help those has been taken advantage of. It's taken a lot of reflection and tough conversations to come to terms with not helping those who may take advantage. (Steve Barrett)

Not being clear with people from the outset. Say you are working with someone who has an ego and you don't set the groundwork on how to interact or work together. These big ego people will always try to gain more ground over you. I've been guilty of sitting back and seeing how things develop in some instances where I should have been more proactive, in hindsight. These people also have to know you are not dependent on them to have a good life, which is a common mistake I see coaches have with athletes (who normally fit the big ego mould!). (Joseph Coynes)

Not standing up for myself in certain situations and, instead, just taking those frustrations to heart every time. It only created more problems and made me feel more and more stressed and angry with situations. Then you get into this chain of negativity where you start venting to all these people in your staff rather than being mature, standing up for yourself and not letting this become a giant problem. Sometimes letting these moments go actually can be just a way to keep feeding those egos because they think it is okay to do or say certain things towards others. (Ivi Casagrande)

It's important to allow big players to stand up and get themselves in the front row. But make sure this doesn't go too far, where they end up stepping on teammates or humiliating someone on the way, which could have a perverse effect. (Frederic Bougeant)

Trying to adapt to absurd and ignorant requirements of high-ego players / coaches, trying in vain to ease their complaints. You end up being dishonest with yourself. (Jesus Olmo)

TAKE AWAY

To recap a short chapter, then, we don't want to get too emotional. We want to maintain our sense of reason, without detaching ourselves from the problem. We need to make judgments about how we handle things, based on the knowledge we have about the people involved, our surroundings and the stakes. And we can't be passive. We have to assert ourselves in this encounter with someone else, taking strength from our understanding and mastery of the situation.

So the last thing we'd want to do is to neglect or dismiss those "functions that enable us to perceive, reason, make judgments, store knowledge and solve problems." You know, that "part of the self that is in contact with the external world," or - since we're talking about a conflict - your view of your self "as contrasted with another self."

Sounds like the all-encompassing "Ego: Don't" is denying our own egos.

Funny, that.

AVOID	KEEP AWAY FROM
Being direct **Getting into a fight for details**	**Talking too much**
Trying to convince them to consider your opinion	**Being reactive and emotional**
	Emails or WhatsApp
Fighting fire with fire	**Talking to them in a language that is not their**
Trying to compete or undermining them **Showing power or lording a role over them**	**Using objective information** **Challenging them whilst other colleagues are present** **Confronting them in public**
egoalsbook.com	egoalsbook.com

8 | TEAM CULTURE: INDIVIDUAL AMBITIONS DRIVING TOWARDS THE TEAM'S GOALS

"We must all hang together, or most assuredly we shall all hang separately."

– Benjamin Franklin

Ask any of the greats what they want, and it will always be the team goal. It's actually a pretty reliable way to distinguish the greats from the very goods: the very goods might get a bit more hung up on the individual stats and honors, but the greats never lose focus on the title.

If you're thinking that this shows how altruistic and selfless the greats really are, put a bookmark here and review Chapter 2.

The team goal motivates the greats because it's the biggest, most challenging goal they can find, one that demands that they surround themselves with players at least as good – maybe even better – than they are. It's why players who lead the league in individual stats and are the uncontested standouts of decent teams will ultimately demand a trade or transfer to a team that has a shot of winning the Stanley Cup, the Super Bowl or the Champions League, even if that means being just one star among many.

Part of what makes the greats great is that there is no daylight between their individual goals and the team goals. They don't see any tension between a collective goal and an individual goal: it's the what, not the who vs. who else, that drives them. When teams become dynasties, this relationship goes both ways: the individuals want the team goals, and the team culture reinforces the individuals' goals.

POSITIVE CULTURES ALIGN AMBITIONS, ACHIEVEMENTS AND RECOGNITION

Sports teams, like any other company, have extensive staffs of increasingly specific specialists. As the overall level of performance goes up, the number of staff members goes up, which means their individual marginal contributions to the team's success go down.

That can be difficult for motivated, ambitious people to accept, especially when they are so close to the people who publicly bring about that success: the players and coaches. High-performance practitioners dedicate themselves to making a significant, if marginal, and perhaps significant only to them, contribution to the team's success. Yet they remain anonymous as a group of 20-somethings and a few teenagers are praised for the abilities that the practitioners helped hone. Some accept this, and some don't.

These dynamics are not unique to sports. We see the same thing when a whiz kid founder becomes the face of a startup, and the lead UX designer and QA manager - the ones who bring the vision into being - have to go home content knowing what they and their project teams did. Many times, they do: they go home content - proud, even - in their behind-the-scenes contribution to success. Eventually, we read not just about the founder, but about the winning culture of the company.

Startups are particularly feted for their workplace cultures, but plenty of books and articles examine the relationship between culture, strategy and success among all types of businesses.

Sports teams, which devote themselves to squeezing out every possible marginal gain, rarely have cultures that facilitate long-term success. Teams like the All Blacks of international rugby and Manchester United under Sir Alex Ferguson (whose books and lectures for Harvard Business School go deep on this topic) stand out because they are so truly exceptional.

Vision is a prerequisite for a team culture. A 2021 survey by Kitman Labs [Buchheit, McHugues & Smith, 2021] found that nearly two-thirds of respondents in high-performance sports identified "Lack of Uniform Vision" as the largest challenge they faced, more than lack of money, time or technology. Even more than lack of buy-in for their methods from the players.

No vision, no culture.

Yet it should be so easy to set the vision for a sports team.

Whereas other industries hire consultants and go through extensive off-site planning sessions to come up with their "definition of victory," sports have a built-in definition of victory, namely... victory. You win the game or you don't. You finish atop the table, on the podium or in the playoff places or you don't. Players set personal best marks and career-best stats, or they don't. Teams, coaches and athletes have a limited set of discrete standards to evaluate themselves and their performance day to day and year to year, and those standards all derive from victory on match day. And when you hit those standards, you trigger bonus clauses and contract extensions.

Pursuing any goal other than athletic victory seems inimical to every reason one could have for wanting to be in sports. Wins and trophies should be the obvious thing that unites every staff member. Why else would we have players eat meticulously-designed diets, do rigorously validated or theoretically sound exercises, wear devices that monitor their nine hours of sleep each night, if not because all those things help the players perform better so the team wins more often?

Well, it turns out that some of those diets are a hot topic in sports nutrition forums. Some of those exercises fit perfectly into an Instagram Story. And those wearables? No journal editor or conference organizer can say no to sleep-monitoring wearables on Champions League winners. Or maybe you just want your boss or the Big Boss to think that you're doing more - for the club, of course, it's all about the club - than your colleagues who are somewhere else when the boss walks through the training room with a board member.

Claiming ownership of success - whether it's inflating your role in the team win or going rogue with what you think is the most important thing you do - is not just self-esteem and ego. It's about survival in an environment that is always competitive and often irrational. A practitioner can be at a team for five years and then lose his job tomorrow, not through any fault of his own, but because there is a new head coach who took the job only if he could fill the staff, top to bottom, with "his guys."

Showmanship can take over when there are betting lines on how long until your boss gets fired.

Yes, some staff probably feel that the best way to survive and advance is to further their own cause at the expense of others as opposed to trying to collaborate. (5)

People who work here for a long time, they believe they are part of the property and sometimes they underestimate the quality and dedication of your work. For me, that's the most negative part of it. (Antonio David Sánchez)

When I see these poor teamwork attitudes, I feel like we are still in the prehistoric age when there was little food available, when you had to hunt for five hours before catching a small rabbit to share with your entire tribe. Or, if you were among the few male lions in the jungle and you had to fight for your life to make sure you would get the best female. This starts with an erroneous belief in a scarcity of work that has to be done - when, in fact, if you have 25 players to train there will always be something to be done, at least at the individual level. More than enough for people to feel important. But some people want to make sure they look busy, are perceived as being responsible for important matters and feel like there are irreplaceable. It is this direct fear of missing out, of losing the job, etc. that completely distorts their approach to teamwork. (Charles Vallejo)

I consult at multiple places, and it is the single biggest issue: coaches / physios / sport scientists all fighting in the name of ego. (Craig Duncan)

As an independent consultant, I experience it when I visit certain corporations, organizations, colleges and professional sports teams, for example. A lot of my conversations with the personnel that work in these sectors is around ego and entitlement, and how to deal with it. (Allistair McCaw)

Athletes, coaches and support staff all have egos of varying degrees. Successful sports performance is an interdependent process, with every stakeholder having a distinct role and scope of practice. Great leadership, alignment to performance goals and great people will facilitate these individual scopes of practice merging towards performance. Unfortunately, because of ego, individuals do not apply themselves 100% to their area. In many instances, they feel they should be the primary decision-maker. Ego makes everyone think they are the top of the tree. Ego interferes with true understanding of their role, and clouds their perception of what others think of their impact. Therefore, ego drives the need to be heard, to have an opinion and an expertise which lies outside their scope of practice. (Stuart Yule)

For their own personal fulfillment and to have a reasonable standard for their performance reviews, each individual needs KPI's that are linked with winning but can be judged independent of the team's results. In sports, this usually comes back to improving the players in some way. But it could also, as in any industry, involve refining the processes and structures that will give the organization the greatest possibility of long-term success - winning later, if you can't win now.

Without these individual measures, teams devolve into a zero-sum-at-best mad scramble for influence and attention. Physios take players out for set piece training and talk about nutritional supplements. Fitness coaches bypass the team's liaison with the front office to ensure they and their workouts make it into an Instagram Story, despite knowing that the team psychologist is trying to make the training room a "private" space for the players. Personal preference - "This player took me clubbing with his supermodel girlfriend and their crew. I better stay on his good side!" - overrides team needs.

At the other extreme, well-defined KPI's become ends in themselves.

Someone is working at a club that regularly goes deep into international tournaments, but they'd rather keynote a conference or publish a raft of research papers than win one of those tournaments because the former directly relates to them while they are only a small part of the latter. A fitness coach pushes a player over a limit two days before a game because the coach fears his job depends on the athlete improving his vertical jump and change-of-direction tests, and not his or the team's performance in a game.

Managing a team entails aligning individual and team goals, regardless of whether you have greats or goods (or not so goods), and regardless of whether your team is the one on the pitch or one of many among the cubicles. Culture can help automate this process, functioning as the invisible hand that channels goals, ambitions and relationships in a high-performance environment.

Culture quietly enforces the standards the leaders set (assuming there are leaders who set standards). When a project succeeds, culture keeps the group celebrating as a team rather than devolving into an argument over whose contribution was decisive.

Ego will always have a role in every workplace. Ours is no different. The players have egos. The staff members have egos. We all have our own personal circumstances that influence our ego one way or the other. You could be a new staff member trying to prove your worth. You could be coming off of a bad decision that led to a mistake and now you are trying to repair your reputation. You could be at the top of your game and success has led to a lack of ambition.

It's the beauty of human interaction. We are all in our own unique place despite our need to be one. And in an environment like ours, where our number one core value is selflessness, we are forced to deal with our own ego volumes, whatever they may be from day to day, and still come together as a group and make decisions for the betterment of others. In this case, our players and our country. (Steve Tashjian)

The ego is always being fed as an athlete: you are the fastest, the strongest, the best. When you transition to coaching, that same level of ego that was an advantage as an athlete becomes a disadvantage as a coach. (6)

The country I work in has a very strong hierarchy in terms of leadership. The person in charge has to be seen to be in charge. They lead and we follow. (Ben Ashworth)

It has and it always will be. The environment has an eclectic group of high level professionals from different nationalities working together - that means this will always happen. The uncertainty of professional sport also means that there is a lot of change. This can be represented as a high turnover of coaching or backroom staff, and, as such, it is important to be comfortable working close to changing environments. This also means that there is a big emphasis on building relationships and trust with people with different sized egos. It is then important to be able to work out which ego is backed up by one's confidence in their own ability, and which is trying to support one's insecurities. (Lee Nobes)

The less you chose the people you work with, the greater the ego involved in the relationships. When people don't know each other and have been put together by a third party, such as in a football club, they can easily imagine the others as threats and being in danger, and that's when they put their reflector on and use their ego to defend themselves. This doesn't happen when working with small staff groups and when people have chosen to work with the other; there, people open themselves more easily for a better collaboration. (Yann Le Meur)

Strong egos often get in the way of team and club development. When personal agendas are prioritized over the benefit of the group, it quickly becomes counterproductive. (Yann Le Meur)

Ego has an impact within every organisation. It is the level of that ego which is the true reflection on whether or not the organisation succeeds as a collective, or if it becomes harder to succeed due to the ongoing "political battles" within some establishments. Different cultures and learning how the level of ego is interpreted is something I am learning within my current global position. What is deemed a high ego level by one country is the norm in another. (Steve Barrett)

There is ego in every decision that is made in the team. From big decisions, such as which athletes will be hired / fired, to decisions in competition by staff and athletes. Do I pass the ball or do I try to score myself? Do I help my teammate win today or do I save my energy and try and win myself tomorrow? (Marc Quod)

LEADERS LEAD THE WAY AND LEAD THE EGOS

"Ego is most dangerous in a team when it's the coach who has the biggest."

— Claude Onesta

The leader's job in these settings is to keep each team member on the appropriate scale and in the appropriate context for understanding their achievements. The fitness coach's extra effort to improve one player has a marginal impact on the team's success, and those outcomes (like the example we're about to give) won't mean much to most people. But within the scope of the fitness coach's work, a 4% improvement in a 28-year old's force production at maximum velocity is a massive accomplishment. The coach absolutely should take pride in it and present it as a case study at the next conference.

Culture just has to be there to ensure the last slide of his presentation isn't a picture of him photo-bombing the trophy lift.

If the coach has a higher ego than the player, it can lead to issues. (Tony Strudwick)

From a management position, it is difficult to work underneath people with a large ego. It doesn't breed a progressive and open workplace, unfortunately. (Adam Johnson)

For me, the most destructive ego in the workplace is the power-hungry leader. The leader that cannot delegate, cannot show weakness, cannot admit mistakes. Ultimately, that is a sign of lack of humility. That can be very destructive, not only to individuals, but, most importantly, to team outcomes. (Jonny King)

I feel it stems from the top. If the senior leadership are defensive, protective and hostile, that filters down to all levels of the organisation. This can lead to workplace bullying, a paternalistic / toxic culture and make people less loyal to the organisation. (8)

Ego is a part of any elite sports environment. How it is handled and managed is the major difference. Much of that is taken from leadership, specifically the head coach, technical / sporting director in any club. (Garrison Draper)

Ego needs to come from leadership. Change a bunch of highly confident individuals centered on their own performance into a sharing mentality oriented toward collective performance. It can only come from above: club leadership, the organizational structure, the coach. It's very hard but it's the only way. (Frederic Bougeant)

Ego is attached to self-image, and I believe it's important to display a healthy self-image and confidence. In a leadership position, it's important to show humility, empathy and confidence. Let's be honest, no one wants to follow someone who doesn't have a healthy and good self-image. (Allistair McCaw)

Leaders who are collaborative, humble and authentic breed positive cultures. This may create a greater sense of loyalty to the organisation, and buy time for the leaders when results are not going to plan. (8)

IT'S ABOUT PEOPLE FIRST

I surround myself with people who I want to work with. Hires and dismissals are very important. Have courage to not hire the right skills from the wrong person. Create a culture where it's OK to talk about culture. Show vulnerability when in leadership roles - it promotes vulnerability and growth in others. (Jeremy Sheppards)

The good thing about being a manager is that you can choose your collaborators. (Frederic Bougeant)

As a manager of a large team, a big ego was my first "no" when interviewing. I turned down some good people purely because it was obvious they were in it for themselves. Employing big egos is a circus. (Colin Lewin)

In order to be really successful its starts back at the recruitment stage. The club need to identify key values and frame of reference for how people should work together. If, despite efforts, people are not willing to commit, then "if you can't change the people, change the people." Make it clear to the people above you who are in charge of recruiting, but keep open the potential of someone else in that role if that could benefit the club. (Johan Swensson)

Our medical and scientific teams are pretty respectful. We would not hire people that are not. We want individuals who fit into the team but also can gain the confidence and trust of the players. (Andrew Murray)

Know how to select the people who are worth giving a s*** about, both co-workers and players. (Charles Vallejo)

STRUCTURE AND RESPONSIBILITIES

Clarify roles and responsibilities and let individuals with big egos engage in leadership roles. But, just as importantly, put them in roles where they need to provide support as well as leadership, and complement that with support activities when warranted. (Dave Martin)

There are always egos involved where people want more or less control or ownership over things. It's natural, especially amongst males!! I think you need to recognise it is natural, but hopefully it can be shaped and made into something positive. To do this, I think you need a management style or paradigm to consistently remind each member that team structure should be flat and open and we all need to be on the same page for all our goals to be achieved. Plus, struggling over turf isn't the most productive use of our time!! (Joseph Coynes)

A healthy balance of humility and the understanding of each individual's role within the department, so the right people are held accountable but there is a shared decision-making process. (Selwyn Griffith)

Work hard!! Frame and define roles to all, whatever their position is. Everyone is important in relation to the overall performance goal - even the bus driver! (Frederic Bougeant)

I think it can be more difficult from the standpoint of having an "inferior" job title to handle aggressive actions directed towards you, but having a good reporting structure and supportive leadership is essential. (Amelia Arundale)

It's of utmost importance to set the boundaries of each staff member's duties and responsibilities. It's the only way to have a cohesive group of people working together. Daily meetings are also required to keep an organization effective. (Alexandre Dellal)

Every staff member needs to have a clear role and find his place in the team. Respect others, respect their work, and they will respect you and your work. (Olivier Krumbholz)

Unclear job descriptions, together with a lack of strength from the management that lets people work outside of their primary area of expertise without any accountability, allows oversized ego to ruin the organisation and create chaos. Job descriptions are everything to me in the context of multidisciplinary teams. Failing to respect the organigram chain of command can't be tolerated. Easier said than done, though, when the staff's relationships with big individual players enter into the mix. (Martin Buchheit)

In my opinion, the clubs should delimit very clearly the purviews of the employees, and give total freedom to them in their areas of responsibility, but not in the others. Divergent opinions are not a problem as long as the professional competences are respected. Clubs are responsible for designating managers with high education in sports performance. Football today is a high-performance sport that must be managed by people with high levels of education and a grounding in science, not just the ex-player's experience combined with low academic education, as it was in the traditional model. (Jesus Olmo)

There are three different situations to consider. First, if you have to work with them and they have "more power" than you: Don't try to convince them. Give them something to win; respect them despite the disagreement. Second, if you have to work with them and they don't have "more power" than you, let them make clear the role they have. Finally, if you don't have to work with them, get them out of the team's work. (Rafa Maldonado)

This can be achieved also when staff organisation (especially, and maybe uniquely, in football) follows a monarchy model (the king being the head coach). With this model, there are no opportunities for individual agendas or "freedom" to make isolated decisions, so the staff works cohesively together. Chain of command is the first principle. And when things don't go well, staff members are eliminated and the head coach's head is the one chopped!! (Alberto Mendez-Villanueva)

Of course, there are some people around with big egos. But the hierarchy is well-defined as well as the specific responsibilities and areas of impact of each person. So, it is quite easy to operate. (Alberto Mendez-Villanueva)

TEAM CULTURE CAN FINE TUNE THE EGO VOLUME

Breaking ego-led processes is critical for creating a culture where everyone feels like they have an opportunity to challenge each other for the betterment of our performance. Developing people is largely about developing their own sense of self-worth / value. At whatever level of an organisation you work in, you should feel like you have an opportunity and a freedom to speak, and that when you speak you will be heard. (Ben Ashworth)

> If the culture is rigid, based on power and hierarchy - the "big dog" mentality - with an intolerance to divergent opinions, it's unlikely that you can speak up and express yourself. There is, in contrast, a high risk of humiliation, of rejection. This is what immediately creates those ego-driven behaviours. The driving energy behind your ego, what can give

you strength and resilience, needs in these situations to be activated to protect yourself, to shield yourself from the others when safety is at stake.

At the extreme of these types of cultures, ego shows up as well in people who have troubles with intimacy and open-heartedness, those who can't show vulnerability. When they can't access their empathy, they use their ego shield to avoid being embarrassed. (Pippa Grange)

In our teams, we pay attention to language. We try to stay curious so we don't skip to judgment. I think this is good for lots of reasons, but two consequences are most certainly that we seem to have fewer fragile egos and don't have big egos steering us.

I don't follow "equal outcome," but try to be very aware of equal opportunity. Possibly as a consequence, my working teams have a higher proportion of women compared to many others, and many are in roles with broad accountabilities and, therefore, leadership. I feel this helps with culture and might positively avoid polarization.

In our teams, we practise contextual leadership. We encourage leadership from the most relevant folks based on the situation. There is no straight hierarchy, but more a hierarchy of accountabilities and responsibilities. Because everyone is aware of these accountabilities for the whole team, we behave in a way where it is an inter-dependent necessity to support each other. This is humbling and tends to promote a healthier level of ego and a supportive environment. (Jeremy Sheppards)

I will always allow everyone to have a forum to speak. No matter what. Staff need to be given an environment where they feel comfortable voicing their opinion. I didn't have that in my early days of working in a team setting. The next part is to find what is important to each person who has to work together, and underpin their opinion with a foundation of an evidence-based practice. (Johann Bilsborough)

Changes in practice patterns or training philosophies, I think, require study and examination of benefits versus risks / detriments. Trying to open dialogue about changes can be helpful, and approach with an open mind. Again, I think a big component comes back to open and trusting communication. (Amelia Arundale)

TEAM CULTURE CAN CHANNEL THE EGOS ORGANICALLY

Sometimes you realize that focusing on changing individual behaviour is going to be either too long or too difficult. If you manage to create a culture that is so strong in terms of values and mindset, it becomes an incredibly powerful torrent that takes and carries everything with it. People don't even question it - they don't have the choice and they just go with it. This is what I call team culture.

— Kevin McLaughlin, VP Strategic Account Management, Kitman Labs

Remember in the 80's, when any guest could come into your house and light a cigarette without even asking you for permission? Could you imagine this happening today? Even asking to do such a thing sounds absurd. While it obviously took time, this is a good example of how culture, and the implicit attitudes that come with it, can drive behaviors.

Collectively agree and set your team's or organisation's values and beliefs. When someone breaks a belief or value, then it's acted on - every single time. Stay true to this. (Ben Ryan)

Should someone in your team have different opinions and drives against your established core values, have a strategy in place for how to deal with it as a group. Create common values for how you want to operate as a team and engage everyone in the bigger picture, the long-term goal. (9)

There are a lot of books and podcasts about self-improvement, dealing with people and leadership related to ego. But you need an environment and a system that supports a non-ego culture. If the ones that are promoted, hired, attain power follow that profile, then is very hard to fight it. (10)

We all know the importance and value of working together, but this is easier said than done. To go over personal agendas, you need to build a framework that goes behind individuals. Define everyone's role, the processes that define how to work together, so that you integrate every staff member with harmony and, above all, efficiency. Without objectivity, it's too easy to invent yourself a role and responsibilities, or to build fake stories to protect yourself. (Martin Buchheit)

I think the creation of a team vision with collaboration is the key to this. That, then, allows alignment to happen. However, differing levels of knowledge limit this process in my opinion. (Paul Delvin)

Often the "game plan" for any particular race is in part to ensure all the riders egos are aligned. Significant time is spent communicating with athletes individually and as a group to "pump up" their ego or otherwise manage their ego to ensure the group is working collectively. (Marc Quod)

Relate everything to the overall project that, by default, can't be reached individually. It's a way to remind them that the collective aim must be stronger than them individually, whatever their role, status and competence. Even though external communication can allow egos to speak out sometimes, in the locker room, the only voice that should remain is that of the team. (Frederic Demangeon)

TEAM CULTURE EMERGES FROM INDIVIDUAL CHARACTER

Ego in the workplace is probably one of the greatest obstacles and barriers to achieving an effective and efficient working environment. When I'm asked "How does one eliminate ego from the workplace?" I always like to answer that question with a smile by saying, "Simple: don't hire it in the first place!"

But what if it already exists, you ask? Well, then, that comes down to the leadership and the question as to why these behaviors are being permitted to continue.

In cultures of excellence, I've learned that great leadership does not stand for problematic egos or disruptive behaviors. One example I can think of is Sir Alex Ferguson of Manchester United, who was known during his time at the club to have quickly - and some might say harshly - dealt with players that he either saw as a problem or future threat to the team's culture. One example was star player David Beckham, who was quickly shipped off to Real Madrid in the summer of 2003. Sir Alex saw David as a potential threat to the club's culture, despite the player being incredibly popular and adored by all the fans.

Poor cultures come down to poor leadership. Poor leadership allows for ego. I have always believed having a winning culture (free of ego and toxicity) starts long before with the leader envisioning what that culture should look like.

If you don't have total clarity in what your culture stands for, then you won't have clarity in finding the right people. The golden question is this: how do you know if we are hiring the right people? It always starts with character. Do they fit the culture? Are they the kind of people you'd want to spend a 10-hour flight sitting next to? Do their values align with yours and those of the organization? What about the standards they hold themselves accountable to?

When it comes to determining character, this is an area I help many leaders and coaches in, especially coaches at colleges and universities, who recruit student athletes in the United States. It comes down to asking the right questions. If you are sitting with a possible recruit who only enjoys talking about him or herself, then that's a red flag. Another one is, do they share their successes and give others credit? By asking the right questions, you are usually able to detect if you could be dealing with a problematic person in the future. First and foremost, a person must fit the culture.

Often, a person can be hired or recruited because of an impressive resume or above average skills, but lack the right character qualities. You can improve skills, but character? That's another ball game altogether.

The big thing is, can they work and get along with others? And do they understand that it's not about them, but more about the team and the greater vision. Ego is a "me," humility is a "we."

And one last thing: always remember that the people you choose will always be more important than the systems you use. (Allistair McCaw)

LEARNING FROM THOSE WHO MADE IT

I am fortunate that currently a lack of egotistical colleagues has had a positive impact. There is plenty of room for competent practitioners, players and coaches in elite sport with moderate egos. (Paul Balsom)

I genuinely do think that at Swimming Australia, leadership, coaches and support staff are generally confident, but not self-centred. It's about the athlete and their successes. Our current culture is good this way. (Tom Vandenbogaerde)

In a national team (at least in the one I've been working last two years) the collective spirit is different. I don't know why, but, as an example, when players don't play they don't get angry as they would at a team. Perhaps it would be worth analysing if other professionals in national teams (who have also been in top teams) comment the same. (Rafel Pol)

I have been fortunate to cross paths with lots and lots of elite athletes and practitioners whose egos were not particularly big nor a source of conflict. In fact, the best of the best are quite often humble and easy to work with, they thank the professionals contributing to their achievements and they share the credit for their success. (Iñigo Mujika)

Being a consultant I would say it clearly depends on the sport and organisation. No doubt, in football (soccer) it's where it's the highest. In tennis, with respect to the experience I have, it's pretty low. There is a high level of trust and fewer people involved, which helps to lower the ego. (Yann Le Meur)

Ego always affects us, but it's much less now as I am a private coach and business owner, who mostly works from home. Athletes I coach trust my opinion, and I have a great relationship with my business colleagues and employees. Ego seems minimal now, which provides a lot of satisfaction and calm in life that I value. (Paul Laursen)

TAKE AWAY

The most important word in football is unselfishness. It's about covering others both on the pitch and outside

— Joseph Montemurro, Head coach, Juventus FC Women

When Zlatan Ibrahimovic dubbed the national team "Zweden," the common response went along the lines of "OMG, this guy's ego is so big that it's taking over entire teams. Entire countries, even!"

But Ibrahimovic knows, maybe subconsciously, which way these things are supposed to flow in a team: from the individual to the group. He's not taking his sense of self-worth, let alone his identity, from team. He has such an abundance of ego that he can share some with others, proudly (of course) displaying his ego largesse through some donations he won't even miss.

Yes, it was a bit goofy because he wasn't even part of that squad, but it was completely consistent with who he is. At every turn, he knows what he wants: he wants to be the best player and he wants to win trophies. To do that, to fulfill his ego's purpose, he needs the team. He needs the performance team to keep his body in top shape, which means he needs the performance team to be the best. He needs his teammates to be at their best because, even though he says he can play at any position, he knows that in a game he needs 10 other men in those positions. He wants to be surrounded by success, because that's how he will succeed.

That ambition combines with an ego like his to create an outflow of spirit, the source of team culture. Whether he's boosting the team's morale or demanding more with one of his "Hey genius!" moments, he is upstream of the team's culture and the group's achievement.

The singularity of the "Zweden" tweet, where an individual tries to infuse his spirit into a team or organization, gets far more attention than the much more common scenario: when the individual relies on the team or organization for his sense of pride, ego or self-worth.

When you combine large ambitions with a less healthy ego, things flow the other way. Such people puff up their sense of purpose in the organization by crowding out others. They steal their sense of accomplishment by swiping credit for others' achievement, they cover up their insecurity by micromanaging their subordinates and they hide their lack of identity behind the organization's logo. They take from the team's culture and distract everyone from its purpose. They're "in it for themselves" because they don't have much to give.

Managing egos within the context of team culture is not about filtering by size but controlling the direction of flow. "Givers vs. takers" is a more important distinction than "big vs. small."

Zlatan Ibrahimovic is a rare individual in the "size" of his ego and his comfort - indeed, his facility - with it. We key in on so much that he does because he is the exception. He shows what many think impossible: that you can be a giver without being self-effacing, that an individual's ego can be the source of team success in a high-performance environment and can actually increase cohesion around the common goal.

9 | ESCALATING CONFLICT: SEPARATING THE CHALLENGES FROM THE THREATS

It happened a lot... It's very difficult... I think that this is obviously a very difficult position to be in...When this happens, it's very difficult for me to handle it... Initially I struggled with it, to be honest - I couldn't understand why they would do things a certain way... Compromising my values and beliefs is the most difficult thing I have had to do in my career... At first, it was very difficult to accept, because sometimes you have the ideal world of an elite team, where you think everyone in the team can have a voice or an opinion, and I believed in the teamwork.

Yes, you're the head of nutrition, the lead sports scientist, the director of player rehab or the high-performance manager, and for most of your career, you've been able to do that job - your job - on your terms. But as you move clubs or your club changes the hierarchy around you, your stint as the hero in your own movie reaches the scene where for every problem you solve you get two smaller ones in return.

After years of being able to do things your way, someone comes in to tell you to do it their way. Your new colleagues or supervisors may see your duties and your place in the structure differently than you and the last regime did. They may have philosophies and methods that diverge from yours - or run directly opposite to yours. Your immediate supervisor may have your back, but if your decisions must go through the head coach or technical director, we all know who really has the last word.

You may have the "better" record in your respective field than they do in theirs. You may even have the better record than the person who will be your new boss. But now, words like "head," "lead," "director" or "manager" in your job title lose all meaning because you're not the head coach or technical director.

The job is to provide the best possible care to your athletes and respect the needs of the coaching team. This is the hardest part, as a coach's perspective mostly revolves around winning at any cost, and evidence-based practice will be neglected. (9)

You do all the right things from Chapters 6, 7 and 8, believe you have reached a resolution, show up to work the next day and find that not much has changed and some things have gotten worse. This whole time you've wanted to think of yourself as Hercules battling the Hydra, but you can't help thinking more about Mickey Mouse vs. the brooms in *Fantasia*. Like those two, you have to recognize the nature of what you're up against before you can regain a foothold towards your purpose.

RECOGNIZE & IDENTIFY

Not every conflict has the same stakes. Even a disagreement that extends across several people, levels or the culture of your organization can have a low-key resolution. Part of our professional development is learning to recognize the nature of the challenge we are facing, and how we react to it.

Does the challenge boil down to adapting your methods to someone else's guiding philosophy, or are you being expected to adopt that philosophy? If so, does it conflict with your deepest professional and personal values? Are you confident enough in your methods to defend them, but also confident enough in your values to adapt your methods as long as the more important elements stay intact?

Many of our respondents talk about there being "more than one way to skin a cat" and how much you can learn by keeping your mind open to the new ideas and strictures in your organization. Having the intelligence to recognize the situation for what it is and the confident ego to not feel threatened by taking a step back usually leads to a positive resolution.

> *"Challenging every opinion that doesn't fit your philosophy for the sake of challenging won't lead you anywhere; and it's also highly probable that your philosophy is not the best, either!"*
>
> *– Nick Poulos, High Performance Manager, Greater Western Sydney Giants*

If you are consistently unsuccessful in dealing with conflict, and persistently clashing with others, perhaps you are tackling the wrong problem, or going about it the wrong way. (Jonny King)

I think that it's about not trying to fight and argue about this point, but maybe about offering solutions for how you can complement their practice. (Adam Johnson)

Accepting that there is more than one way. As I have gained more confidence in my career I have improved in this space. You do not have to get everything right to avoid the sack! Sometimes allowing others to fail is OK if it doesn't harm the athletes / team. (Paul Delvin)

One thing to remember is that there are always different ways to skin a cat - as long as you are not asked to do anything illegal or that would call into question your integrity, you might be forced to do things in a different way. I have always believed that the work that you do, if it is done well and to a high standard, should be able to stand up to scrutiny. Sure, you might have to defend it multiple times, or even have to teach and re-teach to new management. (Adam Douglas)

Remember it is not about me. It is about the team, the organisation and the community. I will go to great lengths to understand why we are changing or doing things in a different way. In the end, if the rationale is sound, it is moral and ethical, and everybody agrees, fall in line. (David Howart)

As long as the quality of the service provided to the players is not compromised, then I do not have a problem doing things differently. (Paul Balsom)

After a few years, I manage these situations better. I think sometimes in big teams you have to accept your job as a specialist, and that some colleagues don´t want to share too much in order to have more power with the manager. But this is fine as long as the boat keep heading in the right direction. (Antonio Gómez)

It's important to understand what is best for the culture of the organisation and which elements are crucial for the success of a high-performance program. While there may be elements you may not agree with at times, if it doesn't impact your ability to perform your role and isn't having a negative impact on the performance program, then you need to be able to assess whether it is something worth challenging or accept that it is better for the culture to allow it to occur. (Selwyn Griffith)

Think first. Finding the reasoning behind change is always an initial goal for me. Whether it is a change in protocol or thought process, understanding the reason why we feel there needs to be change is really important in the process of deciding how to react to the situation. Once the underlying drivers are revealed, then you have decisions to make. (Garrison Draper)

It's also important to try to understand the perspective of the new management team, coach or athlete. If you can understand their point of view it will help you deal with the situation and maybe even find some positives from what was initially viewed as a negative situation. (Nick Grantham)

Together everyone achieves more. TEAM. One of the first head coaches I worked with (who I got to work with twice) would use this phrase consistently. Working around individual egos to come together is how we can gain success.

Ultimately, if we all work within the same organisation, especially within elite sport, our shared goal is for that organisation to achieve success (however that be defined). Working with those people on these common goals helps to accept / deal with / manage all these situations. Something I have learnt from the observations of great leaders I have worked with within my different roles. (Steve Barrett)

ASSESS

It's a problem of motivation, alright?... My only real motivation is not to get hassled. That and the fear of losing my job. But you know, Bob, that'll only make someone work just hard enough not to get fired.

— *"Peter Gibbons," Office Space*

Identifying what's being asked of you is the first step to recognizing whether you're on the verge of a sacrifice or an investment.

As our career goes on, we have a different answer to "What's this worth to me?" than we did at the outset. The cost-benefit equation shifts over the course of a career. Early on, you want to endure. You want to prove you can do it, you want to learn the ropes the hard way and the easy way. In sports terms, you want the positive adaptations that can only come from overload. In the language of ego, you want to be able to back it up.

Hopefully, as you've increased your value and raised your ego accordingly, you've raised your threshold as well.

The prestige of the job might not get you through another year without a co-worker saying "Thank you" or "Great job." Your annual presentations at your field's most influential conference may not make up for the knowledge that your boss is going to take credit for the work you presented. The time away from your family and occasional workplace betrayals start to feel like they are not worth being a recognizable brand, er, individual in an industry that numbers a few thousand worldwide.

The same ambition and endurance necessary to reach the point where the negatives start to accumulate can predispose people to endure even more in pursuit of their next ambition. There might be a sense of inertia - "I've made it this far, why stop now?" - that may even give way to hope: "Besides, I've made it this far, so it's sure to get better!"

Other times, there's an element of fear to it. We're hung up on what we've invested to reach this point and the fear that we'd be throwing it away. These are the "sunk costs," a phrase often followed by the word "fallacy." We think that if we walk away now, or simply say "No" where our younger self would say "Yes," then we've wasted everything we've done to get to where we are. The problem with that line of thinking is that it puts the emphasis of our concern on the past. Any anxiety we may feel about "throwing away the past" should take a back seat to the risk of throwing away any part of our future.

KNOW WHAT YOU WANT OR YOU'LL NEVER GET IT

I'll come back to the level of ego. Sometimes it can be the one who shouts the loudest who gets noticed more and may get rewards for doing so. I'm a big believer that good quality hard work will reward itself. That's the level of my ego. I won't go knocking on someone's door asking them to reward me. I want them to be wanting to come to me and reward me, if at all. Just to hear the words "thank you" from someone you have provided a service to is justification to my own ego that has helped.

Within reviews and reflection periods at board meetings and managerial staff meetings, this has been a constant theme. Even if I don't get thanked, if people can appreciate my colleagues' and my effort and intention, I am grateful. This has been a common trait which has seen me rewarded from a career, academic and networking perspective. (Steve Barrett)

One of my colleagues, who has been working in a top club for 15 years and collaborated with more than 10 head coaches from various backgrounds, told me one day: "In this world, if you want to survive, you need to say yes."

This sentence has haunted me for months, and keeps me thinking today. Since the ideas of people that you haven't chosen to work with are unlikely to perfectly align with yours (and vice versa), this literally says that either you constantly prostitute yourself - or you are out. There is not trade-off - it's a one-way street.

This is pretty difficult to handle when you place the pursuit of your own ideas or simply the willingness to do what you believe in above the simple fact of "holding" the job in itself. (Martin Buchheit)

I personally think that it is important not to compromise your integrity just to keep a job. I have left several jobs for this reason – probably to my professional detriment. If your contributions are not being treated seriously or you are being disrespected on a personal level then I do not think that is a healthy scenario for you to remain in.

The best environments are those where less senior staff and players do not feel scared or intimidated to contribute to the fabric of the club and challenge their superiors (with respect) with the intention of improving the program fundamentals. Working at a club where all the secondary / junior staff just keep their heads down, don't feel empowered and parrot the directions from above is pretty toxic and rarely successful from my experience. (Andrew Young)

WHAT IS BEING CHALLENGED: YOU, OR YOUR WORK?

The first question to ask yourself is whether the disagreement and the frustration comes from you being challenged, or because the program may change and you have concerns about the outcomes. You don't need to be right. The programs? They need to be right. Understanding this can make a complete shift in the way you react and approach the discussions. (Martin Buchheit)

I, too often, tended to feel offended, but I am now working on that. When it happens, I try to zoom out and then zoom in again, reflect and try to see things not only through my eyes but the other person's. I also try to find arguments for what I am doing and why they question my work. Obviously, if they question it just for the sake of it, then it's more difficult to accept the criticisms. (Benjamin Kugel)

At the beginning, I fought and tried to do my way. I tried to convince everybody to my side because I really thought that was the "real side." Not now. "NO ONE HAS TO WIN ALWAYS AND NO ONE HAS TO LOSE ALWAYS." Elite sport is about sharing, teamwork and knowing that if we work together, there are plenty of time and opportunities to put in practice what we think is correct (but always with previous agreement from the staff and players). (Alain Sola Vincente)

My ego has gotten in the way of my learning when I'm challenged and put on the defensive. When I've had to defend what / why I'm doing something, I have more difficulty taking on new ideas that could be valuable. I find it much easier to take on new ideas when they are presented in a constructive way. If combined with non-constructive criticism, or criticism that's valuable but not presented well, I am still working on taking the valuable information and not taking personally the criticism.

I try to be as open as I can, but recognize that I have shortfalls as a young practitioner and can be very sensitive at times to criticism, particularly from people I don't trust. (Amelia Arundale)

I have always erred on the side of going down with what I believe in and fighting for those causes. BUT I always try to listen to the new ideas and understand them, and evaluate them with a level head, as there are many other ways in which we can reach our goals as practitioners and teams. (Garrison Draper)

It all depends on your role and how senior you are. I've been really lucky, but I'd also say I'm a pragmatic person and super aware of the realities of high-level sport and I've seen a lot of different things work. So if, for example, a physical therapist wants to use Active Release Treatment vs. cupping, or an S&C coach wants to use the yo-yo test instead of the 30-15 Intermittent Fitness Test, as long it gets the athlete better, I don't care. And then if I have been told by a superior they want to do it a certain way and I might be a skeptic, I'll happily go out and trial it first. Then, if it doesn't work, you can say "well, we tried your way, would you be open to another way?" in a review process. (Joseph Coynes)

WHAT ARE YOU RESPONSIBLE FOR? WHAT WILL BE ON YOUR CONSCIENCE?

I have discussed this at length with my former colleague, Ricardo Rosa. Ricardo is an incredible practitioner, having worked in Brazil (various clubs and the national team), the Middle East, FC Barcelona and Paris Saint-Germain as Neymar, Jr's, personal physical coach. Above all, he remains one of the nicest people I have ever worked with in football. He always had words for awkward situations, and was always able to see the glass half full with his guiding philosophy.

It all comes down to hierarchy, associated power, decision-making ability and, in turn, accountability. Everything should be clear first-hand. If you aren't on the top of the pyramid, you'll always have to accept someone else's vision and decisions, even when these conflict with what you believe in. Even if you were the president of the club, there would be someone else above you to tell you what to do (the board, investors, etc.).

You need to be prepared to accept this. You will always complain about someone else's decision coming from above you, whatever your position and role! It will always come. Once you accept this, the challenge, then, is to make the difference between what you do to serve the process first (put yourself at the service of others, even when you don't believe in what you are doing, which is, in the end, what you are paid for) vs. doing the things you believe are right, but with the possibility of not acting as a team player and then losing the trust of the people you work for.

In Ricardo's words, follow your heart and God and you'll know which path you chose. (Martin Buchheit)

Clear roles and responsibilities allow for an understanding within the performance department of who is responsible for certain components.

The first thing you must be able to do is make sure you are completing your role to the best of your ability to support the department before challenging other people's opinions. Once this is done, your ability to have open and honest conversations about other parts of the program is easier to do, but you need to address these in a safe environment. All departments will have a hierarchy to a degree. Understanding where you fit in is important to assess who will have the final say among differing opinions. (Selwyn Griffith)

Respect hierarchy. Just try to plant the seed and let them figure it out. (Dylan Mernagh)

The head coach has all the responsibilities and he is the only person accountable for success (and failure). So as simply as that, you have to adapt yourself and work to support him. If you don't like it, that is another discussion. (Alberto Mendez-Villanueva)

I now take those situations with a bit more tranquillity. I always try give my opinion, for them to know what I think. For things to be clear where I stand. At least this allows me to stay aligned to my values and what I really believe in. But I then put myself at the service of the people above who are in charge, shifting the responsibility to them. (Miguel Ángel Campos)

I worked with an assistant coach who was used to say, "The first question to problem solving is: is this really my problem?" It took me some time but now I understand what he meant. Don't think you own every decision, as it's often wise to leave the responsibility to those who really own it. (Martin Buchheit)

When things aren't aligned between yourself and the hierarchy, clarifying responsibilities should allow you to not have to be accountable for things you don't believe in, and in turn stand for your own values. If what you're doing is not your decision but a reflection of the hierarchy's vision, then you are, over time, not completely compromising yourself, right? (Yann Le Meur)

From above, you have two choices: 1. Compromise your values / beliefs and keep your job, or 2. Don't compromise and lose yours. If you were like me, middle-aged with kids, wife and a large mortgage, you just compromise but make sure you are on the record saying something won't work, etc., so when it does not work and they are looking for scapegoats, which always happens, you have some record to "protect" your reputation. (Dan Baker)

You have to accept it and be able to move on pretty quickly, otherwise it will consume you. I've found that it's always helpful to present your side and explain how you would approach a situation. Then if your colleague / coach / athlete decides to take an alternative approach, at least you've had your say. (Nick Grantham)

If I apply something I don't believe in because it is my boss's decision, I make sure he knows my (opposite) opinion and I do it out of loyalty to the man with the highest responsibility: the coach. (David Utrera)

Sometimes, it comes down to lots of differing views, and sitting down to discuss is a good idea. If someone isn't willing to discuss, then I have made it clear that I don't agree with them, and, if anything happens (e.g., injuries), then they must accept responsibility for their actions. (Andrew Wiseman)

Made it clear what I could and could not do professionally. (Andrew Murray)

What I have done is underline that if I´m in charge of a group or specific player I will do it my way, otherwise I refuse to do it and I hand the power over to the person who wants to impose his viewpoint. (Julio Tous-Fajardo)

As a strength & conditioning coach, if a new head coach doesn't allow me to implement what I believe is good, I'll simply clarify my exact role with upper management: am I in charge or just supporting the head coach? I'll always adapt myself for the best of the team, but clarifying responsibilities is the key to work in peace. When responsibilities are clear, it's easier to accept not being listened to when making final decisions. When there is mutual respect, you can even end up doing things you may not completely agree with, and you can still enjoy fruitful teamwork and collective losses / victories, which is what this is all about, no? (Franck Kuhn)

This happens very often when, like me, you work in a club and don't move with a coach, so you have to adapt every time a new staff comes in.

We all have beliefs and we need to be prepared for the fact that others may have different ones, and that they may not be wrong. It's then very important to assess how big the gap is between what you believe in and what they want. If the gap is small, make sure you are not the pebble in the shoe. Take it easy. Keep challenges only for important topics. And you may always learn something. When disagreements are large, focus only on the big rocks and then it's crucial to clarify responsibilities with the hierarchy. Respecting the hierarchy is a very important concept when working in a team, but make sure you do it as a man. (2)

It's pretty simple for me. When you are an assistant, whatever your role (technical, doc, physio, strength coach) you have to be able to suggest and fight for your ideas, but the final decision should always be that of the leader of the project (i.e., head coach). So, from that point of view, you have to be prepared to do those things you don't like, but this is the rule. However, when this happens too often and if it's too painful, then you have to leave. (Paul Quetin)

I would say that we always act in relation to who we are and what we want to achieve and how. Values are central, but not exclusive. The key is to accept the role that our positions allow, not only as we see it ourselves but as it is perceived and accepted by the others. We are all a part of a larger system that needs to function as a whole. Depending on each person's role, we need to give the best of ourselves into this role, be a strong source of information / knowledge and make sure we help the team with our expertise, independently of what others may have to say about our work and what you would have to say about theirs. Project first. A place for everyone, and everyone in his own place. (Sebastien Gardillou)

Eduard Pons, sport scientist, Spanish National Team, former FC Barcelona: It happened to me many times that I had to change roles when the technical staff changed, and often into a smaller role. Overall, even it often hurts at the start, the only option if you want to stay is to center yourself within the overall project: put yourself at the service of the new staff, and help them as much as you can. That's what I have done so far and I think it's worked well.

If the change is a requirement from powers above, then there is no point fighting it. Save your energy and work on what you can change. If there is scope to provide feedback, first make sure your ideas are sound and look for ways to be involved in the discussion and decision-making process (employing Rapoport's Rules helps here). (Marc Quod)

I think a key skill in my role is flexibility. I have worked with a number of managers and they all work differently, from how they structure the training week to the content of the sessions. As a practitioner, I feel my role is to guide the coaching staff and offer feedback to their ideas and processes. Ultimately, if the manager has a certain way of working, then as staff we need to embrace it and accept it. (Scott Guyett)

I work on my specific duties, without trying to work on the overall system / process where the disagreement may come from. It's not always very productive in relation to the team, but at least it's a way to respect the inter-staff dynamic. (Sebastien Gardillou)

As I grew to understand it a little more, I realised you can still do your job effectively by working around it. For example, if management have very different philosophies, then you can work individually with players. (Darren Burgess)

It clearly also depends on your actual role and level of responsibility. It probably relates to your pay check as well. More money = likely more need to shut the f*** up and do what you are asked to do (whether you like it or not). (Antonio David Sánchez)

If you are paying me to do that, we need to discuss. I can manage your expectations. (David Dunne)

SOME CONFLICTS ARE OPPORTUNITIES TO LEARN AND GROW

This, of course, is a common occurrence in sport. During my time working in English football, I experienced a variety of approaches and belief systems from the various coaches and backroom staff I worked with. All of these experiences can add to your melting pot of knowledge and help influence your own philosophy and system.

A positive approach is to try to see it as an opportunity to develop in alternative ways and learn from other people's experiences, even if it just confirms your thoughts against an approach. As Sam Robertson and David Joyce posit in their editorial on bounded rationality: "In the event that a differing view is presented on a certain problem, the other individual may well be in the wrong – however, they may also just be considering the same problem in a different way." It can, of course, be difficult to accept, but if we are not open to other people's ideas and experiences then we, too, are being overcome by ego. (Jo Clubb)

WAIT. See what you might be able to learn from the new staff. (Adam Waterson)

One of the aspects I like most of my job are the options to learn from many people of many places and methodologies and, when it´s possible, try to visit others. Having a brief idea about how we can develop, the first thing I try to know is how the other persons works (could be it´s like a chance to have a masterclass close to you). After that is seeing what is different and trying to know why they work this way. It could be they are right and I can learn, or I could think they are wrong and try to explain my point of view. (Javi Garcia)

I think you need to find the best compromise between what you can do, what you like / don't like to do and what you are ready to do within this context. Often, changing a few things in your work may be beneficial and you may learn from it. Accepting change is a very good way to manage your own ego and move forward. (Sebastien Carrier)

Ask them what works for them, and truly believe in a collaborative approach to the training and development process. You cannot be autocratic, especially with diverse characters who have complex needs and motivations. You will spend too much energy resolving conflict. One size does not fit all.

I learned plenty of lessons when dealing with players who played and prepared for high level competition. We, as coaches, can learn a great deal from players who have reached elite level. I have stolen the phrase off Paddy Upton: use "the collective intelligence model." If a player is world-class, find out what they have done in the past to prepare and remain elite level.

Xavier Rush at Cardiff Blues taught me a valuable lesson. No other player prepared the way he did. He was very diligent, on reflection. At the time, I wanted players to prepare a certain way. That relationship changed my whole mindset on working with alpha players and getting the best out of them. Huge learning curve for me. I definitely think it made me a way better coach. That was 11 years ago. (Chris Tombs)

I knew only one change in management within the professional team and I succeeded in working with the new staff. Of course, it was not easy at the beginning because I lost all my references and I needed to build new relationships with the coaches and, also, a new way to train. Finally, this change was a good thing because it allowed me to open my mind and improve my management and my philosophy of training. (Julien Robineau)

I would always look to give something a chance, as you may learn something new and, if you are stuck with a dogmatic view, then eventually the world will move on without you. You can always caveat that by saying "OK, we will do it your way now but can we come back and review this in a few weeks." If you follow this route then you have to be all in, as players will sniff immediately if you do not wholeheartedly believe you are doing this with their best interests at heart. If there is a realisation amongst players there is a divide in the staff, it will end in disaster. (5)

If this is only for political reasons, I'm super upset. But if this is evidence-based or "for the better," I accept it and try it as an opportunity for learning. (Mathieu Lacome)

THE OPPORTUNITY IS IN THE STRUGGLE

Don't lose self-confidence. Being challenged doesn't mean you're doing things wrong. It's a challenging and transitional period, but resilience should help you to learn from it, for yourself and for the organisation (or another!). Resilience, self-reflection, and hard work are the key to moving on. (Eric Blahic)

I remember an interview from Krzysztof Wielicki - a Polish alpine and high-altitude climber, regarded as one of the greatest Polish climbers in history - that made me reflect at a crucial moment in my life.

He says it all when it comes to handling difficult situations. When talking about the climbers of his generation, he says that their ability to suffer was the key to their success. "The art of suffering," handling stress to survive and climb in difficult environment has helped them to develop new hiking strategies, and find new routes that are now used by everyone. I have tended to use the same approach during hard times with management and colleagues. "What doesn't kill you makes you stronger". I can't agree more. Focusing on "surviving," doing my job well and trying to see the overall situation both as a learning opportunity and a way to (re)define my goal, actions and approach of human relationships. During those moments, it's obviously very hard at all levels. But once the storm is over, and you may need a few months or even years to digest and understand the entire situation, you actually can't be prouder of what you have done and understood, and you realize that those events have changed you a lot, for the better, both as a professional and, more importantly, as a human being (Martin Buchheit)

I've read somewhere that the "best way to deal with disappointment is to take action and stay positive - to become better, not bitter." Our ability to see obstacles not as setbacks but as learning curves and experience is the key for growth. When a challenge arises, or when you disagree with colleagues: stop, put your ego at the door, take a deep breath, accept the situation and assess before acting. (Martin Buchheit)

MAKE A DECISION AND GO WITH IT

Lieutenant Dyke wasn't a bad leader because he made bad decisions. He was a bad leader because he made no decisions.

— Carwood Lipton, "Band of Brothers: The Breaking Point"

Few phrases damn a leader as much as "empty suit" or "blank screen." Leaders don't have to be master motivators or multidimensional strategic thinkers. But they have to be present mentally and physically, they have to know why the group is doing something and they have to know how they will get the group to their goal. Within any organization, whoever is in the executive seat - whether that's for a sports science team of four people or a company of 10,000 - needs to decide. And within the self, our executive - the ego - cannot dodge deciding.

The "executive ego" doesn't need to be loud or large, but it has to be present and capable of doing its job from Chapter 2: know its purpose, identify its values, weigh the options and their attendant costs and rewards, and then choose what to do.

Ego, under any of its definitions, connects reality with the self. Reality - the nature of life - demands we make decisions on our own behalf. Otherwise, it decides for us and we're still left to deal with the consequences.

Knowing those consequences exist feeds the fear that underlies many of the unhealthy egos we've encountered. One of those potential consequences is that you'll be wrong. In fact, if anything, when you come up with a list of possible choices, many more will lead to an undesirable or less-than-desirable outcome than to your ideal end state. Attempting to evade being wrong can quickly turn into evading a decision.

Healthy egos want the challenge that comes with the risk of being wrong. They recognize that every decision they consciously make is a win-win situation: you either get it right, or you have a chance to learn from what you did wrong. If your ego is dependent on always being right (or, worse, perceived as being right by others), you'll avoid the risk of mistakes, double down on being wrong and will never learn from any outcome. On the other hand, if your ego is dependent on living by your values and accomplishing your goals, being wrong can be a step forward.

None of that makes the process, the choosing or the action easy. The best we can often hope for is that the decision is clear so we can make it without fear.

When fear is at the root, it's often misread as an overinflated ego and people stop there. But to move forward you need to think further and uncover what is the fear, this emotional energy that is driving the behaviour. All sources of fear interact with ego a lot.

A sensitive ego shows as overload, but sometimes it can show as a withdrawal. If the ego is too strong, if those fears are so strong, they won't put themselves in a position to be wrong. This is, then, driving them at the opposite to where you want them to be to work collaboratively. (Pippa Grange)

FEAR OF...

Not being good enough?
Not being the title holder?
Not being the best?
Not being recognized?
Missing out?

egoalsbook.com

ESTABLISH YOUR TERMS

Find the win-win. There is always something you can agree on and work towards. This is a stronger starting point than continuing to clash over disagreements. (Steve Ingham)

Agree to disagree. Can you mould the two philosophies into one program? Can you take bits from both to move forward? If they are completely against your philosophy, make a time to sit with them and acknowledge their work, but then spend time showing them your philosophy and how it has worked for you and the athletes you train. (Adam Waterson)

I think that it is important to be able to compromise your beliefs sometimes to establish a relationship. Once you have better foundations from a relationship standpoint, you can then better negotiate around your beliefs and have a greater influence. At the same time, the relevant people in the organization need to be made aware that you are compromising your beliefs to improve relationships. It shows humility and a willingness to work as part of a team. (Ben Ashworth)

Having an open mind to what ideas they bring to the table and staying confident and strong in what ideas you bring to the table. I always try to have an objective reasoning behind what I do, and so being able to discuss differences and perspectives at a high level is important. (Maggie Bryant)

I now always listen to new coaches' wishes and ask myself why they think that way. I try to build a relationship and understanding over weeks, first. Once I feel mutual trust is established I may, at the right time and place, challenge or ask him / her on how and when they would like me to challenge. It takes time, and your previous 10 years of great work counts for nothing!!! It's about building a new relationship and showing empathy and full understanding of their world and how they see things and why. Very little at first about yourself. (Grant Downie)

If you deal with an intelligent person, the best is to talk outside the work atmosphere to find out first if you have common interests in life, cultural issues, etc. Then try to explain in a relaxed way, with sound data and arguments, why you think your viewpoint is more appropriate. But try to generate a win-win situation by reinforcing the strengths of his / her viewpoints. If you deal with a stubborn kind of fellow with no background and no interest in life outside the work but who is a real "dominator?" Get another job. (Julio Tous-Fajardo)

A new manager inevitably brings change and new ideas. Important to develop a relationship early and have good communication, and to gain trust / credibility by doing the core components of your job well. Managers may have particular reasons for doing certain things. For example, one new manager insisted on testing player hydration every morning, which was new. We did not obstruct this, even though it meant a staff member was taken away from important duties to do it. We attempted to understand the manager's rationale / perspective, continued to do it (it wasn't doing any harm) and to build trust with the manager. When the time is right, we can review it - and the trust we built with the manager allows us to make those decisions. If we objected from the beginning, that would have eroded the trust immediately. (8)

1) You have to get yourself on board with them. Let's call it self-preservation. I try to find what their ego is and what they believe they are great at. Initially, therefore, it's about stroking someone's ego a little to make sure you break down those initial barriers and endear yourself.

2) Once you have got into bed with their ego and you're getting support for your methods, it's then about finding their triggers that turn their ego on or off, or makes the ego positive or negative. These need to be noted, as it is ultimately these triggers that I then try to use to get the most from that working relationship. (Duncan French)

I am actually quite relaxed about this situation. Ultimately in sport "the coach is king," and the effectiveness of us "peripheral" staff depends on us understanding how a coach works, and best aligning our work with these practices. On teaming up with a coach I don't know, I have on a few occasions initially compromised standards in order to put myself in a situation where the challenge is to then gradually move the thinking of the coach more towards my own (in my area of work). Overall, I do find this to be quite a successful approach. (Chris Barnes)

I begin by trying to understand their perspective first and learning about why they hold such opinions. Direct challenge generally doesn't work, but with time and a willingness to engage you can begin to influence. With staff who I have inherited, I normally organise a departmental meeting to explain philosophy and methodology with information to support our stance. It also offers staff the opportunity to present theirs and their experiences, especially with a new group of players. (Dave Carolan)

Accept non-negotiables, but try and mould them with your overall philosophy over time through several layers of persuasion. I've never worked with anyone that I wasn't able to influence. (Tom Little)

As I have said - and hopefully as I have matured - I feel I have done a better job of better understanding others' points of view. If there is a genuine attempt on others' parts to do the right thing, and I simply disagree with it, then I feel it is important to have an honest conversation. If the attempt is not honest, or if it is self-serving (which happens far too often in sport), then I do all I can to not let myself be affected by this person, or to remove myself from such situations. (Stu McMillan)

PICK THE RIGHT BATTLES (THE ONES YOU CAN WIN)

You have to choose battles to win the war. There are some battles you can win with good arguments immediately, and then others take time - but all the time you have to keep in mind you may actually NOT be right. Sometimes the new coach has a valid reason for the change and you have to engage and find out the rationale. (Fergus Conolly)

Choose your battles when you can. More importantly, some key advice I received is to "pick your timing, not your battles." You already know your battles at this level, purely based on your experience and coaching philosophy. I choose my timing for battles that seem appropriate. If players' health and safety are at question, I will express my feelings in more of an authoritative tone.

However, dealing with change is not always easy. If the timing isn't right, you may not be in a situation where you can apply your philosophy. I tend to take time when accepting the implementation of change. I will pick my timing with new practitioners, and even other staff, and attempt to explain the benefits and advantage of applying some approaches that I do believe in. (Alex Calder)

You have to accept that there will be times when you need to back down from a short-term "fight" or "battle" to gain headway in the long-term. The ability to recognize "when to go to war" is really important. There are some fights that you just can't win and are not worth getting involved in. I tend to save my energy for when it's really needed! (Nick Grantham)

It happened a few times that even though my plans or options were better than those of the people I was arguing with, there was a political barrier for not accepting what I was suggesting. It was so frustrating. I fought a lot of time, but in the end, I realized it was a waste of time. I learnt a lot from that and now I assess this aspect before going to war. (Andrea Azzalin)

Going to war in the name of your values is often too difficult to handle mentally in the long term: too many people to fight against, with those battles lost in advance. It may be wiser to accept letting it go and looking for alternative work approaches, both in the short- and long-term. That is, either change focus within the job or change jobs. (Yann Le Meur)

Honesty and, again, make it clear you have different opinions than the person, in particular, but, if the situation doesn't change, also to people above. Important, though, is that you don't let this frustrate you. Try to zoom out and focus on what you can do rather than what you can't do at the moment. The hard part is how you deal with it externally (to players, other staff, colleagues, etc). On the one hand, you should show a united frame of reference (to the club), but on the other hand, if this goes against the values and core principles of your own work, it's hard. Maybe have peers or colleagues who are in a circle of trust, so to speak, who can act as speaking partners and guides in what battles to pick and what battles not to pick. (Johan Swensson)

I think it is a question of balance and equilibrium. There must always be time and room for sharing different opinions because we all come from different experiences. Compromising is part of the game, so you have to recognize when it is the right moment to let something go and when it is time to fight. You cannot win all the battles, and it is important to understand which battle is important to fight. (Andrea Belli)

I keep performance at the forefront and aim to have rational thought and processes aligned to this. I also aim to choose what is important and what is not. Therefore, if the situation of change is on something that is not important, then I move on with that change. If there is a conflict and the change is taking us away from performance, I aim to influence over a longer term through education and relationships. (Stuart Yule)

My best strategy is being able to compromise with individuals, whether it be staff or players. For example, if a physiotherapist wishes to prescribe something that I may not find beneficial for the athlete, I will often ask them (in a private setting) to explain the rationale behind the exercise. If I can construct a robust conversation and educate myself in the process, that would be best case scenario. However, if I believe the exercise does not merit a place in the programme, I will try to provide some solutions that align with both philosophies and values. (Alex Calder)

This happens often, and especially when you join a new team that has its "own way" of doing things that are different from your own practice.

In general, if I think it's not going to harm a player, and the player believes it will help him, I will do the (bullshit) treatment, for example, laser therapy, but I will also add what I do believe in: exercise and tissue loading and strength building. That way my colleagues, the player and myself are happy. Then, as I build trust with the player and my colleagues, I might have a conversation about whatever the bullshit therapy is, so maybe I can reduce or eliminate it. I also think with coaches you have to "meet them where they are." In the NBA, player load management is a hot topic that some coaches just don't believe in. So you have to build in player load management concepts and change the name slightly, or just call it "individualized training." (6)

Sometimes you win, sometimes you lose. It's fine. Don't give up - take a different approach to move the needle. Focus on the "low-hanging fruits." (David Dunne)

REMEMBER WHY YOU'RE THERE

People remember you for what you have achieved, not for the number of times you have compromised yourself. (Sébastien Carrier)

If I have a deep belief and supporting evidence that it won't make the team, organisation or community better, then I hold my ground. (David Howart)

I have always come at things from the mindset of doing things with the goal of helping athletes perform their best. Unless my actions become a hindrance to that goal I try to stay true to my beliefs. (Keith D'Amelio)

The best years of my professional times are far behind: behind the spotlights, with smaller teams. We were part of something, creating new things and, more importantly, having fun. (Johann Bilsborough)

If you have strong evidence that what you support is right (from research, experience in other contexts, best practices in the industry) you would be fooling yourself if you do not stick to your ideas. You may just have to be ready to pay the consequences - and here it's an overall cost-benefit approach that you need to think about. (Charles Vallejo)

A season is long and there are many (often unexpected) changes. Be patient and resilient, keep your beliefs in place. You will come back stronger. Your time will come and you'll get back on your feet. (Eric Blahic)

Many people feel strongly when they are in "their moment," but we all know that success is transient and temporary. Failure is never too far away and, for sure, there will be a time they will need to self-reflect and understand what they've done. The truth of today is unlikely to be that of tomorrow. So be patient. (Pierre Mangin)

We need to be open-minded and sometimes cope with their new method even when it doesn't work. But if it doesn't work, then it's the right time to change things - at least you'll have arguments to show your point now. (Gregory Dupont)

If you can't convince the new member of staff about an idea or philosophy they are proposing, you have to sit back and watch it crash. Or, maybe sit back and accept you were wrong sometimes!! (Colin Lewin)

First, seek to understand. There are many ways to deal with circumstances and you can learn other ways to tackle certain circumstances unless they strongly conflict with your personal values. Also, try to do everything you do with the highest integrity, so if things go wrong you can feel comfortable with where you sit. (Darcy Norman)

FREE YOURSELF

The story of the UFC fight between Israel Adesanya and Kelvin Gateluem is worth noting. Adesanya is completely dominated at the start. During the fifth round, when he can barely stand on his feet and looks like he is going to lose the fight, you still can see him whispering "I am willing to die." He then copes with more hits, gradually gets back into the fight, and ends up winning.

This is a good example of both the importance of resilience and the fact that when you don't have anything to lose, you are the most dangerous. It's when you have the freedom to say what you think and can have the greatest determination to change things.

Buy yourself the opportunity to do what you want. Fight this world of fear and scarcity by creating your own freedom.

Being able to leave your job any time, because you have the possibility financially or have other options from whatever you have created for yourself, gives you the freedom of action and thought.

People who don't have this option, on the other hand, will act to keep their job, rather than saying or doing what they really believe in. And there is a big difference here.

When creating your life and creating your freedom to be able to leave tomorrow you are a danger, since you won't be a yes man. People don't like that in the industry. Yes men survive, but they don't change anything. (Keir Wenham-Flatt)

Create your own liberty so that you can act actively rather than passively. Be in a position to leave anytime, so you can distance yourself from the toxic context if needed. Freedom gives you the power and strength to absorb the daily s**t. (Yann Le Meur)

It's very important when you are involved in elite sports to have a dream. What do you want to do for you? What your life is going to be? If your identity is the badge you are wearing on the shirt, one day you are going to get lonely, so it's very important to have and develop something for yourself. (Grant Downie)

We all have different profiles and approaches to life and work. For many people, working in football is the ultimate goal of their life. They don't make the distinction between the actual work, the social status that comes with it and their daily experience. That's all one entity. The problem is that when you have such a narrow life goal and approach, you become a mechanical prisoner of the system: you'll do whatever it takes to keep this job or this kind of job. You then shape your behaviours toward the goal of keeping the job, not toward defending what you think or believe in.

On the other side, having both a clear distinction between work and personal goals, and having the ability and skills to work in different environments, gives you more freedom to say and do what you want.

Wherever I worked in my career, I always had the feeling (and the self-confidence, thank you, my ego) that I could enjoy work and have a happy life somewhere else if I had to leave tomorrow. That gave me the liberty of my opinions, positions and actions. This is, however, interestingly, something that people hate to hear from you, especially if they don't have this liberty!! I lost some relationships by just saying so. (Martin Buchheit)

I often refer to the following idea that I got from a colleague, Francois Duforez: "Learn how to be here without being here. Know how to float rather than fighting against the waves and current. Know how to let it go, be still and be patient." (Yann Le Meur)

It's of extreme importance to have a life outside of your profession. (Adam Waterson)

Have a life outside of sport. Be more aware of the wider world and learn from other domains. (Fergus Connolly)

There is no point to fight when the battle can't be won. I can't be bothered letting people who I don't feel are legitimate decide things for me. So I step back. I simply focus on my work and the things I can control and have an impact on. That could be working on projects within or outside the club. This helps me to concentrate my energy where I see a clear outcome, and more importantly preserve my mental health. (Yann Le Meur)

It's obviously much easier to accept and be accountable for decisions you took rather than those someone else took for you. I, therefore, try to make as many decisions as possible on my own (Olivier Krumbholz)

TAKE AWAY: FROM EGO TO YOLO

"There are only so many hours in a day" is a common way people think through their daily trade-offs. It's as useful as any cliché can be. If nothing else, it reminds us that we can't just linger in the world of having preferences and priorities: we have to act on them by choosing.

But it can be dangerously short-term, if we find ourselves only thinking in terms of hours in the day. Expand the adage out to a more meaningful scale and see how those preferences, priorities and choices change. Instead of sighing to yourself "there are only so many hours in a day," remind yourself that there are only so many days in a lifetime.

When it comes to weighing our self-esteem against our progress towards our purposes - matters of happiness and fulfilment - the executive ego is a useful reminder of two things: life is short, and YOLO. You Only Live Once.

YOLO is normally dropped casually, maybe a bit swaggishly, to explain away some hedonism or mildly regrettable impulse.

Coming from the ego, YOLO is a reproof. Ego's detractors are right - just not in the way they think - when they say that the ego is, or that it makes you be, selfish. The ego is constantly looking at the balance sheet and the shortening road ahead, and every so often chides you: "You only live once. Is this all we're getting out of it?"

Are you really going to let this internationally-recognized logo on your "insiders-only" jacket, shirts, pants and accessories cover up the fact that this high-profile job is making you unhappy and you can't even do the job you want to do there?

When everyone else is getting so much more out of you than you are getting from your own efforts, is the selfish thing to stay and be leeched or go and be you?

If you'd rather have your spouse for a lifetime than your job for the next Olympic cycle, what's the selfish thing to do? Does a string of failed relationships really sound like something the achievement-driven ego, one that Just. Can't. Handle. Failure., will be OK with?

Even if you've never given this much thought to ego, ethics and your work, if you are making trade-offs, are they setting you up to live well or are you layering new regrets upon old? Sacrifices or investments?

The ego is not a self-destruct mechanism. When the ship hits the iceberg, it doesn't matter if the ego, the soul, the spirit, the id or whatever else was the helm - they're all going down together.

If the ego is the most selfish of the lot, it'll be the most persistent and maybe the loudest voice saying "You only live once. Get it right."

10 | PUTTING THE "I" BACK IN EGO: FOLLOWING YOUR VALUES WHEREVER THEY LEAD

This is the book Martin wished he could have read 20 years ago. This is the chapter he needed to be writing at the turning point of his career.

We've talked about several gaps over the course of this book. We opened Chapter 3 with a look at the early-career deficit between what we think we know and what we actually know. In Chapter 8, we identified a characteristic that separates the all-time greats from the year-to-year really goods: for the greats, there's no daylight between their individual goals and their team's goals. And a recurring theme throughout the book is the idea of a well-developed ego being a reality check: *do* you have the chops to back it up, or is there a gap between your ego and the world with which it interacts?

For some people in high-performance environments, as they reduce those three gaps over the course of a career, another one starts to open up: an expectation gap, between what we wanted and thought this job would be, and what it is.

High-performance sport offers its shares of temptations: money, fame, prestige, professional respect and the watered-down versions of the same (social media clout, professional puffery, basking in reflected glory).

It also offers some great professional perks: top of the line equipment and technology, a full staff of specialists as your colleagues, nearly unlimited budgets and players who bring to life the pinnacle of human performance. You get to work with the best gear and the best people in the most advanced sporting environments on earth. Meanwhile, your graduate school classmate - or, perhaps, your co-author - loads up his car with resistance bands, cones, medicine balls, rolls of tape and 5-foot lengths of plastic pipe to take to public high school tracks every morning.

Those temptations and perks do more than offer a stark choice between work environments. At times, they can corner you into choosing what's more important: the well-appointed setting, or your reason for being there in the first place.

High-performance work lends itself to situations that cut to the core of our professional identity. Some will challenge our identity, while others challenge our self-respect. Both can rattle our entire career progression to that point.

Our ability to recognize, assess and respond to those situations depends on how we have developed our ego in the years before.

"Garbage in, garbage out" was our take away from Chapter 2. In Charles Babbage's day, computers were that linear, and "garbage out" was the end of the process. More advanced software is based on recursion: the garbage out loops around and becomes the garbage in for the next time through the cycle.

Ego development is similarly recursive.

If your ego craves the seat four rows directly behind the head coach, you'll be willing to put a player at risk with a method that will keep you in your new manager's good graces. If your ego is addicted to being at a "big club," you'll have your athletes doing a "beach muscle" workout instead of meticulous, low-impact movement work when the owner entertains a prospective kit sponsor at the training ground on GD - 2. When your ego would rather have viral Instagram posts than the anonymity of a season free of major and non-contact injuries, you'll do whatever it takes to make sure you're in the background of a trophy lift - *whatever* it takes.

On the other hand, you may be in the job for the right reasons and want what's best for the mission, but you may not have the final word (or the first word) on how you do your job.

The people in authority are not always among the all-time greats. Their individual goals have nothing to do with the organization's goals, so there is no common ground between you and them. They may see your specialized knowledge or the relationships you've developed as a threat to their standing. The increasingly frequent and acrimonious disagreements you have with them are not about the best way to achieve a shared goal, but whose individual goal gets to be everyone else's goal.

This is where you move past the day-to-day concretes of the previous chapter into the more foundational conflicts. A supervisor not only disagrees with your way of doing something, but demands you do something that you honestly believe is wrong, professionally or ethically. A new manager orders you to implement a procedure that you have opposed for years on record in journals and blogs that all your peers have read... and now you will be forced to take responsibility with your players, coworkers and maybe the press for the outcome of that procedure at your club.

An immature ego won't know what's being asked of it. A weak ego won't be able to stand up for itself. A fragile ego can't bear to lose everyone else's approval.

Those same egos will be just as complacent on matters of self-respect.

Chapters 3 and 5 shared stories about practitioners looking for a moment of fame or praise and getting humiliated instead. Here's another:

Martin: Pre-season friendly match. For different reasons, I didn't have players' usual shakers for their post-match protein drinks, so I had to prepare the mix in a separate bottle and then give them the drink in paper cup. We had done that for a while and it always worked well. That day, I probably didn't shake the bottle enough so there were a few lumps remaining. While drinking from his cup, a player called my attention, waited for me to watch him and then poured his drink on the ground.

Let's be honest: fame, admiration, money and prestige are not nothing.

But is that what brought you into the field of sports training or medicine, and from there into the high-performance side? Are they enough to keep you in the profession and at that level?

If so, you'll think that such incidents are just part of the job, something you have to endure along with the sleepless nights and stomach pain as the price of the fame, adulation, money and prestige - and the bullet on your CV and blue checkmark on Twitter.

On the other hand, if you chose a career in high-performance sport for the sport, the science, the performance, the teamwork and the relationships, you can separate the job from the trappings.

Recognizing the gap between what we want, what we expect and what we find can lead to feelings of disappointment and maybe failure.

Were we wrong to want those things? Maybe, if we didn't enter the field and take the job for the right reasons. If we never aligned our ego, we might have sought the wrong things and are now disappointed not from falling short but by having attained them.

Were we foolish to have high expectations? No, because high-performance sport attracts competitive people with high standards. But our standards may not be others', and an immature ego will fall in line with theirs than hold the line of your own.

Are we justified in feeling disappointed? Yes. Now what will your ego have you do about it?

Problems can grow when the choices that are imposed on you are not aligned with your own perspectives and values. When clubs have put in place departments and systems to guarantee a minimum level of stability, it's important to speak out and refer this problem to the appropriate person in the hierarchy so you both understand why those changes are on the table and clarify responsibility. Dialogue is compulsory, and you can't leave just when your ego is challenged. (2)

In this world, where there are a lot of fake relationships and self-aggrandizement at the expense of others, you need to have it clear with regard to your own integrity. What is more important? It all comes down to individual sources of motivations. The logo on the shirt, the dream job in the view of people on the outside and the money and fame that comes with it? Or being honest with your own values, keeping your integrity or preserving your mental health?

The reality is that it's an illusion to have them all, and for many practitioners, having the logo on their shirt is a good enough reason both to endure a lot of frustrations and to eat some s***. End result is they don't have much problem compromising themselves and even betraying others to be able to wear that logo for as long as possible. (Antonio David Sánchez)

For many things in life, there is the content and the form. While the form can always be modulated, the content needs to be examined pragmatically, especially if it's well-considered, objective-oriented and not used to satisfy your own ego.

The problem arises when someone imposes on you content that is not in agreement with your own work philosophy. You won't be able to look yourself into the mirror if you apply it.

The other option is to work on the form (politics) and keep doing what you believe in, but then be prepared to perform with high risks: only the end results will talk for you. If there is success, people may recognize your work and it may be your chance (which is still only a possibility, especially with others' egos not willing to recognize your value). But if there is failure, then you are immediately and definitely out!! (Sébastien Carrier).

CHOOSE INTEGRITY OVER LOYALTY

A few times I have been trapped in a pretty uncomfortable situation. We were doing things I disagreed with, and having an amicable relationship with the people in charge made the discussions I was trying to have very complex. On one side, I felt I should speak up in the name of my integrity, transparency and professionalism. On the other side, these people were rather looking for an ally, support from my side, which meant everything but questioning their decisions. In these moments, when stakes are very high, even a high level of trust doesn't guarantee the ability and openness to have such crucial conversations. The first few times it happened, I simply said what I had to say, but almost every time I lost my relationships with them. I started to question myself: was I going too far in the name of my values and my integrity?

I realized these relationships often meant a lot for me, either personally or for my ability to do my work properly. Trying to learn from that, I changed the approach when I found myself in those situations again. I gave a few insights about my perception of the work, but overall kept silent. Most of time that allowed me to preserve the relationships, but I always ended up feeling very bad and I really hated it. I wasn't myself, and couldn't look at myself in the mirror. I tried to think and focus on other things that I was directly in charge of to regain the feeling of autonomy and ownership. It's a quick fix, and it helped a bit on the short term, but looking back I am not very proud of myself. So, however you look at the situation, whatever the decision you make, the reality is that it sucks. I would say now that the starting point for how to behave is how much your values are under attack vs. how much do you really care about the person you disagree with and how much do you need a functional relationship in the job. This is how I weigh the decision with a kind of cost / benefit approach – but easier said than done. (Martin Buchheit)

I have been in a very difficult situation in this context. I didn't believe anymore in our work, and the way we were approaching some key training aspects at the club was going against my philosophy – but my loyalty to the coach obliged me to stay silent. I was stuck, and even started to hope that the coach would leave so that I could work as I wished! I tried to find partners to survive, but the season was going along and the coach was still with us. I started to tell the players my opinion on some of those key aspects. When the coach heard that, he pulled me out of the team. But then one week later, he was fired!!

A new general manager came in, and he heard from the player that I had spoken to behind the other coach's back. So I had no support anymore, and I eventually got fired, too!

Lessons from this is that if you really want to keep your job you have to stay silent, and that there is no way players will board an unstable ship with you. They always choose the boat with the largest sails.

But the most important question is: What do you want for you? Wait until the storm is over (staff change so often, I could have simply waited for the coach to be sacked) to stay for the sake of it, or stick to your values, resign and summon the courage to go out on your own? (Benjamin Kugel)

I listened to the head coach's advice and turned down a coaching role somewhere else. I had the trust and potentially the ego to listen. He then didn't offer me the promotion that he had promised. I should have moved on, but remained loyal. That loyalty was not reciprocated. He left for a way better job that year and almost crippled my career (Chris Tombs).

STAY TRUSTWORTHY, EVEN WHEN THEY ARE NOT

Trust is a big one for me. But you often work with people you don't trust. I have learned that sometimes it's not about trust, it is about being part of something bigger than yourself and being a good teammate: it's about helping the players and the team. You sacrifice things, but you help and support others. In the NBA, the staffs are huge and growing, and there is a lot of ego. You deal with it, or you don't. (10)

I build trust by never criticizing in front of others, by trying to reinforce the things I do agree with him on, and by showing him that I am dedicated to the health of our team. I am also not attached to any of my own opinions too strongly. I have learned from past experiences that many things I was attached to as treatment methods 10 years ago are no longer the best option, and I'm sure I will be wrong again many times. So I try to stay open minded and separate my opinions from my own self. (6)

Trust for me comes with having no alternative agendas, while having positive relationships with people and aligned goals. My job is to support performance and everything I do is aligned to this. There will be mistakes, but learning and improvement will take place. I review and reflect on my processes continually. This enables to me identify where I need to work harder or have more focus. Detailed planning, review, communication, relationships and aligning my interventions to what matters to others (i.e., on-field performance), rather than pursuing what matters to me blindly, I believe helps maintain the trust of others. (Stuart Yule)

Be available and reliable: if you tell your colleagues or the players you will do something, do it. That's the basis of trust, whether you agree with people or not. It took me a lot of time to understand why I couldn't trust one of my colleagues. I realized it was because I could never know if he had finally done what he had said he would do, and why he was doing it or not. Since that day, I always respond to queries by a simple "yes, I'll do this by xx." And if I am late, no worries, I just say that I need more time to do so. And when the work is done, I simply notify people that it's done. It's simple, but it at least gives people a first level of understanding about your reliability. The rest hopefully comes after. (Martin Buchheit)

I'm open about my values with my team. The behaviours that support these values are defined, and I discuss this. By doing so, I then can ask my colleagues to hold me to this standard - to HELP me live those values. We apologize and define when our behaviours don't match those values. We don't shy away from debriefing, in strong detail, where we went wrong. We take ownership. Trust comes from being that reliable person, including being reliable in admitting your mistakes. This, then, leads to the whole team feeling safe to admit mistakes. The more mistakes you make and catch, the faster you are learning. (Jeremy Sheppards)

Including everyone in the process. Being inclusive rather than exclusive always helps to nurture relationships and build trust. You could be preparing a return-to-play plan, planning a new testing battery or writing a paper: the people around you will always appreciate being (or at least feeling) involved. This will directly stroke their ego, and they will implicitly understand that their opinion matters to you. For you, it won't cost much to have them on board, but for them it will mean a lot. It's a big win for a little cost. (Martin Buchheit)

It wasn't a case of one day someone telling Nick (Broad) "This is your role." It was a case of a smart, driven guy evolving and almost creating this role. And he didn't do it at the expense of anyone else - he did it in an inclusive way, which I always appreciated.

– Mike Forde, sports executive and talent development consultant [Austin, 2019]

COMMUNICATE WELL, KEEP ALL CHANNELS OPEN AND PRESERVE THE RELATIONSHIP

I find it helps to be consistent and clear in my values, and to keep messages simple so there is no doubt why I support certain ways of working. I feel differences of opinion can be healthy, and the way you deal with them is a measure of you as a professional practitioner. (Chris Barnes)

This can be a productive situation as you also don't want to be surrounded by "yes men." It ultimately comes down to soft skills: communication, building relationships, trusting each other, etc. It sounds like a cliché but is vital in professional sports. The old adage is that "we have two ears and one mouth so that we can listen twice as much as we speak." If we are speaking more frequently than this, perhaps it is our ego doing the talking. Instead, get to know your peers and their journeys, try to understand how their experiences have shaped their opinions, and, on reflection, why they may differ from your own. (Jo Clubb)

Communication, and no talking behind backs or backstabbing. Try every day to maintain some conversation. It's better to be inside the tent pissing out than to be outside the tent pissing in. (Colin Lewin)

Praise that person when they do good work. Don't just "attack" when they do something you disagree with - this devalues your argument, and others may also view this negatively. (8)

Maintain good lines of communication: face-to-face, regular informal / formal meetings, telephone, email. Avoid passive aggression. Phone calls trump emails unless you need something in writing, no WhatsApp. Do not let the communication suffer when disagreements arise - absence of communication leads to resentment and distrust. (8)

My personal strategy is to have everybody on-board and informed of everything I do, and keep my professionalism in a straight line with my personal values. I´m not going to lie to you, and I have learnt that it is impossible to make everyone happy, anyway. (Antonio Gómez)

Keep the contact and the connection. Don't hide yourself behind your "shield of values." This refers to a protective mechanism when, in the name of our values that are not aligned with the others, we disengage with these people. "I don't want to be fake, so I'd rather not speak / engage with them." True, maybe, but in the end, you unconsciously exclude yourself from possible collaboration and end up in a situation that is opposite to what you need. Because you protect yourself emotionally from this person, you could even be perceived as arrogant, someone who thinks he can do everything by himself, someone not willing to engage. The reality is that if it's about work, you need to think big picture and engage a minimum to get the work done and done well. (Martin Buchheit)

I try to maintain a good relationship and lines of communication with colleagues, so that they know when to escalate issues to me. Allowing them to maintain some autonomy in their own practice is crucial for their well-being and job satisfaction. (8)

I think you have to be honest and open, and communicate even in uncomfortable situations. I think you also have to trust that those around you will do the same. I think setting culture and precedent in times where there is less stress means that in times of stress they are already in place. I think procedures / protocols are also helpful for guidance. (Amelia Arundale)

Keep asking questions to uncover their beliefs. At the very least, you will learn something!! At the end of the day, I think human trust is built upon how much a person believes someone else knows about them and their beliefs. If you can understand where they are at, how they got there and why they are doing it, you cut past the bullshit of ego and can start having a healthy discussion around the actual topic your opinions diverge on. That builds trust, in my experience. (David Howart)

Again, you have to find the common ground. For sure, there are many more things you have in common with someone than things you disagree on. These may not be anything to do with your professional opinions, but bigger things outside of work. If you can find and build on the commonalities then it will build trust and probably a better platform from which you can have disagreements. (5)

Take a step back and use empathy to understand the other person's situation. Then communicate like crazy. Assumptions sink ships. Don't ever assume someone's intentions, because it is impossible to do so. When times are "bad," communicate more. Understand the values of others. Give them a chance to understand yours. It's the common ground that will create trust. That's what creates safety. Now your conversations will have more transparency and depth, because opinions usually don't have much depth. And they are most dangerous when we state our opinions as fact without evidence. So I try to give context to my opinions. "I don't think that will work and this is why." And if I have no context, and my opinion is coming from a gut feeling, I will say so. That's only fair.

Remember these are human interactions that require the two people to feel a connection before they can trust each other. Statements that imply you think someone is wrong, with no proof, makes you look like an idiot that can't be trusted. (Steve Tashjian)

Demonstrate trustworthiness. Meet them where they are. Understand the person and what makes them hold their opinions and display their behaviours. (David Joyce)

STAY RESPECTFUL EVEN AT MOMENTS OF MAXIMUM HONESTY

Martin: Laurent Blanc was called "the President" for many reasons reflecting his leadership skills. But he is maybe not the type of leader you would expect if you only see him from the outside.

Working with him over the years, from the spotlight of PSG to the somewhat anonymous Al-Rayyan of the Qatar Stars League, has taught me that the most important aspect of human relationships is mutual respect. And the respect that others have for you comes from the respect you show them. Whether he was talking to Zlatan and Thiago Silva, players from the French National Team that he coached for two years or Abdelaziz Hatim Mohamed, he always started by telling them that respect was central to everything.

I have seen Laurent disagree with a lot of people, but he has never disrespected anybody. I have lost count of the times when he has been in a heated conversation, but kept saying "Don't get me wrong, I have nothing against you, although I disagree with what you think or say." There are many things that Laurent taught me, but this is probably the most efficient "strategy" to use when you have to go through an uncomfortable discussion. And beyond helping you work out your problems, it makes you a better person.

Look, it's OK to have a difference in opinions. In fact, that can be very healthy in a work environment or relationship. The key thing is how those conversations are approached and handled. (Allistair McCaw)

I think it's important to have difficult conversations and to have them repeatedly. Disagreements are not harmful. Arguments are not harmful. Disrespect IS harmful. (Colin Lewin)

Try to have the heartfelt meaningful conversations with the new staff member when they are still in their honeymoon period. Remember that being a new staff member in a leadership role in elite sport is super hard because players and coaches will have formed allegiances with former staff. Let the new leaders know how you feel and respect their authority and try to help them look good to higher management without becoming a "people pleaser" without a perspective. Try not to talk bad about someone behind their back, but also give colleagues a chance to vent. Tricky balance. (Dave Martin)

Be clear, be transparent. And be honest. And always be professional with the athletes. Never say "I am only doing this because the manager wants me to!" That makes you are a part of a potential problem. (Tony Strudwick)

Always be honest and open. You will not always gain everyone's trust. My strategy has always been to be direct and have the "hard" conversations behind closed doors. Trust takes time and it's earned, so you must be patient. (Johann Bilsborough)

Authenticity. Be honest, be authentic, be open about why and what you think. If you have that, you can always agree on something and find a way. If you don't have authentic teams, you're always in a threatening situation. (Fergus Conolly)

I'll always push for my ideas but without imposing on others. How we say in Spanish "tener mano izquierda." It means being able to behave appropriately in all situations while balancing what's really important or not, so that you don't lose energy and your position on things that don't really matter. (Eduard Pons)

I believe we should be able to disagree while not losing the trust of others. If the disagreement is based on structured facts, logic and evidence, at least your competence will have to be acknowledged. (4)

Establish rules of engagement! We are going to go into a room together behind closed doors and we will disagree. Good debate, argument or whatever you want to call it, but when we are done, we will reach a consensus agreement. Once we leave that room, it is that one message that we deliver to everyone. (Ben Ashworth)

I explain that, while I don't believe in it, it doesn't mean that it is not effective or useful, it's just not for me. I find it easier to do that than dismiss it completely. (Colm Fuller)

I believe the ability to talk openly and not leave things to accumulate under the carpet is key, and everything that can be said or done early to avoid the situation escalating is always welcome. I tend as much as I can to have those open discussions with as much humility and empathy as possible to defuse potential bombs, but the reality is that not many people are ready to have those discussions!! (Martin Buchheit)

I think the best way is to always be open and honest. For example, if a manager works a certain way and you don't believe it is the best way of working you can disagree and explain your rationale. But, at the same time, you need to show support and solidarity towards the manager.

You are never going to agree with every decision the manager makes or with how every colleague works. It is important there is openness and flexibility. I usually address this with a "wait and see" approach. Don't make any knee jerk reactions, and be prepared to see if the new way of working is actually more effective / efficient than the previous way of working. There have been plenty of times where I have disagreed with a process / opinion, only to find over time it is actually a better way of working. (Scott Guyett)

Being open and honest. It might not make it an easy working relationship, but I have found it develops better long-term relationships. Sometimes we are too happy to say yes. Having open conversations to try to work around these scenarios has been best for me. Even when I've worked with colleagues who can't speak the same language as me at first, going and learning part of their language or helping them to learn my language is important. I have worked with a couple of managers who brought different cultures and different levels of understanding to the language. Helping them to embrace the culture of the organisation, while embracing their culture, are my strategies. There is no better strategy in my eyes then being a good human being, first and foremost, and building a relationship with someone. It might only be a mutual relationship of working together, but we are striving to achieve the same goal. If it is a new head coach, I am there to help them to get the most out of the staff and players to ensure the team gains success. I don't think this has looked the same with any two staff members I have worked with. (Steve Barrett)

Understanding someone's perspective is different than agreeing with someone's perspective. Be clear in meetings that "I think I understand what you want to do, but I need to let you know I still don't feel comfortable going the way you want to go. With that said, I have spoken my mind and I am happy to support you 100%, and if all goes poorly I will not say, "I told you so." Equally, if all goes well you deserve credit. Humor can help as long as it doesn't link to sarcasm. Overall, it is an emotional business. You need to feel comfortable being uncomfortable and you need to be resilient when your ego gets walked all over. Don't ever go out through social media, public presentation or the media to vent your frustrations. (Dave Martin)

CONTROL WHAT YOU CAN: LIVE YOUR VALUES BY DOING YOUR JOB WELL

The best recommendation has been to focus in what really is important and also focus in the things you can control. If you match these two points - things that are important and things you can control - you can really worry about situations that depend on yourself, not the situations or conflicts someone else wants to make. (Antonio Gómez)

If the service that is being offered to the players is not compromised, then working with colleagues with divergent opinions can be rewarding. However, it is important to stay true to your own personal values, morals and ethics. (Paul Balsom)

My primary focus is the health and performance of our players, and that's the thing I care about the most. If players are healthy and playing well, I really don't care who gets the credit, because I am happy inside. If my colleague who I disagree with also has the same goal as I do, then it's going to be fine. We are trying to get to the same place, but by different paths. (6)

I'll allow time and space to see it from their perspective. I will present my case for an alternative approach to the situation. Ultimately, I will accept the decision taken by the rest of my team or senior member of support staff, if the majority have agreed on a specific course of action, even if it differs from my recommendation. (Nick Grantham)

To me it's pretty straightforward. I'll always try to defend my ideas with as strong a set of arguments as possible. But once the final decision is made (by the head coach, for example), in front of everyone I'll always do as if the decision was mine. (Miguel Ángel Campos)

I guess that the chain of command goes from up to down. If you are down you accept what is imposed by up. It is perfectly possible that how you believe things need to be done is perfectly wrong! (Alberto Mendez-Villanueva)

If you consistently act in the best interest of the club, people will recognise this over time. Lots of the great managers adapt their outlooks based on the unique circumstances of each club. (Tom Little)

By being 100% professional and doing the work I am allowed to do as perfectly as possible. (Inigo Mujika)

WHY CALL THEM VALUES IF YOU'RE WILLING TO GIVE THEM AWAY?

Know yourself. What are your values? Who you are as a person is who you are as a coach. You don't have "work values" and "personal values." (Jeremy Sheppard)

It's hard to trust others when values don't align. I think the most important thing to do is stay professional, and stay close to your core principles and values. (Allistair McCaw)

It is not realistic to think that you will always trust everyone you work with, or have the same opinions as others. However, not compromising on your own personal values is another matter. I believe that standing by your personal values is one of the most important things we can do. (Andrew Gray)

Values? You don't compromise on values! Until they are tested, they are just verbal preferences - but there will always be a time when you are willing or compelled to test them.

Then it depends on the goal. Pre-season physical testing: is it really important? If it serves the greater good, it's OK. But it has to be two-way traffic. If you always have to compromise and they never do, then it's a no go. When you have your non-negotiables clear, then it's simple. (Keir Wenham-Flatt)

I will not be someone's puppet. I have certain values that I respect above all others. Honesty and integrity being two of them. I am an honest communicator and will not be Machiavellian to keep a job. You can still respectfully communicate without alienating yourself, especially with senior managers or high level players. It's about connecting, as I previously stated. (Chris Tombs)

That is the million dollar question! Some are slaves to the hierarchy, "yes-men," if you like - puppets! This slows progress. I don't think I could be one of them. For me it will never be about surviving or staying in the shadows. I will always strive for progression, development and success, however small the "wins" or "gains" are. I will always stay true to my core values and principles. I am happy to put my neck on the line. Small wins keep the team moving forwards! If the team is moving forwards, and the boat is moving faster, then I believe that is how you build trust with your peers and athletes. (Charles Vallejo)

Sometimes sticking to your values is more important than anything. If you can't stay aligned with them, ask yourself if it's worth trying to chase this trust? (Frederic Demangeon)

Never surrender to demands against your ethics or methods. I don't think you must maintain the trust of people who do not respect you and your work because they are not educated and don't understand it. Low-educated people's trust is not trustworthy. (Jesus Olmo)

If you believe in your values, and have a sound philosophy - don't back down easily! You will gain more respect. (8)

It obviously becomes very difficult when the choices we have to make are drifting outside of our own values. But if you don't speak up, it's worse, since you remove the possibility of remaining aligned to your own beliefs. So, speak up – always. (2)

Until which point can you compromise your ideas? It's more a matter of ranking what is really important or less so, and picking your battles. Some of them are not worth risking breaking trust and, in turn, a relationship! (Paul Quetin)

I think you just need to recognise the differences of opinion openly, and then, at the same time, be open to other ideas. Then, as long as you act in line with what you are suggesting or your values system, i.e., others see you as being consistent to what you say your values are, you should be fine. (Joseph Coynes)

First and foremost, I would never do anything that would go against my own personal morals and values. Second, it is important to establish common ground which you can then build off of. I am sure the correct answer lies somewhere in the middle between the two opinions. I think the trust ultimately comes from the ability of both parties to not dig in, and slightly push their egos aside either to find either the common ground or break new ground where both opinions can be valued. I guarantee you there is lots of learning that can happen from everyone when egos are acknowledged and set aside. (Adam Douglas)

I think meeting people halfway becomes really important in those situations. How to find other creative ways to get the job done even though there are limitations with certain staff not allowing you to do so. It is important, though, to keep true to yourself at the same time, standing up for what you think you believe in but being flexible enough to maybe re-create the way you do things to align with what people want. Especially if we are talking about your boss or the leadership of your institution, there are some non-negotiables you might have to be flexible standing up for if you really want to be part of that culture. That might be worth analysing, and reflecting risk or rewards on being part of a culture that might not align with your values. It depends on your end-goal, financial situation, family scenarios, etc. However, it is important that above all you don't let those things affect your happiness and passion coming to work every day, or not letting all these things divert from your true values and things you believe in. (Ivi Casagrande)

Honesty and humanity, linked to our values and what we really believe, should lead our decisions, not our ego. If you manage to function like this, there is not even the need to control your ego. It doesn't even have a say. (Frederic Demangeon)

If you fail, do it by being faithful to your principles. (Rafel Pol)

EGO EMERGENCIES: PROPER PLANNING TO PROTECT YOUR VALUES

First, I never compromise my authenticity, my values, or my ethics. I made a promise to my family that if I was ever asked to do so, I would leave the situation.

That being said, this is how I have handled it in my career:

1. I took a step back and revisited my responsibility to the team (always team first). "What's my role?"

2. I seek to show the new head coach / management team that I have integrity and can be trusted. If they don't trust you, they won't listen to you.

3. I give their methods a chance, making sure to collect data and evaluate their methods in an unbiased way

4. Come from a place of empathy during conflict. It's their ass on the line.

5. Once I have trust, I present data. But I always use the following mindset: "Boss, this is what I am seeing …. This is my opinion based on data … I don't agree, but in the end, boss, it's your decision."

6. I wait until I have a solid level of trust before I aggressively dig in my heels on issues. (Steve Tashjian)

I think this all depends on how you manage to build initial relationships, which then leads to building trust. The complexities of this challenge increase if the person with the divergent opinions works in the same department as you. The complexities would increase further if the staff member had been appointed as part of the manager's backroom staff. There is a fine line between being compliant and allowing someone to undermine you.

Some of the questions I'd be asking myself initially are:

How compliant do they appear? Do they seem like someone who is willing to listen?

How hard am I willing to fight this?

What are the potential battles I am likely to face if I am going to fight this?

How hard am I going to go to fight this?

How likely am I to win this battle?

If the answer is very unlikely, what is your strategy going to be to try to make small wins that will eventually have a positive effect on this issue. That is, if you are prepared to continue in this way. If you are, you need to commit to it and ask some questions of yourself:

Actually, how different are their methods / values to mine?

How much of my opposition to them is due to my own ego about my position in the department?

How much of my opposition to them is due to my ego and how I look in front of other staff and players?

What are the positives of their methods, can I learn anything from them?

Are their methods the best in the world? Probably not, but whose are? Are your methods proven to be better?

If it is an inter-department issue (increased complexity):

Understand them, but make sure you get your say and ensure it's a two-way process.

I don't think there are many teams or individuals in the world doing things completely differently. If this is the case, pick your battles. When you pick your battles, try to provide evidence to your argument without being accusatory. I often feel this job is half clinician / half politician!!

-Don't be surprised if some divergent opinions is due to a lack of knowledge with the person who you have the different opinion. Then it is a calculated, education process but again doing it in the right way!!! (with Politician hat on!!)

-Finally, if this is an inter-dept issue, its likely you might have had some input to the appointment (if you are the head). They have to realise that the buck has to stop somewhere. If the buck stops with you, it is important that they know you have listened but you have to make the decision that is right for the athlete even if it doesn't agree with their point of view.

2- If it is a staff member who has been brought in as part of the coaching staff:

This is similar to the above - unfortunately, they are in a very strong position and unless you have back up from a very strong sporting director behind you, you have to try to work on making the relationship work. How hard you fight it depends on 1- how important is the cause for you in relation to your values and 2- how much you really want to take the risk to lose your ground since which such persons you have to know that it's impossible almost to win. (Lee Nobes)

When opinions diverge, it depends on what it is about, of course. We can disagree on details. But when it's touching values, core principles or factors that seem nonnegotiable for you, this is the challenge.

If you have the support from the club and directors, you should have enough power to go through your ideas. But if it's not the case, you have to act on your own and find your own strategies to both survive and keep doing your job. That's when it becomes tricky and, to me, there are only two options here.

The first option is engaging your key stakeholders to better understand what they want from you, to go 100% on the most powerful person's side (likely the manager), put your own ideas in the bin and tell him you'll die for him, whatever happens. This gives you some strength and comfort on a daily basis, at least until he gets sacked. A lot of people can do that. Me, personally, I can't, for two main reasons: 1) I believe too much in my own ideas (which is related to my ego, as well), and 2) I can't fake it - honesty is too big a value for me.

The alternative is to try to stick to your own ideas with integrity. You'll still have to make a lot of compromises, though, and work more on the relationship side of things to make players and staff happy, before focusing on your "real" job. Players consistently want to feel cared about and loved. They want to be seen as individuals. Staff all want to be recognized and have a progression plan in place, which is hard to achieve in football. This is where establishing the WHY is so important to understand what people want out of the job. This focus on people management is very important when you are in a leadership position. It's an underrated aspect of the job. it's exhausting, and you're walking on eggs since it can escalate at any moment. I have been in situations when I had to compromise my integrity permanently to try to maintain these key relationships. But how far can you go? You may need to have the confrontation, the hard conversations, knowing it's going to make the relationship worse than before. When it becomes unacceptable or when you reach a threshold that you define as a point of no return, you may just need to leave. You can't sell you soul. (9)

WHEN THE LOGO HIDES EVERYTHING

Most of us don't have numbers on the back of our work clothes, but our employer's logo can tempt our vanity just as much as a "prestige number" like the No. 9 or 10 jersey can for a soccer player. The people who walk around with their employee access badge on a lanyard around their neck hours after leaving the office care more about us knowing who they work for than who they are (assuming they know who they are independent of the name and logo on that lanyard). The logo stands in for the ego, which leaves you serving the logo instead of representing it.

As the former CEO of Sunderland said in the Netflix documentary: "When you're in football, you want to get out and when you're out, you want to be part of it." This is what a lot of people say, yes. But believe me, life can be very good outside of football, and so good that you may not be willing to come back. How good is it, to own what you do? To enjoy your days? It's incredible how once you are outside you finally see the light - because while you are in, your ego is so much flattered that you can't see this. You can't see what life is about: being happy should matter more that the logo. But when you are in you can't see this. The logo hides everything. (Jesus Olmo)

From the outside, the bigger the club, the shinier it looks. But there is so much bullshit you can't say. You have to be prepared to lie publicly when people ask questions about your job. I guess how you cope with this depends on your personality. (Keir Wenham-Flatt)

One of the assistant coaches I was sharing the office with would say to me, almost every day, commenting on another conflict with a colleague or about someone in the staff who didn't act as team player: "Did you see that? Is this something you could have imagined before joining? We just can't tell people from the outside what actually happens here, we would look like fools, don't you think?" (Martin Buchheit)

Working in the big leagues is exciting but there can be a price to pay for working daily in an environment that rewards people with big egos, perfectionism, workaholics and sociopathic behaviours. I loved my time working in the EPL but it did teach me about what is really important in life and who my real friends and trusted colleagues are. (Andrew Young)

People associate your expertise with the badge on your shirt, so if you can't see further than that, if you can't walk away from chasing the recognition of others, your peers, you'll be forever stuck in those types of positions. But are you really enjoying it? Are those jobs good for you? It's a constant roller coaster. Or better, it's like golf. You miss, miss and miss again, so you are about to quit. But then you hit a birdie and keep on for 5 more holes. You complain about missing out on too many social events, friends, weddings, and family birthdays... and then you have a big win over the weekend and you forget all the shit you were complaining about - then right back on for a few more days or weeks... (Keir Wenham-Flatt)

I found myself staying for the wrong reasons: money, comfort, a "different" and interesting life, the people you meet a bit everywhere, the (legitimate?) respect you have from others, recognition from your peers, nice hotels, travels around the world. But nothing related to either the core of my work or anything related to growth in terms of being either a better professional or a nicer human being. (Antonio David Sánchez)

I was never looking for a resource on how to deal with ego as I was not prepared for how big some egos can be. I think one of the more difficult and sometimes disheartening parts of elite sport is how often it isn't about the athlete but other factors (marketing, attendance, $$, politics). I was completely unprepared for that reality when stepping into the professional sports world. That is the piece I wish my mentors and advisors had better prepared me for with conversation and discussions on how some decisions are made. (Garrison Draper)

I had been dreaming since I was 12 to be able to work with the best players possible in the world, and assumed that the greater the level, the greater the work quality, the greater the need for precision, that working at the top would mean collaborating with top professionals, delivering top programs to athletes and becoming a top practitioner yourself. But soon you realize that there are so many factors that you could not even fathom from the outside that constantly compromise your ability to run the best program for the athlete in relation to their health and performance: decisions based on economic or political strategies, peoples' attitudes toward personal vs. team success. This means that you end up very often choosing the least bad solution rather than the optimal.

I managed to find some excitement and fulfilment in developing this ability to "do what is best when it can't be optimal," but when you have the pursuit of excellence inside of you, it's very difficult to handle over long periods of times the frustration inherent in these contexts. This is often why some people enjoy working in sub-elite environments or in less mediated sports. They can really focus on executing their vision of high performance. But can you then still call this high performance?! Many practitioners remain happy and stay in their "elite" jobs forever, but they likely find fulfillment somewhere else than in the core aspect of their job: fame, money, recognition and adventure vs. participating in a top program and delivering high quality sessions. It's a pity, but do we really have to choose between elite level of play and sub-elite program vs. sub-elite level of pay and elite program? (Martin Buchheit)

The best applied sports science was when we actually got to collaborate with externals and people within to produce something that actually impacted what we did on the field. Not just for a research paper. What a great time. It didn't get better than that, and it was 10 years ago. Instead, the politics got worse, we lost every single good person from that club and uprooted all the evidence-based practices we spent so long developing (Johann Bilsborough).

Do you really have an impact? Most strength coaches' impact on a club is like taking your finger out of a glass of water - it's like you were never there once you're gone. (Keir Wenham-Flatt)

Elite sport is a very strange business overall, since this is where, on one side you have the largest financial and human resources to, in theory, support innovation and change to improve practices, but on the other side you find the greatest level of stagnation, protectionism and reluctance to change. So it's a bit like when you find yourself trying to give water to a donkey that is not thirsty. Whatever amount of water you put in front of him, he won't drink. I found myself too often preparing this bucket of water, as I was paid for this, but then most of the time I ended up drinking the water myself. (Martin Buchheit)

In elite sports, a lot of key positions are occupied by ex-players. Their knowledge of the culture and network are clear assets, but Tim Sweeney (the director of Epic Games, the studio that developed the video game Fortnite) spent his life coding and learning how to program – he is not an ex-gamer. John Philip Jacob Elkann, chairman of Ferrari, graduated with a degree in management engineering – he is not an ex-pilot. Are you really ready to work for people with no understanding of what the core of your job is? (Martin Buchheit)

The nepotistic nature of the business means you can be gone in an instant no matter how well you're doing. For the most part, you're being hired and evaluated by people who can't even define what it is you do, let alone measure it, so your survival depends on how much they like you more than any performance metric. (Keir Wenham-Flatt)

Football is monarchical. Things need to go straight and people who have opinions contrary to the king's generally have their head chopped off. To work, and more importantly to keep working in football, you have to accept this to fit in – especially if you are not one of the king's servants!! This means accepting people to make decisions for you, doing what you are told to do and shutting up. If you are looking for a democratic system, keep walking. (Charles Vallejo)

The best physio of the club just got sacked for "political" reasons: "Sorry, this is football."

A player you have been working with for five years leaves the club without making the time to say goodbye, yet you had breakfast together the same day: "Sorry, this is football."

The coach just cancelled the pitch training this morning to do an indoor video session while you have two schools of disabled kids coming to watch the training session: "Sorry, this is football."

You were expecting a pay raise for three years, your manager promised it will be next September... and then HR tells you that it is not for this year: "Sorry, this is football."

A player yelling at a kitman who took six seconds rather than the expected four seconds to bring him his towel at half time: "Sorry, this is football."

You have been working for years to build a project, and without any notice or explanation, the management cancels everything: "Sorry, this is football."

"Sorry, this is football." How many times I have heard this sentence? This is the one-size-fits-all answer to everything that people can't explain: irrational decisions, irrelevant actions or poor attitudes. Again, it's probably a cultural thing... either you are in, you adhere and accept, or you are not and you need to be prepared to forget rationality, common sense and often the respect of others. (Antonio David Sánchez)

TRADING ON A BORROWED EGO

Often the animal world provides striking analogies to human behaviours. The cuckoo shows how a pretty, pleasant song bird can be a ruthless parasite.

The female cuckoo doesn't lay her eggs in her own nest. She looks for an unattended nest of a smaller species, removes one of their eggs and lays her own egg in its place. That way, she doesn't have to bother feeding her chicks. Following in the mother's footsteps, when the cuckoo chick hatches, <u>it ejects the other eggs or hatchlings</u> to get everything for itself.

Sound like anyone you know?

Football reveals people. It's when they have the power, when they are on the top of the ladder that you see who they really are. The good guys remain who they were, the others change completely, full of themselves and toxic. They select their "friends" and only consider the other "important people." What is interesting is to see how this second class of people behaves the day they are sacked. It's hilarious. Imagine you were smoking in your room when you were 12 and then your mum just comes in… (Charles Vallejo)

When on duty, big egos are needed - both for athletes and staff. However, when the work is done, many drop the mask and become very different people. (Dave Carolan)

Elite sport, and in particular professional sport, tends to involve high turnover of personnel. It is highly competitive and there is a constant threat of losing your job. People are often protecting themselves, sometimes at the expense of others. (Ben Ashworth)

Ego is part of a survival mechanism, and besides living in the wilderness or life and death situations, sport is probably the next prevalent area where public opinion and criticism are paramount. I think people will hide behind their ego to not admit that they do not know the right answer. I think this is common in jobs that are of high demand or higher pay. People will do what they have to keep them, and that's where ego gets in the way. They end up being there for themselves rather than what the job intended in the first place. (Darcy Norman)

Yes, very much so. Working in elite sport is full of egotistical people. It's very hard to show vulnerability in elite sport because it's a cutthroat business. I've been in situations where the staff will not admit faults because of the consequences it may bring. This is unfortunate in the work space because it's everyone trying to undercut the others to help themselves (Maggie Bryant).

Elite sport world is full of ego. Every professional tries to protect himself, his job and his position. There are many people ready to take your place, many players ready to guilt you because of their problems, many injuries (many injured athletes with elite contracts) ready to "kill you" if anything goes wrong. (Alain Sola Vincente)

In a context of scarcity (not many positions available with such a large amount of fame and money), often people end up putting their own interest first – surviving and keeping the job – over personal relationships. Long-term friendships may have different meanings and can easily be destroyed, depending on whether working interests are shared or not. The ability to keep your seat warm, play politics and deploy slaughtering strategies are very well developed in this world. Longevity, again, is often more a product of your survival strategies (puffing up your importance, trying to look good and being liked) than the quality of your strength program or nutrition advice. At a certain stage of your career, you have to ask yourself if this context is what you really want on your daily plate. (Charles Vallejo)

To impose your ideas, you have to have sponsors, someone to go to the mat for you: the head coach, for example. If you don't have this, things are almost impossible. The main question remains: do you really want to fight every day with players who want to do what they want, fight with every single staff member, each fighting to get their part of recognition and part in the decision?

If you think seriously about enjoying the journey and being happy, is this really what you want? Why would you want a job like that? (Antonio David Sánchez)

When I took the job, I knew it was going to be hard, but I had such a great motivation for it, that I was ready for all the sacrifices. On Day 1, it was the best job of my life, the one I always wanted. Two weeks later, I just wanted to leave. The rate at which your motivation degrades in this world is incredible. You just want to do your job well, and be respected for that. It's such a relief when you leave... (Johann Bilsborough)

When asking people what are the most important character traits required for a long career in elite sports, terms like endurance and resilience come often. I initially thought that this made sense given the long hours, the constant travels required, etc. But the reality is that this should be seen in the capacity to eat a lot of s*** on a daily basis, deal daily with poor human behaviors (people who have never been told no) and tolerate denigrating attitudes and threatening acts of some colleagues! If you are not able to flush this quickly enough, then the s*** accumulates and this becomes too much to accept. You then need to either find other things to do or eventually leave. (Charles Vallejo)

If you are comfortable with yourself you can accept criticism and have open relationships. If not, you close yourself and no one can talk to you. This is what happens with many staff who can't deal with insecurity. To protect themselves, they put their ego in front.

The consequence of this is that you can quickly feel very alone. It becomes impossible to tell others what you think. You don't want to share your thoughts, and you ultimately prefer being on autopilot. Many do it to survive, but it's living half alive.

When you try to have these conversations, you look like you are too opinionated, someone difficult to work with who can't shut the f*** up. You're outside the norm and people are not comfortable with this.

To me, the single most important things in life is relationships. But in football it's not always the case. (Andrew Young)

If your work doesn't allow you to develop as a person, feel happy and comfortable, for sure you need to make a change. Does the life you have make you happy?

We too often don't make the time to reflect on our current situation, and since we have the badge on the shirt, we think that everything is OK and that we are doing the right things. But, in reality, we may be lying to ourselves and overlooking what's under the carpet: the daily frustrations and battles, fake or even toxic relationships, compromised mental health. We need to reflect more and find our own space to thrive!! This sometimes means changing the focus of your work or your role, but often the real solution is to move on... if we have the lucidity and courage to do so. But further than that, can WE decide to leave such a job? (Antonio David Sánchez)

Sometimes I have thought about leaving my dream job or my passion, because of the difficulty of dealing with some people, or when some roles devalue my work. Those factors can be your personal challenge to continue in this business. (Charles Vallejo)

...AND SOMETIMES... YOU JUST NEED TO LEAVE

This book came together while Martin was in the process of leaving what was, on paper, in the public's eye, by any conceivable measure, his dream job at the pinnacle of his profession. Despite the very different circumstances, this is something George had some experience with. Twice in 18 months he had left a job that he thought was everything he was looking for. More than that, the first of the two was an organization of his own making.

George: After I folded up the team, I was texting with one of our athletes who had moved away to attend grad school. She asked me if this meant I was done with coaching, with track & field, with sports as a whole - any of it. I replied by paraphrasing an American general from the Korean War:

> *Retreat hell! We're not retreating, we're advancing in a different direction.*

— *General Oliver P. Smith, United States Marine Corps*

I kept every door and option open, obviously not knowing that after leaving that other putative dream job a year or so later that I would have a fruitless and unfulfilling year out of the sports world. The one thing I knew at every step of that advance in a different direction is that the values and ambitions that brought me into the sports industry were the same ones that led me out of those two situations. There was no point to me staying in situations that worked counter to what I wanted to achieve and how I wanted to progress.

It's not the job, it's the work. And it's not even the work, it's the why and what for of the work. When those are disconnected or missing, you're working against yourself. You're sacrificing yourself. What kind of egoist would I be if I did that?

Retreat? Retreat hell! Retreating would have meant staying put.

I've thought of that conversation, quote and two-year period many times as I watched the reaction in the sports performance world to Martin's decisions over the short time he and I have worked together.

"Why did Martin Buchheit leave a full-time job in pro sports?" one podcaster asked him. Leave? Leave hell! Martin is more fully into pro sports, sports science, the sports profession, than ever before - and, for the first time in years, our industry is getting the full benefit of a satisfied and, therefore, truly productive sports scientist. As for me, I'm not working at "the level" I did before, but the athletes I'm working with now match me ambition for ambition, value for value. Is there a better formula for coach-athlete success and a coach's fulfilment?

I have always been willing to put my energy into things in which I believe and that I have expertise in. If I feel that the change will not allow me to follow my beliefs, it's preferable to leave and look for another project. (Alexandre Dellal)

Of course, I remember new head coaches arriving with new ideas that were completely different from my own. My response was to be supportive and try the new ideas. Maybe other ideas are better than mine. However, if I felt I compromised my values as a person or as a sports scientist then I have two options: Challenge the coach in the right way, or leave! If you compromise your ideas and values for too long you lose your own sense of purpose. I did both! (Tony Strudwick)

First, I struggle personally. Then, I try to understand, adapt to some of the things and keep working to change what I can if I can with my daily work. I think adaptation is a big one, until the moment you don't believe in the project or the people. Then I prefer to move somewhere else. (10)

Conflict is central to and required for change. If you do what everyone does, you may manage to isolate yourself from the risk of failure, but at the same time, you pull yourself away from the opportunity to create and innovate. Have the ego and self-confidence to be able to do it and say it - you push hard and you can actually leave if you're pissed / unhappy…. that means it's important to you!! (Keir Wenham-Flatt)

You have to accept that this is the best way forward for the team / club, etc., or move on.

I'm lucky. It's been a long time, but I remember. It was a swim club. As I was struggling to accept some of the actions, I heard the expression "the standard you are willing to walk past is the standard you are willing to accept." I realized I wasn't willing to be associated with some standards, and so I stopped working with them. I'm glad I did. You can't always just walk out on something if you don't like it - there are always things you won't agree with completely. But, you need to know your non-negotiables. (Jeremy Sheppard)

If it is something that is unimportant, or only relatively important, I try to discuss and negotiate to come to a compromise that satisfies both parties. If the disagreement is of a fundamental nature and no consensus is possible, I leave. (Iñigo Mujika)

I set a limit. Because of ego? No! Because of accountability. I prefer to die with my ideas than make mistakes with others' beliefs. I have a range in which I can adapt. Outside of it, I prefer to leave. (David Utrera)

I can adapt the work dynamics of my department to a new coaching team, but I have never tolerated major interference in how things are done in the area under my responsibility. That is probably why I am not inside a football team right now, and probably never will be. (Jesus Olmo)

If you have too many non-negotiables you simply can't achieve, it may be best to move on. (Tom Little)

Mmmmm, this stage of my career, if it's outside my moral belief I will move on. (Craig Duncan)

If you can't deal with it, you must step aside. Otherwise you will risk your honesty and professionalism.

It depends on my personal situation and the uncomfortable level of work. If I'm not happy and I can afford to do it, I leave the club. If not, I'd try to find motivation to work (other departments, players, etc).

Earlier in my career, when there was a change in manager at one of the clubs I worked at, I was forced to deliver what I felt was wrong and there was a subsequent and dramatic increase in injuries that affected the performance of the team. I made the decision that I didn't want to be associated with such a way of working and left my role. My colleagues are still there and the manager has long gone. (Damian Roden)

My motivation has always been to do what I thought was the right thing - feeling I knew better than whoever was directing me otherwise. (Stu McMillan)

I lost a job (mutual parting, I guess, depending on how you want to spin it) because I vehemently disagreed with the high-performance manager's approach, to his face, behind closed doors. I always towed the line with the players, but I guess it probably showed my heart wasn't in that program. I LOST MY JOB - no other job to go to (at the time). But I don't regret it, and I didn't at the time. That program was not right for me. My ego was part of it. It was tough to have no job, but I found another one, eventually, and that opened up some fantastic opportunities for me. (7)

I have left big jobs because I couldn't walk past a standard or value I believe in. It's very important to have your own personal guardrails in what you can and cannot accept; and you need to make difficult decisions sometimes as a result. When you have change in your organisation then you need to manage that and discuss those guardrails and values straightaway.

Sucking it up and trying to deliver this program was the hardest year of my career. I learnt a lot from the experience, but it was tough. I decided that was not why I got into this industry. By the end of the year I had decided that I would rather work in a gym as a personal trainer than stay working for the new high-performance manager, who I believed was egotistical and abusive to the players. I legitimately felt like our program was doing harm. I hated it. I had to leave. (7)

At a certain moment of my career I realized I wasn't a kid any more, willing to sacrifice whatever it takes to keep the job. I found myself thinking too often "How can you accept this without saying anything?" or "This is not you. You can't accept this." With age and experience, I knew better what I really wanted at all levels of life, and compromising myself for non-essential purposes, like preserving a job, was the last thing I wanted to do. And on the top of this, probably because of my strong ego, it became impossible to keep doing the things that others were imposing on me. I felt that those persons were in no position to tell me what to do. It was clearly time to leave. (Charles Vallejo)

Unfortunately, I have a level of integrity that at some point will be challenged and will not be broken over something that I feel strongly about. I lost a job because, at one stage, I was not prepared to be a coach's puppet. The irony is he called me six months later and told me that I was right and he should have kept me on as a coach in the organization. Validation, I suppose, in some respects. (Chris Tombs)

To me, there is some line here. If you are so divergent that you can't agree on fundamentals, I don't think it's healthy to be on the same performance team, serving the same group of athletes. This may be different in an institutional setting, where you serve different athletes. On differences that don't cross this philosophical line, I think it is healthy to respectfully disagree and come to a common understanding. Sometime the disagreement is so strong that two people on a team can't compromise with one another (I have been in this situation), but it is still respectful. It's just complete disagreement. In this case, the leader of the team needs to make the decision and everyone needs to get on board. If staff can't do that, they don't belong on that team. (7)

You may wake up one morning and have it all figured out. Whether it came naturally or following a longer introspective process doesn't matter, but you may realize that you may not be made for this life, and that there are too large mismatches between your values and those of the people around you. Not the sport itself, not the high-performance side of thing, but the culture of the sport, or at least this environment. The codes of this group of people may not be for you. (Antonio David Sánchez)

One of the greatest challenges in life is managing to be happy in the context of difficult people, like when working with people you haven't chosen. When the amount of energy I am willing to invest to manage these relationships is unlikely to produce change, and if working with these people compromises my quality of life and challenges my integrity in a way I am not willing to accept, I can move. It's difficult, but it's important to take responsibility for this decision and not to blame others for who they are. We should remain honest with ourselves and be agents of our own choices. The worst thing is to see ourselves as victims of others. Understanding this is the first step toward freedom and happiness. (Martin Buchheit)

As a final observation – in early 2014, I was the Head of Fitness and Sports Science for the Australian National Team (Socceroos) preparing for the FIFA 2014 World Cup in Brazil – my lifelong dream to go to a World Cup. Two months before Brazil, my father was unexpectedly diagnosed with terminal lung cancer and given only months to live. I immediately resigned my position with the team so that I could provide daily palliative care for my father in Canberra. I was never going to go to Brazil with the chance that my father might pass whilst I was away. Some of the staff and coaches did not understand my decision and my father wanted complete privacy. I cared for my father every day for five months. He died on 18 September 2014. The final conversations and time that I spent with my father were wonderful and irreplaceable – comfortably better than going to a World Cup. Everyone makes their own decisions but I am not completely sure how many of my professional colleagues would have made the same decision.

This experience put everything starkly in perspective for me and was life changing. It taught about what is really important in life and what really defines you as a person. (Andrew Young)

I have found myself counting the months I should stay in a position, justifying it with everything other than the reason for which I actually should stay. When you realize that you are not doing the right things anymore. What would be my legacy if I was to leave tomorrow? Would I want my son to be trained by me? If it's a clear no, then the response is simple. Go. (Keir Wenham-Flatt)

How to assess YOUR SITUATION?

1 Does this give me enough money to live how I want?

2 Does the job help me personally in my life, and social relationships?

3 Does this help move me forward professionally?

4 Do I feel a sense of purpose? Do I make a difference?

egoalsbook.com

IF YOU HAVE...

4 of them, never leave.

3 only leave to get the 4th... make sure you keep

2 looking for another job that gives you more.

1 only, slap yourself in the face because you shouldn't be here!!

egoalsbook.com

IT'S NOT IN THE BOOKS – YOU NEED TO LIVE IT

When you ask me if I would do things differently? Probably not, because you learn from it, and scars don't come from books. (Keir Wenham-Flatt)

The single most important thing that I take from all these years working in this unusual environment is how much it teaches you about yourself. It is such a unique working environment and is a great life learning experience on so many levels.

You live this unique experience by yourself and it is often very hard for outside people to understand. It's a journey and I think that you come out of it a wiser person. (Andrew Young)

So it's definitely worth the struggle. If you had told me what I will have to go through, I wouldn't have believed you. The reality is that you have to live it all the way to understand it. It's pretty hard, but the process and reflection required to adapt to and strive in this environment make you become a better person overall. And it's only after that development that you can make the best decision for yourself. (Martin Buchheit)

TAKE AWAY

No one starts their career planning for the day they leave their dream job. No one embarks on two decades of school and work, looking ahead to the moment when the talk of their industry will be "LOLWUT, he quit? Who does that? Whatever." No one looks forward to meeting their new colleagues and asking "What are your personal agendas that have nothing to do with the real reason we're all here?"

But not enough people start their career knowing that there are goals bigger than the logo on your jacket or your business card; that there are sources of pride more deeply held than your status in the field; that ego is not some image you choose to broadcast about yourself. That someday they may have to choose between their job and their work, their ego and someone's else logo. That they may have to ask themselves not "Is this worth it?" but "Am I worth more than this?"

Then, after answering those questions, assessing your self-worth to be higher than what you (and hundreds of your peers) thought was the apex of your profession, having the confidence - having the ego - to walk away. Knowing that you'll be the subject of whispered "That's the one who bailed on Silicon Valley and moved to Grand Rapids. Guess she couldn't hack it."

But then again, no one starts their career knowing the things that you can only learn when they happen to you.

The best anyone can do is be ready for as much as possible. Our hope - our EGOal for this book - is that people at any stage of a high-performance career will recognize the importance of a healthy, self-sufficient ego to their professional happiness. Healthy, so it stays connected to reality, including the reality of other people. Self-sufficient, so that the immense drive it provides pursues your ambition rather than chasing someone else's desires for you.

> As human beings, we are the only species on the planet that strives to be better. As a social animal, we also strive to be accepted by others. You add extraversion as a personality style, social history, life experiences, sense of being rejected. The coupling of all these provides our constant and core drive for improvement and recognition.
>
> In addition, modern life has made it too concerned with looking successful, which amplifies everything. We should go back to the principled questions:
>
> Is this serving me and others?
>
> Is this drive serving me and my fulfilment? (Pippa Grange)

The ego, at its best, is an object of admiration, even if you're the only one admiring it. High-performing egos bring people into high-performance environments. As necessary, ego will lead them out when the place is no longer worthy of the person.

CONCLUSION

Ego has created the best things in sport but also the worst. (Darcy Norman)

Ego is like fire. You can use it to cook your dinner, or you can let it burn down your house! (Keir Wenham-Flatt)

Take out all of the package deals, misrepresentations, provocatively titled best-sellers, flamboyant superstars and overcompensating co-workers, and ego will probably still end up with a negative connotation for most people. Something that requires that much hard work always will, even when the upside is immense.

It doesn't take long in any high-performance environment to learn that there are many more ways to lose a game, tank an investment, write code that crashes or make a flawed argument than to get it all right. Let's just say we had much more material from our contributors for Chapter 3 than for Chapter 2.

> A certain amount of ego, well managed, can be positive and help you perform at your best. The problem is triggered when it causes a person to do things only thinking about the image they project, that the most important thing is what others think even if it goes against their own convictions.
>
> Then he can distance himself from reality, from who he really is, from his essence and even from what unites him with important people.
>
> In short, the ego, disproportionate and poorly managed, is very expensive and difficult to maintain, because it is insatiable, and in the end opens a vacuum that is never filled except at very specific moments. (Juan Carlos Álvarez Campillo)

Martin: This journey of writing the book, along with some work in parallel on myself over the past year and a half, has helped me to better understand the positives and negatives of the ego landscape in the workplace. More importantly, I have learned a lot about mine, as well.

I know better that, to give my best and to be successful in my personal and professional lives, I need this clarity both about my own ego, what I want to achieve and why, and how to better deal with others' egos. Without this clarity, you find yourself navigating in a foggy, orbital journey, disjointed from reality and what you should really be doing. Competing interests and battles to satisfy everyone's egos often tend to override our initial objectives and derail us from doing things right.

Overall, it's first about being aware of it. It's about the volume. Knowing when to push and when to pull. Finding the balance. Placing the bar at the right level with enough humility and empathy to show you're not a d**k and are happy to listen, putting yourself at the service of others, if needed. Having the ability to accept that sometimes you can be wrong and need to learn gives you the required distance to be in control and not just be reacting to what happens to you. Knowing your strength but keeping control of your emotions, actions and reaction.

But I also discovered that, with this level awareness, a well-channelled ego can be your strongest weapon to achieve great things. In fact, we shouldn't put the bar too low, because we need to keep moving forward. We should seek and maintain the credit that others give us. Position yourself as you really are in relation to your true value, showcase your strengths and what you bring to others. And keep writing papers and books to change the world!!!

Finally, because I also know better what I'm capable of and what my real value is, I even have a greater confidence and estimate of it today. I realized that standing for my values and the things I believe in is my priority. I have such an ego - I believe in my value so much - that I can't compromise my values for the sake of anything, like keeping a relationship or a job. This has been a game changer for me.

My vision and mission is clear: **having an impact with humanity and integrity**, nurturing a strong impactful ego, but not at all costs. Only with the required level of humility to keep growing and, above all, have respect for others.

George: Until I was on my second or third phone call with Martin, I had never heard the contemptible statement "ego is the enemy." If you've read this far, you can imagine my anger at learning that it was the title and theme of a best-selling book; and, perhaps, my disappointment, sympathy and - yes - more anger at how widespread that idea is amongst leaders in my field.

Part of why I was so determined to come on board this project was the opportunity to use the arena of sport to illustrate how vital ego is to our lives. The higher one's ambition, the higher one's level of performance, the greater the need for an appreciation of ego.

As Tara Smith says in "On a Pedestal - Sport as an Arena for Admiration," sport gives us so many moments where we joyously confer our admiration in exchange for someone else's achievement. I actually took a break from writing this section to watch the last 20 minutes of the English Championship promotion play-off final. I had no particular interest or affinity for either team. I just wanted to see the celebrations, knowing what it means for a team to "go up" for the first time. If, through this book, I could expand sport's "ego sanctuary" into the life of someone who works off the pitch, field, track or court - letting them know it's OK to look at themselves the same way we fans look at winning teams - then I will have done something worth admiring in myself.

Some of the stories I heard from Martin in our chats were even more appalling than the ones we included in Chapter 3, or those that make headlines in the sports media. I have little doubt our readers in tech, law, medicine, finance, entertainment or any other high-performance environment can think of some anecdotes that make ours look gentle.

In light of that, if I could offer one piece of advice, it's this: Take pride in your ego. At the end of the day, it's the only friend you've got.

If the readers get at least 20% of the value that we gained for ourselves while writing, we'll be honoured and fulfilled. - Martin & George

egoalsbook.com

CONTRIBUTORS

- About 9 anonymous incredible practitioners, and
- Martin Buchheit, sport scientist, strength and conditioning coach, researcher, performance consultant, Kitman Labs and Lille OSC; formerly PSG, Aspire Academy and some cool pro and national handball teams.
- George Perry, athletics coach, sports writer and businessman.
- Adam Douglas, sport scientist and strength coach, Catapult Sports and Hockey Canada, former NHL strength coach.
- Adam Johnson, Physiotherapist, Stoke City Football Club.
- Adam Waterson, Australian strength & conditioning coach working with LA Galaxy in the MLS. Previously with professional football teams in Australia and Asia.
- Alain Sola Vicente, strength & conditioning coach and physiotherapist in different professional soccer clubs.
- Alberto Mendez-Villanueva, Performance Manager, Qatar National Team; researcher, former Senior Sport Scientist at Aspire Academy.
- Alex Calder, Head of Sports Science, Houston Dynamo FC.
- Alexandre Dellal, strength & conditioning in soccer, sport science researcher; formerly Olympic Lyon and OCG Nice.
- Allistair McCaw, author and speaker. Team culture, mindset and leadership consultant.
- Amelia (Amy) Arundale, physiotherapist and researcher, Red Bull Athlete Performance Center, former Brooklyn Nets.
- Andrea Azzalin, Head of Fitness for the Ukraine Football Federation; former Head of fitness at Fulham, Nantes, Leicester, Greek National Team, Monaco and AS Varese 1910.
- Andrea Belli, Performance Sport Rehabilitation and RTP specialist, FC Internazionale Milano; formerly Lazio, Qatar National Football Team and 32nd America's Cup campaign with Italian Sailing Team.
- Andrea Scanavino, athletic trainer; after a long tenure at three of the main Serie A teams, for some years he has been involved with Zenit St. Petersburg and the Italian National Football Team.
- Andreas Beck, performance coach with a sport science background. Head of Physical Performance, Prevention and Rehabilitation, Eintracht Frankfurt; former Borussia Dortmund and FC Nürnberg.
- Andrew Gray, Founder & Director, Athletic Data Innovations; High Performance Manager, Australian Rugby League clubs (NRL) over last two decades.
- Andrew Murray, Chief Medical Officer European Tour, Ryder Cup Europe. Ex-endurance athlete.
- Andrew Wiseman, Director of Performance OL Reign, former Head of Performance and Strength & Conditioning in different football (soccer) teams including Real Salt Lake, Exeter City and Celtic FC.
- Andrew Young, physiotherapist and fitness coach. Formerly Fulham FC, Australia National Teams, AFL and various consultancies including Usain Bolt.
- Antonio David Sánchez, Performance coach with 35 years of experience in elite sports across Europe, USA, Middle East and Asia.
- Antonio Gómez. Fitness Coach at Poland National Team PZPN; former Sport Scientist and Strength & Conditioning Coach, FC Barcelona, Liverpool FC.
- Ben Ashworth, physiotherapist turned Director of Performance. Formerly Arsenal, EIS and Premiership Rugby.

- Ben Ryan, Olympic Gold Medal winning coach and performance expert. Formerly England and Fiji 7s Head Coach.
- Charles Vallejo, sport science pioneer, nutrition and manual treatment specialist, worked a bit in all sports.
- Chris Barnes, football scientist for many years, works for several top clubs in the EPL and the UEFA.
- Chris Tombs, Performance Lead Seattle Seawolves. Formerly Leicester Tigers, Cardiff Blues and Northamptonshire Cricket.
- Claude Karcher, handball coach, strength & conditioning coach and sport science; 25 years with professionals and young talents.
- Colin Lewin, 23 years at Arsenal Football Club, 10 years as Head of Medical.
- Colm Fuller, Head of Physiotherapy, Sports Surgery Clinic, Dublin; have worked with Irish national rugby team, Munster Rugby and Kerry GAA in the past.
- Craig Duncan, Human Performance Strategist, Performance Intelligence Agency; formerly Head of Sport Science, Football Federation Australia.
- Damlan Roden, Director of Performance RSC Anderlecht, worked in many clubs around the world, especially in the UK and the MLS.
- Dan Baker, strength & conditioning coach and educator. Worked more than 20 years with pro rugby league and union.
- Darcy Norman, Kitman Labs, US Men's National Team. Physical therapist, performance coach, athletic trainer. Formerly Bayern Munich, DFB, AS Roma and EXOS.
- Darren Burgess, performance coach from Melbourne Demons, formerly of Arsenal, Liverpool, Socceroos and Port Adelaide.
- Dave Carolan, sports scientist and app developer! Millwall FC now; Norwich City, Birmingham, Derby, London Irish before.
- David Dunne, Performance Nutritionist with the European Tour and British Canoe, pursuing a PhD in Technology, Behaviour Change and Nutrition.
- David Howarth, Head of Athletic Performance for Connacht Rugby in Ireland; worked previously in a number of team and individual sports as a strength & conditioning coach and sports scientist, including Oklahoma City Thunder (NBA), rugby and surfing Australia and MMA.
- David Joyce, sport strategy and performance consultant. Two decades' worth of making mistakes in elite sport around the world, working in many sports including AFL and football across Australia, Europe and China.
- David T. Martin, Professor, Exercise Science, Australian Catholic University; Chief Scientist, Director of Performance, Apeiron Life, former Australian Institute of Sports and NBA 69ers.
- David Utrera, strength & conditioning coach, physiotherapist. Back and forth between rehab and performance. Aspetar, Aspire, clubs like OGC Nice, UD Almeria and FK Krasnodar.
- Duncan French, Vice President of Performance at the UFC Performance Institute, former Director of Performance Sciences at University of Notre Dame, Technical Lead for Strength & Conditioning at the English Institute of Sports, and head strength and conditioning coach at Newcastle United FC.
- Dylan Mernagh, First Team Sport Scientist at Queens Park Rangers FC.
- Eduard Pons, sport scientists, Spanish National Team, former FC Barcelona.
- Eric Blahic, assistant soccer coach; formerly PSG, Bordeaux, Sochaux, Guingamp and French National Women's team.

- Fergus Connolly, performance coach who works with elite performers in professional sport, special forces and business. Former University of Michigan, San Francisco 49ers, Welsh Rugby Union and Performance Consultant to Rugby, EPL, NFL, NBA, AFL.
- Franck Kuhn, strength & conditioning coach, French Basketball Federation with Men's National team and SIG Strasbourg; former CSP Limoges, Poctob Handball, Roumanian Federation and SIG Strasbourg again.
- Frédéric Bougeant, world citizen, handball coach in France, Russia, Africa... on the road for the 22 past years.
- Frédéric Demangeon, handball coach, Head of Player Support at the Centre of Excellence in Strasbourg, in charge of professional coaches' education at the French Handball Federation, and research on motricity preferences.
- Garrison Draper, Performance Director, Philadelphia Union (Major League Soccer).
- Gregory Dupont, performance manager and researcher, former Real Madrid, French National Team, Lille OSC and Celtics FC.
- Grant Downie, OBE, consultant in medical and performance solutions. Spent 32 years in elite football in varying roles, including Man City, Middlesbrough FC, Rangers FC and the FA.
- Iñigo Mujika, endurance and team sports physiologist, coach and academic.
- Ivi Casagrande, sports scientist / performance coach with a strong passion for growing the women's game and sharing / learning with coaches and athletes from all over the world.
- Jack Nayler, Head of Performance, RB Leipzig, formerly Chelsea, PSG, Real Madrid and Celtic Glasgow.
- Javi Garcia, GK coach for 20 yrs in various top European clubs including RCDE Espanyol, Sevilla, Swansea, PSG, Arsenal and Villarreal.
- Jeremy Sheppard, Integrated Support Team Lead for Canada Snowboard, and Senior Advisor to the Canadian Sport Institute. Prior to this he has worked with Surfing Australia, Australian Institute of Sport, Australian Volleyball, Queensland Academy of Sport, and professional teams in the National Football League, National Rugby League, and Australian Football League. His vocation around "doing cool things with cool people."
- Jesús Olmo, sports injury doctor and Health and Performance Director at Football Science Institute; formerly Real Madrid CF and Spain Rugby.
- Jesus Perez, PSG assistant head coach, sports scientists, former Tottenham, Southampton, Espanyol, Almeria, Rayo, Murcia, Saudí National Team and many more.
- Jo Clubb, performance science consultant; formerly Buffalo Bills, Buffalo Sabres, Brighton and Hove Albion, Chelsea FC.
- Joël Trebern, Founder of JHT Performance, cognitive and psychology consultant, working with the French Football Federation, the French Institute of Sports and many pro clubs in football (soccer).
- Johan Svensson, Football Fitness Coach, Swedish FA, formerly AIK Fotboll.
- Jonny King, rehabilitation physiotherapist in high performance sport.
- Joseph Coyne, formerly UFC, Chinese Athletics Association, and Chinese Olympic Committee.
- Johann Bilsborough, Director of Performance & Rehabilitation in the NFL. Previously worked in the AFL, NBA and NRL.
- Juan Carlos Álvarez Campillo, sport psychologist working with players and coaches, Spanish National Football (soccer) Team, Sevilla FC and other European league teams, national field hockey and Olympic athletes.
- Julien Robineau, Strength & Conditioning Coach for Rugby XV and 7s, FFR.

- Julio Tous-Fajardo, strength and power coach with the soul of a basketball coach. Formerly FC Barcelona, Juventus FC, Italian National Team, Chelsea FC and Inter Milan FC.
- Ian Beasley, Sports Physician, Aspetar. Medical Consultant, Global Performance Team, City Football Group, Manchester; former chief officer for the English FA and Team GB for the London Olympics. Worked in many teams in the Premier League including Chelsea, Fulham, Arsenal, West Ham, and Bournemouth.
- Karim Hader, over 15 years as conditioning coach, performance manager and researcher. Currently Performance Scientists at KitmanLabs, former Head of Performance at PSG Academy, and strength and conditioning coach with Aspetar in Qatar.
- Keir Wenham-Flatt, strength & conditioning specialist, worked for a decade with elite level rugby and college football in five different countries.
- Keith D'Amelio, performance and sports scientist in basketball, formerly Toronto Raptors and Boston Celtics.
- Lee Nobes. Head of Physiotherapy, Liverpool Football Club. Former Head of Physiotherapy, Manchester City FC.
- Luis Suárez Arrones, Head Fitness Coach at FC Basel, Senior Lecturer at Pablo de Olavide University; formerly Tianjin Quanjian FC, ACF Fiorentina, Qatar National Football Team, Real Betis.
- Maggie Bryant, Director of Rehabilitation for LA Clippers.
- Mathieu Lacome, Chief Performance and Analytics Officer at Parma FC, former Head of Research and Innovation at PSG and Sport Scientist at the French Rugby Federation. Failed footballer turned into a sports performance specialist to help others become more successful than him.
- Maurizio Fanchini, Head of Performance at AS Roma, formerly with US Sassuolo, FC Inter.
- Marc Quod, great coach, insightful sport scientist, and leading high performance manager...oh, wait... worked for the Australian Institute of Sport, Aspire Academy, multiple World Tour cycling team.
- Michael Caulfield, sport psychologist for teams and coaches, putting the person before the player or coach.
- Miguel Ángel Campos, Strength & Conditioning Coach Cádiz CF, previous Granada CF, Levante UD, Algeria National Team and many other pro teams in Spain.
- Nick Grantham, performance specialist and coach to Olympians, professional athletes, and sports teams the world over.
- Olivier Krumbholz, Head Coach of the Women French National Team, 2x World and 1x European Champion, Olympic Champion in Tokyo.
- Paul Devlin, Lead for Amazon Sport in Australia trying to enable sports to maximise their potential through technology and cloud. Over 20 years playing and high performance coaching in rugby league and union in UK and Australia.
- Paul D. Balsom, now officially 50% Brit and 50% Swede and 50+! Spent all of his professional career working in football with diverse groups of players and staff, including Leicester City, the Swedish National Team and the UEFA.
- Paul Laursen, physiologist, sport scientist, endurance coach, entrepreneur.
- Paul Quetin, National Strength & Conditioning Coach for the French Tennis Federation, working with Davis and Fed cup teams for over 20 years.
- Pierre Lassus, 13 years of strength & conditioning in pro rugby (Bayonne) and football (soccer, PSG), consulting in football and endurance sports.
- Pierre Mangin, former PE teacher, Martin's handball coach at the Strasbourg talent training centre, first division men's handball, French Handball Federation and coach for the Youth Women National team.

- Pippa Grange, psychologist, culture coach and author, Head of Culture at Right to Dream Group. Former Head of People and Talent Development for the Football Association, Cotton Group and the Australian Football Association.
- Rafel Pol, physical coach Spanish National Team, former FC Barcelona.
- Rafael Maldonado, fitness, rehab and injury prevention coach.
- Scott Guyett, assistant manager at Brisbane Roar (Australia A-League), former Head of Sport Science and Strength & Conditioning Crystal Palace Football Club and UEFA Pro Licence coach.
- Sébastien Carrier, Director of Performance at Coach Corner, strength & conditioning with the French Ski Federation for three Olympic games, working with Alpine downhill skiing and SkiCross; former Grenoble Ligue Magnus Ice Hockey.
- Sébastien Gardillou, National Coach for the French Handball Federation working with youth and senior teams, as well as a few clubs including Nice and Metz. World and European Champion, Olympic Champion in Tokyo. Former PE teacher, as well!
- Selwyn Griffith, Head of Strength & Conditioning, Melbourne Demons Football Club; previously Brisbane Lions Football Club.
- Steve Barrett, Ph.D., former Director of Sport Science and Research Innovation, Hull City.
- Steve Ingham, Founder, Supporting Champions.
- Steve Tashjian, High Performance Consultant, Head of Performance US Men's National Team; formerly Columbus Crew and Everton.
- Stuart McMillan, Lead Short Sprint Coach and CEO: ALTIS.
- Stuart Yule, Head of Strength & Conditioning, Scotland National Rugby Team; former Glasgow Warriors, English and Scottish Institute of Sports and Falkirk Football Club.
- Thierry Omeyer, best handball goalkeeper in history.
- Thomas Little, Performance Coach, Preston North End; formerly Manchester City. Founder, heroPro.
- Tom Vandenbogaerde, Lead Physiologist, Swimming Australia. Fifteen years' experience working closely with Olympic athletes and their coaches.
- Tony Strudwick, Head of Performance, Arsenal Academy, former Head of Performance for Sheffield United FC, Wales National Team, Manchester United, Blackburn Rovers and West Ham.
- Yann Le Meur, sport scientist and entrepreneur, working for AS Monaco, Daniil Medvedev and the French Agency of Sport.
- Yann-Benjamin Kugel, performance coach with PSV, former German national team and some other soccer teams.

ACKNOWLEDGMENTS

Martin

The universe, unambiguously because we don't control things as much as we think (or wish).

My mum Christine. Simply the best mum on earth, of course. With her unconditional love and support during all those years, she has genuinely guided me in the pursuit of my dreams and pushed me to turn my ambitions into reality – nurturing and valuing the hard work – but always with the right manners and respect of others. She has constantly been present during the moments that counted to build my confidence and in turn, my I-dentity, as a (failed pro) handball player, a diligent student and now, a workhorse and a proud dad.

My wife Jenn, who has been on my side since even before I needed to read such a book. Since I have always shared everything with her, she has been the person the most influential to me as I developed into a more adult person: she is the one who supports me in all my projects, but also the one that really keeps me grounded. She is my reality check. A nice dose of ego, of course, but with her it's ALL about the others: our families, our two fantastic kids, Ysia and Lelio, and our friends. On the handball court, she was an exceptional and incredibly competitive player, but she never even thought about showing off. She had already figured out how to play the ego volumes and, therefore, may not even read this book 😊.

My grandad, papi René, who was the first to teach me the reality of the Dunning-Kruger effect when I was a kid, but in a very simple way. I still remember the two of us listening over and over to Jean Gabin: "Maintenant je sais" (But know I know). Both Jean Gabin and René already knew it all!

My friend Benjamin Boulnois for asking so many times "why do you need to do all this?" with the respect for who I am and, importantly, without any judgement.

Craig Duncan, Allistair McCaw and Fergus Connolly – I had followed for a long time the work of those three greats minds, via their books, at conferences and on social media. They helped me a lot to develop as a person. It's then with them that I discussed the premises of this book. Their strong encouragements gave me the confidence that those 18 months of hard work would be worth it, and COVID made the rest of it.

Many of my former colleagues in the different work environments I have been in. Our sometimes complicated interactions and the difficult situations I have been in made me reflect a lot about myself, and pushed me to first make contact with many of the contributors of the present book, seeking for advices and guidance on how to navigate in my journey with both my ego and those of others. So without these colleagues, you were not reading this book either.

Eric Reira, life coach, with whom I interacted deeply and consistently throughout the process of the writing of this book. He helped me to better understand myself, and as I was uncovering new pieces about my ego, the book was shaping in parallel, together with George's extraordinary inputs.

George. It's been an incredible encounter. How could I have ever imagined that posting a job on Upwork, looking for a bit of help for editing this book project, would turn into such a rich experience? I discovered a great author that kept surprising me month after month, but above all I have now another friend, a clever, well-minded, sympathetic, modest, passionate and pro-Ego American. He doesn't use Trello and get pi**ed off sometimes for details, but he is such a nice person and so good at what he does, that you just have to accept this. After having tried to kill my ego that I thought had caused me too much damage, George has helped to bring it back home, but within a better shape. I am grateful to him for this, too.

George

My parents gave me an early love of reading, and my sister gave me a youthful appreciation for the joy of the English language. Those hours trying to speak as pretentiously as possible to help her study her SAT flashcards and, later, to lampoon some aspects of academia propelled a lifelong love of consuming and producing words.

If not for the relentless optimism, bottomless experience and unfailing mentorship of David Hannah, there's no way I'd have the experience in the sports industry nor even the desire to stay in it long enough to meet Martin and contribute to this book.

Ajitesh Rasgotra opened the first door for me to get paid for writing about sports. The idea of nabbing a few bucks for writing and editing blogs about Chelsea FC was crazy enough, let alone everything that's come since. Aj also showed me that you don't ever need to meet your coworkers to have a productive team and a great friend, something that would be useful a few years later.

I have the greatest respect for entrepreneurs and innovators. Beerud Sheth, Srini Anumolu, Odysseas Tsatalos and Stratis Karamanlakis co-founded the companies that became Upwork. If not for them, I'd be just another reader of something Martin wrote.

Sometimes you need someone to listen and give you non-verbal feedback: a wag of the tail, a puzzled head-tilt, an enthusiastic nose to the back of your leg. Prudence has been an outstanding sounding board during hundreds of miles of walks and many animated, oft profane whiteboard sessions in my office, even if she's asleep or howling in the other room.

I've never understood people who talk about having to choose between their "home life" and their "work life," as though the values and desires of one conflict with the other. Then again, not many people are as lucky as I am on that front. No one knows the pros and cons of my ego better than Kat. Hopefully, what I've gained from writing this book will lead to more pros and fewer cons. She deserves that, and a lot more.

The biggest downside of working independently is that when you're the only person in the room, you're the smartest person in the room. I never want to be the smartest person in the room. In most of what I do, I don't have co-workers or bosses to interact with, to give me critical feedback, to push back and challenge me to get better, do better, know more, explore the details and then, just when I think I've figured it out, say "I still think we can do a little bit better" and let me discover that, yes, we can. All that changed in spring of 2020. Martin invited me to work with him on his most personal project to date, and held me to his incredibly high standards every day. For all of his reputation as a coach and scientist, he's also a master motivator and manager. He ensured I always lived up to the project, which at times meant working harder than I've ever worked to reach that level. He gave me no room for error but endless room to explore. And he eventually relented and let me take a stereotypical free-wheeling writer's approach to my work, free of his beloved Trello cards. I know how much that pained him, and I am grateful. Grateful, that's the word I was looking for. He took a chance on a brash, ego-loving blog writer. I hope I've ended up as the co-author he wanted, and that this book is what he dreamed it could be.

REFERENCES

- Austin, S., *Nick Broad: Remembering a performance pioneer.* *https://trainingground.guru/articles/nick-broad-remembering-a-performance-pioneer*. 2019.
- Batistuta, G., *El poder de la disciplina | TEDxEstaciónEwald*. 2020.
- Blanchard, S., *A vision of high performance sport - Plinths and Platforms.* *https://plinthsandplatforms.com/2019/07/31/a-vision-of-high-performance-sport/*. 2019.
- Blondet, C., *Julien Benneteau, capitaine de l'équipe de France de Fed Cup, a su créer un collectif. Journal l'Equipe*. 2019. 11 Nov.
- Bourbeau, L., ego - *The Greatest Obstacle to Healing the 5 Wounds*. 2017: Les Editions E.T.C. INc.
- Buchheit, M., *The 30-15 Intermittent Fitness Test: accuracy for individualizing interval training of young intermittent sport players*. J Strength Cond Res, 2008. 22(2): p. 365-374.
- Buchheit M. *The 30-15 intermittent fitness test: 10 year review*. Myorobie J. 2010; Sep(1),p.1-9.
- Buchheit, M., *The Noble Ranks of Performance Roles - Who's a king - who's a duke?* Sport Perf & Sci Reports, 2019. May(60): p. 1-7.
- Buchheit, M., McHugues, D. & Smith S. *Kitman Labs Performance Intelligence Research Initiative: A Survey to bring research on the field*. Sport Perf & Sci Reports, 2021. Feb(135), p. 1-6.
- Dale, S., *Heuristics and biases: The science of decision-making*. Business Information Review 2015. 32(June): p. 93-99.
- Dennett, D.C., *Intuition Pumps And Other Tools for Thinking*. 2014: Editors W. W. Norton Company.
- "Ego." Encyclopaedia Brittanica, *https://www.britannica.com/topic/ego-philosophy-and-psychology*. Accessed 12 June 2021.
- "Ego." Merriam-Webster, *https://www.merriam-webster.com/dictionary/ego*. Accessed 12 June 2021.
- "Ego." Psychology Dictionary, 28 November 2018, *https://psychologydictionary.org/ego/*. Accessed 12 June 2021.
- Fridman, L, host. "Michael Malice and Yaron Brook: Ayn Rand, Human Nature and Anarchy." *Lex Fridman Podcast*, 24 April 2021. *https://podcasts.apple.com/us/podcast/178-michael-malice-yaron-brook-ayn-rand-human-nature/id1434243584?i=1000518884261*
- Holliday, R. *Ego is the Enemy*, 2016.: Portfolio.
- Molina, R., *Cavani, el matador*, 2017: Editions H. Image.
- Nadal, T., *El valor del esfuerzo | TEDxMalagueta*. 2018.
- Onesta, C., *L'égo, un frein ? https://www.youtube.com/watch?v=tzAY2cp-pPM*. 2014.
- Perrottet, T. *The Naked Olympics*, 2004. Random House.
- Rand, A., "The Metaphysical Versus the Man-Made." In *Philosophy: Who Needs It*, 23-34. Signet 1984 (Original work published 1973).
- Taylor, S., *The Fall: The Insanity of the Ego in Human History and the Dawning of A New Era*. 2005: The Bothy, John Hunt Publishing Ltd.
- Schmitt, Le Bal des Egos, 2014. Editions Odile Jacob.
- Smith, T., On a Pedestal-Sport as an Arena for Admiration. Sport, Ethics and Philosophy, 2018. 14(1), p.4-25.
- Thiebart, A., Au plus prêt du serial Kylian. *Au Cœur du Club, Paris Saint Germain*. Feb/March, 193, 2019. p20.

- Thiebart, A., Au plus prêt du serial Kylian. *Le magazine officiel, Paris Saint Germain.* Jan/Feb/March, 02, 2020. p20.
- Wenger, A., *USI Events - Qu'est-ce qui nous rend meilleurs ?* 2019.

RESOURCES

Listed below all books and podcast recommended by the interviewees, together with direct links for access. The numbers into brackets (e.g., 3x) indicates how many time the content was recommended.

RECOMMENDED BOOKS

English
59 Lessons: Working with the World's Greatest Coaches, Athletes, & Special Forces by Dr. Fergus Connolly (2x)
7 habits of highly effective people by Stephen Covey
Antifragile: Things That Gain from Disorder by Nassim Nicholas Taleb (3x)
Behave: The Biology of Humans at Our Best and Worst by Robert M. Sapolsky
Black Box Thinking: The Surprising Truth About Success by Matthew Syed (2x)
Blink: The Power of Thinking Without Thinking by Malcolm Gladwell
Blowing the Bloody Doors Off: And Other Lessons in Life by Michael Caine
Born To Win: The Power Of A Vision By John Bertrand
Branches: A Philosophy of Time, Event and Advent by Michel Serres
Business Adventures: Twelve Classic Tales from the World of Wall Street by John Brooks
Captivate: The Science of Succeeding with People by Vanessa van Edwards
Change Maker: Turn Your Passion for Health and Fitness into a Powerful Purpose and a Wildly Successful Career by John Berardi
Conscious Coaching: The Art and Science of Building Buy-In by Brett Bartholomew (2x)
Crucial Conversations: Bridging the Awkward Spiritual Gap: Starfish Movement by Dr. Dan Grider
Crucial Conversations: Tools for Talking When Stakes Are High by Joseph Grenny, Al Switzler, Ron Mcmillan (3x)
Dare to Lead: Brave Work. Tough Conversations. Whole Hearts by Brené Brown
Develop Your Leadership Skills: Fast, Effective Ways to Become a Leader People Want to Follow by John Adair
Dichotomy of Leadership by Jocko Willink and Leif Babin
Digital-Influence by Dale Carnegie
Ego is the enemy by Ryan Holiday (10x)
Eleven Rings: The Soul of Success by Phil Jackson (2x)
Factfulness: Ten Reasons We're Wrong About the World - and Why Things Are Better Than You Think by Hans Rosling
Food for Thought by Nina Savelle-Rocklin
Game Changer by Fergus Connolly, Phil White
Good to Great: Why Some Companies Make the Leap and Others Don't by Jim Collins
Grit: The Power of Passion and Perseverance by Angela Duckworth
Being Happy by Tal Ben-Shahar
HBR's 10 Must Reads Boxed Set By Harvard Business Review
How to Have Impossible Conversations: A Very Practical Guide by Peter Boghossian, James Lindsay
How to Win Friends & Influence People by Dale Carnegie (4x)
I Thought It Was Just Me (but it isn't): Making the Journey from "What Will People Think?" to "I Am Enough" by Brene Brown
Informed: The Art of the Science of Preparing Athletes by Paul Gamble
It Takes What It Takes: How to Think Neutrally and Gain Control of Your Life by Trevor Moawad

Jonathan Livingston Seagull: The Complete Edition by Richard Bach
Leaders Eat Last: Why Some Teams Pull Together and Others Don't by Simon Sinek (3x)
Leaders: Myth and Reality by Stanley McChrystal
Legacy, what the All Blacks can teach us about the business of life by James Kerr (4x)
Self-Made Millionaire Mindset: The success secrets of self-made millionaires by Fredrick Omobude
Linchpin: Are You Indispensable? by Seth Godin
Living on the Volcano: The Secrets of Surviving as a Football Manager by Michael Calvin
Living the 80/20 Way, New Edition: Work Less, Worry Less, Succeed More, Enjoy More by Richard Koch
Long Walk to Freedom: The Autobiography of Nelson Mandela by Nelson Mandela
Made to Stick by Chip and Dan Health
Make Your Bed: Little Things That Can Change Your Life...And Maybe the World by Admiral William H McRaven
Management in 10 Words by Terry Leahy
Managing the Difficult Emotions by Mary Nhin
Man's Search For Meaning by Viktor E. Frankl (2x)
Meditations by Marcus Aurelius (3x)
Mindset: The New Psychology of Success by Carol S. Dweck (3x)
Never Split the Difference by Tahl Raz Chris Voss
Nudge: Improving Decisions About Health, Wealth, and Happiness by Richard H. Thaler and Cass R. Sunstein
Pep Guardiola: The Evolution by Marti Perarnau
Persuasion: The Art of Influencing People: by James Borg
Pig Wrestling: The Brilliantly Simple Way to Solve Any Problem... and Create the Change You Need by Pete Lindsay
Power Cues: The Subtle Science of Leading Groups, Persuading Others, and Maximizing Your Personal Impact by Nick Morgan
Practicing the Power of Now: Essential Teachings, Meditations, and Exercises From The Power of Now by Eckhart Tolle
Pre-Suasion: Channeling Attention for Change by Robert Cialdini Ph.D
Principles: Life and Work by Ray Dalio (2x)
Psychology: Themes and Variations by Wayne Weiten
Sacred Hoops: spiritual lessons of a hardwood warrior by Phil Jackson
Shackleton's Way: Leadership Lessons from the Great Antarctic Explorer by Alexandra Shackleton
Snakes in Suits: When Psychopaths Go to Work by Paul Babiak
Social Psychology 13e by David Myers
Start with Why by Simon Sinek (2x)
Strangers to Ourselves: Discovering the Adaptive Unconscious by Timothy D. Wilson
SUMO Your Relationships: How to handle not strangle the people you live and work with by Paul McGee
Switch: How to Change Things When Change Is Hard by Chip Heath and Dan Heath
Talking to Strangers by Malcolm Gladwell
Team of Teams by Gen. Stanley McChrystal, Tantum Collins, David Silverman, Chris Fussell.
The Art Of War by Sun Tzu
The Beginner's Guide to Stoicism: Tools for Emotional Resilience and Positivity by Matthew Van Natta
The Book of Beautiful Questions: The Powerful Questions That Will Help You Decide, Create, Connect, and Lead by Warren Berger
The Boy, the mole, the fox & the Horse' by Charlie Macksey
The Brain That Changes Itself: Stories of Personal Triumph from the Frontiers of Brain Science by Norman Doidge
The Captain Class: A New Theory of Leadership by Sam Walker

The Chimp Paradox: The Mind Management Program to Help You Achieve Success, Confidence, and Happiness by Steve Dr. Peters

The Courage to Be Disliked: How to Free Yourself, Change Your Life, and Achieve Real Happiness by Ichiro Kishimi and Fumitake Koga

The Culture Code: The Secrets of Highly Successful Groups by Daniel Coyle (4x)

The Daily Stoic by Ryan Holiday (3x)

The Elephant in the Brain: Hidden Motives in Everyday Life by Kevin Simler and Robin Hanson

The Fifth Discipline: The Art and Practice of the Learning Organization by Peter M. Senge

The Gold mine effect by Rasmus Ankersen

The Great Mental Models - General Thinking Concepts by Shane Parrish and Rhiannon Beaubien

The Laws of Human Nature by Robert Greene (2x)

The Life-Changing Magic of Not Giving a Fuck: How to Stop Spending Time You Don't Have with People You Don't Like Doing Things You Don't Want to Do by Sarah Knight

The Monk Who Sold His Ferrari: A Fable About Fulfilling Your Dreams & Reaching Your Destiny by Robin Sharma

The Obstacle Is the Way: The Timeless Art of Turning Trials into Triumph by Ryan Holiday (3x)

The Power of Nice: How to Negotiate So Everyone Wins - Especially You! by Ronald M. Shapiro

The Power of Now by Eckhart Tolle

The Subtle Art of Not Giving A Fuck by Mark Manson (3x)

The Talent Lab: The secret to finding, creating and sustaining success by Owen Slot

The Top 200 Secrets of Success &The Pillars of Self-Mastery by Maxwell Harris

The Undoing Project: A Friendship That Changed Our Minds by Michael Lewis

Thinking in bets by Annie Duke

Thinking, fast and slow by Daniel Kahneman (5x)

To Sell Is Human by Daniel H Pink

Total Competition: Lessons in Strategy from Formula One by Ross Brawn and Adam Parr

Turn this Ship Around by L. David Marquet

What They Don't Teach You at Harvard Business School: Notes from a Street-smart Executive by Mark H. McCormack

Way of the Peaceful Warrior: A Book That Changes Lives by Dan Millman

French
Aucun de nous ne reviendra de Charlotte Delbo
Confiance et Leadership by Ali Armand
La Méthode par Edgar Morin
Les experts de Claude Onesta
Psychologie de la motivation de Paul Diel
Quand les décideurs s'inspirent des moines de Sébastien Henry
Révélez le manager qui est en vous de Patrice Fabart
Petit précis du bonheur de Anna Quindlen
Sept graines de lumière dans le cœur des guerriers de Pierre Pellissier
Un cancre dans les étoiles de Thomas Sammut

Spanish
Anatomía del miedo de Jose Antonio Marina
El poder de confiar en ti de Curro Cañete
El viaje al poder de la mente de Eduardo Punset
La primera vez que la pegué con la izquierda: "7Ps" para brillar de Imanol Ibarrondo Garay

RECOMMENDED PODCASTS

English

A bit of Optimism with Simon Sinek (2x)
Against the Rules with Michael Lewis
Akimbo with Seth Godin (x4)
Alan Watts Podcast
Art of Coaching Podcast with Brett Bartholomew (2x)
Art of Sharm with AJ Harbinger & Johnny Dzubak
Being Well Podcast: Discovering Your Emotional Intelligence with Daniel Goleman
Cautionary Tales with Tim Harford
Creative Confidence Podcast with Suzanne Gibbs Howard and Coe Leta Stafford
Dare to lead with Brene Brown
Don't Tell Me The Score with BBC
Dover calling with Peter Cocks & John Orchard
East Sleep, work, repeat with Bruce Daisley (2x)
Finding Mastery with Michael Gervais (8x)
Harvard Business Review Originals
Hidden Brain with Shankar Vedantam
Jocko Wilink's Podcast (4x)
Jonathan Haidt 's Podcasts
Ken Blanchard Leadercast Podcast
Leaders Performance Podcast from The Leaders Performance Institute
Leadership with John Maxwell
Leave your Mark with Scotty Livingston
Life Advice That Doesn't Suck with Mark Manson (3x)
Making Positive Psychology Work Podcast with Michelle McQuaid
Making Sense with Sam Harris (5x)
Mastermind High Performance Sports with Antony Hudson (2x)
No Ego with Cy Wakeman
No Stupid Questions with Stephen J. Dubner and Angela Duckworth
Pacey Performance (x5)
Philosophize This with Stephen West
Positive University Podcast with Jon Gordon
Revisionist History with Malcolm Gladwell
Supporting Champions with Steve Ingham
Take Command with Dale Carnegie
The B&N podcast with Admiral William H. McRaven
The Daily Stoic with Ryan Holiday (4x)
The High Performance Podcast with Jake Humphrey
The Human Performance Podcast with Dr Craig Duncan
The Joe Rogan Experience with Joe Rogan
The knowledge project with Shane Parrish (x5)
The learning leader show with Ryan Hawk
The learning leader with Ryan Hawk
The MAGIA Mindset with Shawn Alvari
The mastery sessions with Robin Sharma
The Psychology Podcast with Scott Barry Kaufman
The School of Greatness with Lewis Howes
The Strength Coach with Anthony Renna and Michael Boyle (2x)
The Talent Equation Podcast with Stuart Armstrong
The Tim Ferriss Show (3x)
Training Ground Guru Podcast

<u>Unlocking Us with Brené Brown (3x)</u>

Spanish
<u>Ezen Inside con Alex De La Vega</u>
<u>Pep Marí</u>

French
<u>Je ne sais quoi Le Podcast de Diana & Clémence</u>
<u>Le gratin par Pauline Laigneau</u>
<u>Le sens de l'info de Michel Polacco et Michel Serre</u>
<u>Objectif Performance de Julien Astouric</u>
<u>Personnages en personne de Charles Dantzig</u>
<u>Thinkerview</u>

Printed in Great Britain
by Amazon